Lecture Notes in Computer Science

Vol. 23: Programming Methodology. 4th Informatik Symposium, IBM Germany Wildbad, September 25–27, 1974. Edited by C. E. Hackl. VI, 501 pages. 1975.

Vol. 24: Parallel Processing. Proceedings 1974. Edited by T. Feng. VI, 433 pages. 1975.

Vol. 25: Category Theory Applied to Computation and Control. Proceedings 1974. Edited by E. G. Manes. X, 245 pages. 1975.

Vol. 26: GI-4. Jahrestagung, Berlin, 9.–12. Oktober 1974. Herausgegeben im Auftrag der GI von D. Siefkes. IX, 748 Seiten. 1975.

Vol. 27: Optimization Techniques. IFIP Technical Conference. Novosibirsk, July 1–7, 1974. (Series: I.F.I.P. TC7 Optimization Conferences.) Edited by G. I. Marchuk. VIII, 507 pages. 1975.

Vol. 28: Mathematical Foundations of Computer Science. 3rd Symposium at Jadwisin near Warsaw, June 17–22, 1974. Edited by A. Blikle. VII, 484 pages. 1975.

Vol. 29: Interval Mathematics. Procedings 1975. Edited by K. Nickel. VI, 331 pages. 1975.

Vol. 30: Software Engineering. An Advanced Course. Edited by F. L. Bauer. (Formerly published 1973 as Lecture Notes in Economics and Mathematical Systems, Vol. 81) XII, 545 pages. 1975.

Vol. 31: S. H. Fuller, Analysis of Drum and Disk Storage Units. IX, 283 pages. 1975.

Vol. 32: Mathematical Foundations of Computer Science 1975. Proceedings 1975. Edited by J. Bečvář. X, 476 pages. 1975.

Vol. 33: Automata Theory and Formal Languages, Kaiserslautern, May 20–23, 1975. Edited by H. Brakhage on behalf of GI. VIII, 292 Seiten. 1975.

Vol. 34: GI – 5. Jahrestagung, Dortmund 8.–10. Oktober 1975. Herausgegeben im Auftrag der GI von J. Mühlbacher. X, 755 Seiten. 1975.

Vol. 35: W. Everling, Exercises in Computer Systems Analysis. (Formerly published 1972 as Lecture Notes in Economics and Mathematical Systems, Vol. 65) VIII, 184 pages. 1975.

Vol. 36: S. A. Greibach, Theory of Program Structures: Schemes, Semantics, Verification. XV, 364 pages. 1975.

Vol. 37: C. Böhm, λ-Calculus and Computer Science Theory. Proceedings 1975. XII, 370 pages. 1975.

Vol. 38: P. Branquart, J.-P. Cardinael, J. Lewi, J.-P. Delescaille, M. Vanbegin. An Optimized Translation Process and Its Application to ALGOL 68. IX, 334 pages. 1976.

Vol. 39: Data Base Systems. Proceedings 1975. Edited by H. Hasselmeier and W. Spruth. VI, 386 pages. 1976.

Vol. 40: Optimization Techniques. Modeling and Optimization in the Service of Man. Part 1. Proceedings 1975. Edited by J. Cea. XIV, 854 pages. 1976.

Vol. 41: Optimization Techniques. Modeling and Optimization in the Service of Man. Part 2. Proceedings 1975. Edited by J. Cea. XIII, 852 pages. 1976.

Vol. 42: James E. Donahue, Complementary Definitions of Programming Language Semantics. VII, 172 pages. 1976.

Vol. 43: E. Specker und V. Strassen, Komplexität von Entscheidungsproblemen. Ein Seminar. V, 217 Seiten. 1976.

Vol. 44: ECI Conference 1976. Proceedings 1976. Edited by K. Samelson. VIII, 322 pages. 1976.

Vol. 45: Mathematical Foundations of Computer Science 1976. Proceedings 1976. Edited by A. Mazurkiewicz. XI, 601 pages. 1976.

Vol. 46: Language Hierarchies and Interfaces. Edited by F. L. Bauer and K. Samelson. X, 428 pages. 1976.

Vol. 47: Methods of Algorithmic Language Implementation. Edited by A. Ershov and C. H. A. Koster. VIII, 351 pages. 1977.

Vol. 48: Theoretical Computer Science, Darmstadt, March 1977. Edited by H. Tzschach, H. Waldschmidt and H. K.-G. Walter on behalf of GI. VIII, 418 pages. 1977.

Vol. 49: Interactive Systems. Proceedings 1976. Edited by A. Blaser and C. Hackl. VI, 380 pages. 1976.

Vol. 50: A. C. Hartmann, A Concurrent Pascal Compiler for Minicomputers. VI, 119 pages. 1977.

Vol. 51: B. S. Garbow, Matrix Eigensystem Routines – Eispack Guide Extension. VIII, 343 pages. 1977.

Vol. 52: Automata, Languages and Programming. Fourth Colloquium, University of Turku, July 1977. Edited by A. Salomaa and M. Steinby. X, 569 pages. 1977.

Vol. 53: Mathematical Foundations of Computer Science. Proceedings 1977. Edited by J. Gruska. XII, 608 pages. 1977.

Vol. 54: Design and Implementation of Programming Languages. Proceedings 1976. Edited by J. H. Williams and D. A. Fisher. X, 496 pages. 1977.

Vol. 55: A. Gerbier, Mes premières constructions de programmes. XII, 256 pages. 1977.

Vol. 56: Fundamentals of Computation Theory. Proceedings 1977. Edited by M. Karpiński. XII, 542 pages. 1977.

Vol. 57: Portability of Numerical Software. Proceedings 1976. Edited by W. Cowell. VIII, 539 pages. 1977.

Vol. 58: M. J. O'Donnell, Computing in Systems Described by Equations. XIV, 111 pages. 1977.

Vol. 59: E. Hill, Jr., A Comparative Study of Very Large Data Bases. X, 140 pages. 1978.

Vol. 60: Operating Systems, An Advanced Course. Edited by R. Bayer, R. M. Graham, and G. Seegmüller. X, 593 pages. 1978.

Vol. 61: The Vienna Development Method: The Meta-Language. Edited by D. Bjørner and C. B. Jones. XVIII, 382 pages. 1978.

Vol. 62: Automata, Languages and Programming. Proceedings 1978. Edited by G. Ausiello and C. Böhm. VIII, 508 pages. 1978.

Vol. 63: Natural Language Communication with Computers. Edited by Leonard Bolc. VI, 292 pages. 1978.

Vol. 64: Mathematical Foundations of Computer Science. Proceedings 1978. Edited by J. Winkowski. X, 551 pages. 1978.

Vol. 65: Information Systems Methodology, Proceedings, 1978. Edited by G. Bracchi and P. C. Lockemann. XII, 696 pages. 1978.

Vol. 66: N. D. Jones and S. S. Muchnick, TEMPO: A Unified Treatment of Binding Time and Parameter Passing Concepts in Programming Languages. IX, 118 pages. 1978.

Vol. 67: Theoretical Computer Science, 4th GI Conference, Aachen, March 1979. Edited by K. Weihrauch. VII, 324 pages. 1979.

Vol. 68: D. Harel, First-Order Dynamic Logic. X, 133 pages. 1979.

Vol. 69: Program Construction. International Summer School. Edited by F. L. Bauer and M. Broy. VII, 651 pages. 1979.

Vol. 70: Semantics of Concurrent Computation. Proceedings 1979. Edited by G. Kahn. VI, 368 pages. 1979.

Vol. 71: Automata, Languages and Programming. Proceedings 1979. Edited by H. A. Maurer. IX, 684 pages. 1979.

Vol. 72: Symbolic and Algebraic Computation. Proceedings 1979. Edited by E. W. Ng. XV, 557 pages. 1979.

Vol. 73: Graph-Grammars and Their Application to Computer Science and Biology. Proceedings 1978. Edited by V. Claus, H. Ehrig and G. Rozenberg. VII, 477 pages. 1979.

Vol. 74: Mathematical Foundations of Computer Science. Proceedings 1979. Edited by J. Bečvář. IX, 580 pages. 1979.

Vol. 75: Mathematical Studies of Information Processing. Proceedings 1978. Edited by E. K. Blum, M. Paul and S. Takasu. VIII, 629 pages. 1979.

Vol. 76: Codes for Boundary-Value Problems in Ordinary Differential Equations. Proceedings 1978. Edited by B. Childs et al. VIII, 388 pages. 1979.

Lecture Notes in Computer Science

Edited by G. Goos and J. Hartmanis

108

Graph Theory and Algorithms

17th Symposium of Research Institute
of Electrical Communication, Tohoku University
Sendai, Japan, October 24–25, 1980
Proceedings

Edited by N. Saito and T. Nishizeki

Springer-Verlag
Berlin Heidelberg New York 1981

Editors

N. Saito
T. Nishizeki
Dept. of Electrical Communications
Faculty of Engineering, Tohoku University
Sendai, Japan 980

AMS Subject Classifications (1979): 68E10, 05C15, 05C38, 68D90
CR Subject Classifications (1981): 5.32

ISBN 3-540-10704-5 Springer-Verlag Berlin Heidelberg New York
ISBN 0-387-10704-5 Springer-Verlag New York Heidelberg Berlin

Printed in Germany

Printing and binding: Beltz Offsetdruck, Hemsbach/Bergstr.
2145/3140-543210

PREFACE

This volume contains the papers presented at the symposium on "Graph Theory and Algorithms", held in Tohoku University, Sendai, Japan, October 24-25, 1980.

The symposium is the seventeenth in a series of the annual meetings which have been held at Research Institute of Elecrtical Communication (Tsuken), Tohoku University for the past sixteen years on various research topics, mostly reflecting the evolving work of the Institute. The Seventeenth Tsuken Symposium aims to bring together researchers interested in graph theory and algorithms, and to promote a better understanding of the new active area.

These Proceedings contain all the nineteen invited papers presented at the Symposium except one : "Threshold sequences" by P. L. Hammer, T. Ibaraki and B. Simeone, which will appear in a journal soon. We are grateful to the chairmen and authors for their contributions to the success of the Tsuken Sympsium.

The foreign guest speaker C. Berge delivered the special address entitled "Some common properties for regularizable graphs, edge-critical graphs and B-graphs". The paper is also contained in the Proceedings. We wish to thank him for his contribution to the Symposium.

The papers included in these Proceedings were not formally refereed. It is anticipated that most of them will appear in a polished and completed form in scientific journals.

We wish to thank Professor T. Takahashi, Director of Research Institute of Electrical Communication for his support and encouragement and for his welcome to the Symposium. We thank our colleagues for their generous assistance in organizing the Symposium, especially for Mr. S. Miyata for his handling of the business aspects of the Symposium.

Finally, the help of the Springer-Verlag in the timely publication of this volume is highly appreciated.

March 1981

N. Saito

T. Nishizeki

TABLE OF CONTENTS

*speakers

DIVIDING A SYSTEM INTO ALMOST UNIDIRECTIONAL BLOCKS

Wataru Mayeda

Coordinated Science Laboratory
University of Illinois
Urbana, IL 61801 U.S.A.

(Dept. of Integrated Arts and Sciences
Hiroshima University
Hiroshima 730, Japan)

Abstract. When a system is divided into blocks B_1 B_2..B_k..B_m such that the existence of failure in B_k will not interfare required performance of blocks B_1 B_2... and B_{k-1}, then these blocks are called unidirectional blocks. To determine failure elements in a system, unidirectional blocks B_1 B_2... will be tested one by one in the order to find a block containing failure first, then diagnose the block to locate failure elements. It is easily seen that this process is simpler than testing a system as a whole to determine the location of failure elements by one procedure. Unfortunatley, most of systems can not be divided into unidirectional blocks. However, it is possible to divide a system into almost unidirectional blocks B_1 B_2...B_k...B_m such that the existence of failure in B_k will interfare only slightly to the performance of preceding blocks B_1 B_2...B_{k-1}.

Introduction

As huge quantities of printed circuits are utilized in wide area, diagnosis of electrical networks becomes an extremely important task. Especially, for those high priced printed circuits, it is more economical to fix those printed circuits when failure occured than renew them. This situation leads to start research on automatic system diagnosis. Since it is not advisable to remove elements in a printed circuit for diagnosis, usually information for diagnosis are only those obtained by measurement of voltages at available nodes. However, sources for such measurements can be either voltages or currents.

Value of Terminal Transmission

Printed circuits for analog networks usually consists of several blocks of different performances such as local oscillators, mixers and amplifiers. Also each of these blocks may consist of several smaller blocks. For example, an amplifier usually consists of several simple amplifier circuits in series. Hence when a failure occurs, it is reasonable to test each block for the existence of a failure, first. Once, a faulty block is found then, the second step is to determine location of failed elements in the block. To accomplish this procedure, a system must be divided into suitable blocks.

Let $B_1\ B_2 \ldots B_k \ldots B_m$ be blocks which form a system. Then, these blocks are called unidirectional blocks if a failure of block B_k will not interfare a required performance of blocks $B_1\ B_2 \ldots B_{k-1}$ for all $k=2,3,\ldots,$ m. They are called almost unidirectional blocks, if a failure of block B_k will have almost no effect on a required performance of $B_1\ B_2 \ldots B_{k-1}$ for all $k=2,\ 3,\ldots,$ m. Consider an electrical network N containing nodes $0,1,2,\ldots,$ n with 0 being the reference node. Let v_j be a voltage at node j when a source voltage v_i is connected from node i to the reference node 0. Then a value of transmission from i to j symbolized by α_{ij} is defined as

$$\alpha_{ij}=F(v_i,v_j)$$

For example, $\alpha_{ij}=v_j/v_i$, $\alpha_{ij}=|v_j|/|v_i|$, or $\alpha_{ij}=v_j^2/v_i^2$. By taking i and j equal to 1, 2,..., n. with $i\neq j$, we have $n!/(n-2)!$ α's. Using α_{ij} as a weight of edge from vertex j, we have an oriented graph G corresponding to a given electrical network N. As an example, a graph G in Fig. 1 (a) is obtained from an electrical network N in (b) with $\alpha_{ij}=v_j/v_i$.

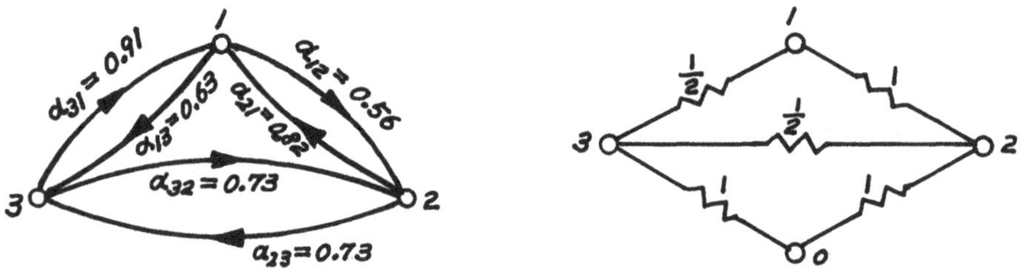

(a) Graph G (b) Network N

Fig. 1 A network N and corresponding graph G.

Let g_p be a subgraph of G. Also let vertex i be not in g_p. Then a value of α_{ig_p} from vertex i to subgraph g_p is defined as

$$\alpha_{ig_p}=\mathrm{Max}\{\alpha_{ip};\ p\in g_p\}$$

Note that α_{ig_p} is the largest value of transmission from i to p for all vertices in

g_p. Also note that when α's are not real numbers, we must define a way of ordering α's. When we consider an amount of signal being transfered form a node i to a block of a network N, each node in the block will receive from a source at node i, we take the largest amount of signal reached at a node among all nodes in the block.

Let g_i and g_p be subgraphs of G which have not vertices in common. Then a value $\alpha_{g_i g_p}$ of transmission from g_i to g_p is defined as

$$\alpha_{g_i g_p} = \mathrm{Max}\{\alpha_{ip}; i\in g_i,\ p\in g_p\}$$

This is equivalent to taking a value of transmission of signal between blocks as the largest amont of transmission between nodes belong to these blocks.

Finally, we define a value of terminal transmission τ_{ij} from vertex i to vertex j is defined as

$$\tau_{ij} = \mathrm{Min}\{\alpha_{g_i g_j};\ \text{all } g_i \text{ s.t. } i\in g_i,\ j\notin g_i,\ g_j = \bar{g}_i\}$$

where $\bar{g}_j$ is the complement of g_j obtained by deleting all vertices and edges connected to these vertices in g_j.

Note that, in general, values τ_{ij} and τ_{ji} of terminal transmission will be different. Hence, for a graph G of n vertices, there are n!/(n-2)! terminal transmission τ's.

Let $\{\tau\}$ be a collection of all terminal transmissions of G. Suppose the values of all terminal transmissions are positive real numbers. Then from the smallest one, we can order them as

$$\tau_1 \leq \tau_2 \leq \ldots \leq \tau_u$$

where u=n!/(n-2)!. By the definition of τ_{ij}, one of α's in $\{\alpha_{g_i g_j};$ all g_i s.t. $i\in g_i$, $j\notin g_i$, $g_j=\bar{g}_i\}$ has the value equal to τ_{ij}. Let $\alpha_{g_i' g_j'}$ be the one which is equal to τ_{ij}. Let S be a cutset such that by deleting all edges in S from G, we have subgraphs g_i' and g_j'. This cutset S is called a corresponding cutset of τ_{ij}. For convenience we use the symbol $S(\tau_{ij})$ to indicate such a corresponding cutset of τ_{ij}. If there are several $\alpha_{g_i' g_j'}$ in $\{\alpha_{g_i g_j};$ all g_i s.t. $i\in g_i$, $j\notin g_i$, $g_j=\bar{g}_i\}$ which are equal to τ_{ij}, there are several corresponding cutsets of τ_{ij}.

For convenience, we say that two cutsets S_p and S_q do not intersect each other if deletion of all edges in S_p and S_q from graph G produces exactly three connected subgraphs. Consider two values τ_i and τ_j where $\tau_i \leq \tau_j$. There are corresponding cutsets $S(\tau_i)$ and $S(\tau_j)$ having an important property shown by the following theorem:

Theorem 1: If cutsets $S(\tau_i)$ and $S(\tau_j)$ do intersect each other, there exists another corresponding cutset $S'(\tau_j)$ of τ_j which does not interesct with $S(\tau_i)$.

Proof: Let the values of transmission corresponding to τ_i and τ_j be α_{pq} and α_{rs} respectively. Let g_a, g_b, g_c and g_d be four connected subgraphs obtained by deleting all edges in $S(\tau_i)$ and $S(\tau_j)$.

Case 1: Suppose α_{pq} and α_{rs} are connected from g_a as shown in Fig. 2.

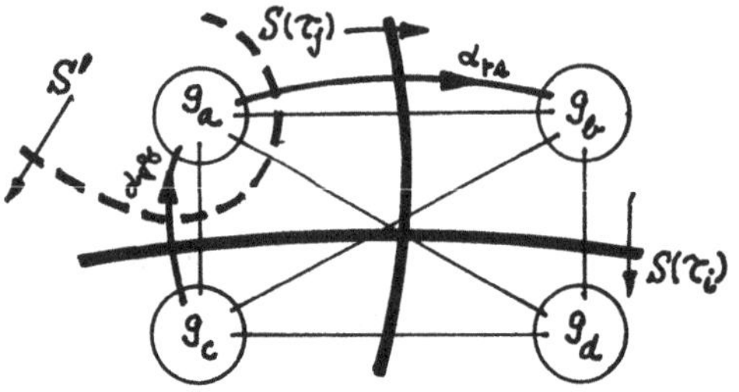

Fig. 2. $S(\tau_i)$ and $S(\tau_j)$.

It is clear from the definition of τ_i that α_{pq} is the largest among the weights of all edges directed from g_a and g_b to g_c and g_d in $S(\tau_i)$. Also α_{rs} is the largest among the weights of all edges in $S(\tau_j)$ directed from g_a and g_c to g_b and g_d. Since $\tau_i \leqslant \tau_j$, $\alpha_{pq} \leqslant \alpha_{rs}$, consider a cutset S' in Fig. 2 which contains both α_{pq} and α_{rs}. The largest weight of edges in S' directed from g_a to g_b, g_c and g_d is clearly α_{rs} which is equal to τ_j. This means that there exists a value of transmission $\alpha_{g_a\bar{g}_a}$ in $\{\alpha_{g_ag_b}$; all g_a s.t. $i\in g_a, j\notin g_a$, $g_b=\bar{g}_a\}$ which is equal to τ_j. Note that $\bar{g}_a$ consists of g_b, g_c, g_d and all edges connected between them. Hence S' is a corresponding cutset of τ_j and S' does not intersect with $S(\tau_i)$.

The same results can be obtained when the location of α_{pq} and α_{rs} are different from those of Case 1.

When $\tau_i=\tau_j$, it is possible to have a situation that corresponding cutsets $S(\tau_i)$ and $S(\tau_j)$ are identical. In such a case, we like to state that the corresponding cutsets of τ_i and τ_j do not intersect each other. Hence, we define that identical cutsets do not intersect each other. By extending the previous theorem, we have

<u>Theorem 2:</u> Suppose any two of $S(\tau_1)$, $S(\tau_2)$,...,$S(\tau_r)$ do not intersect each other. Also suppose $S(\tau_{r+1})$ intersects with some of $S(\tau_1)$, $S(\tau_2)$, ... and $S(\tau_r)$. Then there exists another corresponding cutset $S'(\tau_{r+1})$ of τ_{r+1} which does not intersect with any of $S(\tau_1)$, $S(\tau_2)$, ... and $S(\tau_r)$.

There are relationship among τ's given by the next thoerem.

<u>Theorem 3:</u> Let g_i and g_j be connected subgraph of G obtained by deleting all edges in $S(\tau_{ij})$ and $i\in g_i$. Then for any pair of vertices $p\in g_i$ and $q\in g_j$,

$$\tau_{pq} \leqslant \tau_{ij}$$

Proof: From the definition of τ_{ij}, that is,

$$\tau_{ij} = \mathrm{Min}\{\alpha_{ij} \text{ ; all } g_i \text{ s.t. } i \in g_i,\ j \notin g_i,\ g_j = \bar{g}_i\}$$

There exists a value α_{ij} in $\{\alpha_{ij}$; all g_i s.t. $i \in g_i$, $g_j = \bar{g}_i\}$ such that α_{ij} is equal to τ_{ij}. Consider the definition of τ_{pq} where

$$\tau_{pq} = \mathrm{Min}\{\alpha_{pq};\ \text{all } g_p \text{ s.t. } p \in g_p,\ q \notin g_p,\ g_q = \bar{g}_p\}$$

Since $p \in g_i$ and $q \in g_j$, α_{ij} is in the collection $\{\alpha_{pq}$; all g_p s.t. $p \in g_p$, $q \notin g_p$, $g_q = \bar{g}_p\}$. Because τ_{pq} is the minimum among values in the collection, τ_{pq} can not be larger than $\alpha_{ij}(=\tau_{ij})$.

Note that when τ_{ij} is the smallest among all values of terminal transmission,

$$\tau_{pq} = \tau_{ij}$$

for all $p \in g_i$ and $q \in g_j$.

Semicut and Terminal Transmission

A corresponding graph G of a network N is an oriented graph. So we orient a cutset $S(\tau_{ij})$ from g_i to g_j which are two connected subgraphs obtained by deleting all edges in $S(\tau_{ij})$ and $i \in g_i$. We form two disjoint subsets of $S(\tau_{ij})$ called semicuts as follows:

$s_{ij}(\tau_{ij})$: collection of all edges connected from g_i to g_j in $S(\tau_{ij})$

$s_{ji}(\tau_{ij})$: collection of all edges connected from g_j to g_i in $S(\tau_{ij})$

It is clear that

$$s_{ij}(\tau_{ij}) \cup s_{ji}(\tau_{ij}) = S(\tau_{ij})$$

and

$$s_{ij}(\tau_{ij}) \cap s_{ji}(\tau_{ij}) = \phi.$$

By defining $V[s_{ij}(\tau_{ij})]$ as

$V[s_{ij}(\tau_{ij})]$ = the largest value among the weight of all edges in $s_{ij}(\tau_{ij})$, we can see that τ_{ij} is equal to $V[s_{ij}(\tau_{ij})]$.

Hence,

Theorem 4: Value τ_{pg} of terminal transmission is equal to

$$\tau_{pq} = \mathrm{Min}\{V(s_{pq})\ ;\ S_{pq} \in \{S_{pq}\}\}$$

where $\{S_{pq}\}$ is a collection of all cutsets separating vertices p and q. Note that a cutset separating p and q means that two connected subgraphs g_p and g_q obtained by deleting all edges in the cutset satisfy that $p \in g_p$ and $q \in g_q$.

The proof can be obtained directly form the definition of τ_{pq}. By this theorem, if we calculate $V[s_{ij}(\tau_{ij})]$ for all cutsets in G, we can obtain all values of terminal transmission. As an example, $V[s_{ij}(\tau_{ij})]$ of graph G in Fig. 1 (a) is shown in Fig. 3 from which we can obtain every τ_{pq} as

$\tau_{12} = \mathrm{Min}\ \{V(s_{1,23}),\ V(s_{13,2})\} = \mathrm{Min}\ \{0.63, 0.73\} = 0.63$
$\tau_{13} = \mathrm{Min}\ \{V(s_{1,23}),\ V(s_{12,3})\} = \mathrm{Min}\ \{0.63, 0.73\} = 0.63$
$\tau_{23} = \mathrm{Min}\ \{V(s_{2,13}),\ V(s_{12,3})\} = \mathrm{Min}\ \{0.82, 0.73\} = 0.73$
$\tau_{21} = \mathrm{Min}\ \{V(s_{2,13}),\ V(s_{23,1})\} = \mathrm{Min}\ \{0.82, 0.91\} = 0.82$
$\tau_{31} = \mathrm{Min}\ \{V(s_{3,12}),\ V(s_{23,1})\} = \mathrm{Min}\ \{0.91, 0.91\} = 0.91$
$\tau_{32} = \mathrm{Min}\ \{V(s_{3,12}),\ V(s_{13,2})\} = \mathrm{Min}\ \{0.91, 0.73\} = 0.73$

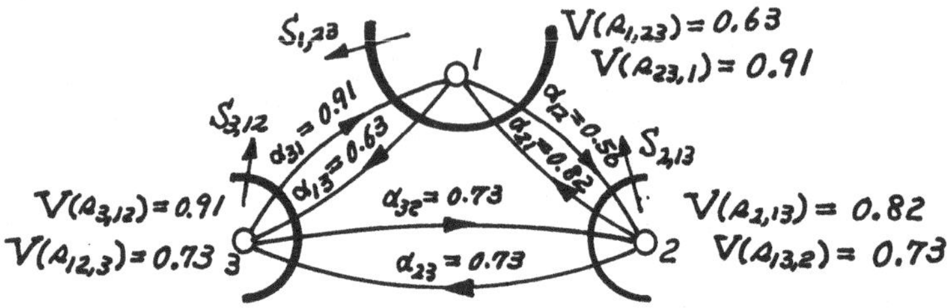

Fig. 3 $V[s_{ij}(\tau_{ij})]$

One way to show all values of terminal transmission is to use a matrix called a terminal transmission matrix symbolized by $T = [\tau_{ij}]$ where

$$\tau_{ij} = \begin{cases} d & \text{for } i = j \\ \text{value of terminal transmission from } i \text{ to } j & \text{for } i \neq j \end{cases}$$

As an example, of a graph in Fig. 1 (a) is

$$T = \begin{array}{c} \\ 1 \\ 2 \\ 3 \end{array} \begin{array}{c} \begin{array}{ccc} 1 & 2 & 3 \end{array} \\ \begin{bmatrix} d & 0.63 & 0.63 \\ 0.82 & d & 0.73 \\ 0.91 & 0.73 & d \end{bmatrix} \end{array}$$

The properties given by those theorems indicate that a terminal transmission matrix has an identical property as a terminal capacity matrix of a communication net[4]. That is, T can be continuously principal partitionable. As an example, T given previously can be continuously partitionable as

$$T = \left[\begin{array}{c|cc} d & 0.63 & 0.63 \\ \hline 0.82 & d & 0.73 \\ \cline{2-3} 0.91 & 0.73 & d \end{array}\right]$$

Determination of Almost Unidirectional Blocks

In order to examine the existance of failure by testing blocks one by one starting from block B_1, then B_2 and so on, undesired signal from a block B_k caused by presence of failure should not influence measurement of block B_j for $j<k$. In other words, value τ_{kj} of terminal transmission from a vertex in B_k to a vertex in B_j should be 0 (or sufficiently small). Hence we need to divide graph G into unidirectional blocks (or almost unidirectional blocks). When unidirectional blocks exist, we can see easily that some of τ_{ij} are 0. Hence

Theorem 5: Unidirectional blocks exist if and only if there exists semicut s whose value V[s] is 0.

Let semicuts s_1, s_2, ..., s_k be those whose value $V(s_r)=0$. Let cutsets S_r correspond to semicut s_r for r=1, 2, ..., k. Then by deleting all edges in these cutsets, graph G will be divided into connected subgraphs. These subgraphs indicate blocks which form a unidirectional blocks.

We can state Theorem 5 differently by the use of a terminal transmission matrix. When a matrix is principally partitioned as

$$\left[\begin{array}{c|c} A & C \\ \hline D & B \end{array}\right]$$

then C is called the resultant upper off diagonal matrix. D is the resultant lower off diagonal matrix and A and B are resultant main diagonal matrices. The name "principal partition" comes because diagonal elements of A and B are diagonal elements of an original matrix. Furthermore all entries of the resultant upper off diagonal matrix consists of identical entry whose value is the smallest among all entries except diagonal elements of given matrix. Continuously principal partition of a matrix means to principal partitioning of a matrix and principal partitioning of all resultant main diagonal matrices produced by previous principal partition. Hence, Theorem 5 can be rewritten as

Theorem 6: If and only if continuously principal partition to a terminal transmission matrix, there are upper off diagonal matrices whose entries are 0, then there exist unidirectional blocks.

As an example, suppose a terminal transmission matrix is principal partitioned as

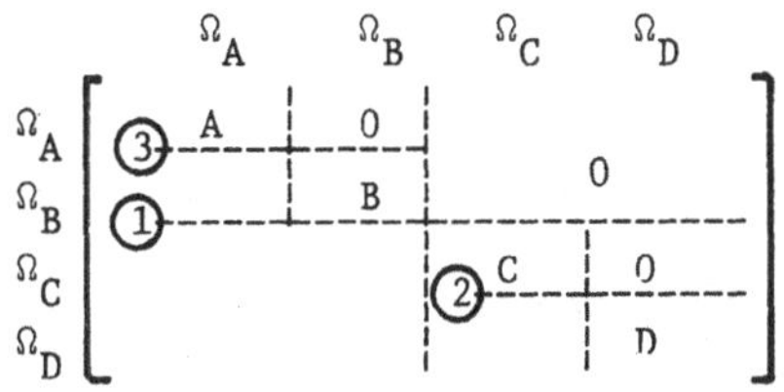

The first principal partition indicated by ① gives cutset S_1. The second principal partition indicated by ② gives cutset S_2 and the third gives S_3. Let g_A be a subgraph containing vertices in Ω_A, g_B be a subgraph containing vertices in Ω_B, g_C containing vertices in Ω_C and g_D containing vertices in Ω_D. It is clear that when all edges in cutsets S_1, S_2 and S_3 are deleted, four connected subgraphs g_A, g_B, g_C and g_D will be produced. It is also clear from partition ① that value τ_{ij} from any vertex i in g_A and g_B to any vertex j in g_C and g_D is 0. Let N_A, N_B, N_C and N_D be corresponding subnetwork of g_A, g_B, g_C and g_D respectively. Then $\tau_{ij}=0$ means that signal from N_A or N_B will not reach to any part of N_C and N_D. Thus we can place blocks N_C and N_D before N_A and N_B to make a sequence of unidirectional blocks. By principal partition ②, we can see that τ_{pq} from any vertex p in g_C to any vertex q in g_D is 0. Similarly, by partition ③, τ_{rs} from any vertex r in g_A to any vertex s in g_B is 0. Thus a sequence of unidirectional blocks is N_D N_C N_B N_A.

The difference between unidirectional blocks and almost unidirectional blocks is that instead of $\tau_{ij}=0$ from a succeeding block to a preceding block, we have $\tau_{ij} = \varepsilon$ where ε is very small. Thus Theorems 5 and 6 can be rewritten for the existance of almost unidirectional blocks by changing 0 to ε. How small ε should be depends on a method of diagnosis.

Conclusion:

Here, we introduce a method of forming unidirectional blocks and almost unidirectional blocks of a network from a corresponding graph consisting of edges which indicate values of transmission. Since value of transmission from node i to node j is not depend only on a component connected between them but depend on almost all components in a network, a corresponding graph does not resemble structually to a given network which would be a disadvantage of this mathod. However, a corresponding graph can be obtained easily by data from suitable measurements. Hence this method may be suitable enough for helping diagnosis of large scale analog networks.

References

1. T.N. Trick, W. Mayeda & A.A. Sakla, "Calculation of Parameter Values from Node Voltage Measurements", IEEE Trans on Circuits and Sys., vol. CAS-26, No. 7, pp 446-473, July 1979.

2. T.N. Trick, W. Mayeda & A.A. Sakla, "Determination of Component Values From Node Voltage Measurements", Proc. of 1979 ISCAS, pp 878-881, July 1979.

3. S. Shinoda, Y. Kajitani, K. Onaga and W. Mayeda, "Various Characterizations of Series-Parallel Graphs", Proc. of 1979 ISCAS, pp 100-103, July 1979.

4. W. Mayeda, Graph Theory, John Wiley & Sons, 1972.

5. K. Onaga & W. Mayeda, "A Boolean Theory of Network Flows and Matrices to particle Transmission and Clustering', Networks, vol 9 pp 249-281, 1979.

A LINEAR ALGORITHM
FOR FIVE-COLORING A PLANAR GRAPH

N. Chiba, T. Nishizeki and N. Saito
Department of Electrical Communications
Faculty of Engineering, Tohoku University
Sendai, Japan 980

Abstract. A simple linear algorithm is presented for coloring planar graphs with at most five colors. The algorithm employs a recursive reduction of a graph involving the deletion of a vertex of degree 6 or less possibly together with the identification of its several neighbors.

1. Introduction

A coloring of a graph is an assignment of colors to the vertices in such a way that adjacent vertices have distinct colors. Although the problem of coloring a graph with the minimal number of colors has practical applications in some schedulings [1], it is known to be NP-complete even for the class of planar graphs [3].

We present here a linear algorithm for finding a coloring of a planar graph with at most five colors, that is, 5-coloring. We denote by n the number of vertices of a graph throughout this paper. Based on the well-known Kempe-chain argument, one can easily design an $O(n^2)$ time algorithm for the purpose by employing a simple recursive reduction of a graph involving the deletion of a vertex of degree 5 or less possibly together with the interchange of colors in a two-colored subgraph. Lipton and Miller have given an O(nlogn) algorithm for the problem by removing a "batch" of vertices rather than just a single vertex [4]. Their algorithm and its proof are a little complicated. In this paper we give a simple linear algorithm for the purpose. The algorithm does not use the Kempe-chain argument, but uses a recursive reduction of a graph involving the deletion of a vertex of degree 6 or less possibly together with the identification of several neighbors of the vertex. We prove that the algorithm runs in O(n) time. Hence the computational complexity of our algorithm is optimal within a constant factor.

2. Outline of the algorithm

We first define some terms. Let G=(V,E) be a graph with vertex set V and edge set E. We consider only a simple graph G, that is, a graph with no multiple edges or loops. A graph G is planar if it is embedable in the plane without edge crossing. The neighborhood N(v) of a vertex v is the set of all vertices which are adjacent to v. The degree d(v) of a vertex v of G is the number of vertices adjacent to v. The deletion of a vertex v is an operation on G which delete v together with all the edges incident to v, and the resulting graph is denoted by G-v. Let u and v be two vertices of a graph G. A vertex-identification (or simply identification) ⟨u,v⟩ is an operation on G which identifies u and v, that is, removes u and v and adds a new vertex adjacent to those vertices to which u or v was adjacent. Our algorithm frequently uses these operations in recursive reductions of graphs.

The outline of the algorithm is as follows. Suppose that G is a given planar graph. We construct a new planar (simple) graph G' from G by deleting a vertex v of degree 6 or less possibly together with some other modifications, and then color G' with 5 colors by recursively applying the algorithm. We extend the 5-coloring of G' to a 5-coloring of G by assigning to v a color not used to vertices in N(v). In order to guarantee that there remains such a color, we construct G' so that G' contains only four vertices in N(v), as follows. If v is of degree 4 or less, then we simply set G'=G-v. If v is of degree 5, then we construct G' from G-v by identifying a pair of nonadjacent vertices in N(v). Note that there exist such a pair of vertices since G is planar (see Lemma 1), and that the resulting planar graph G' has no loops. The pair of vertices of G will be assigned the same color as the vertex substituting for them in G'. Finally, if v is of degree 6, then we construct a planar graph G' from G-v by identifying either three pairwise nonadjacent vertices in N(v) or two pairs of nonadjacent vertices in N(v). Lemma 2 in Section 3 guarantees that there exist such vertices. Note that we must select two pairs of vertices appropriately so that G' is planar.

We use adjacency lists to represent a graph G. All the operations in the algorithm, other than vertex-deletions or vertex-identifications, require O(n) time in total. Clearly the deletion of a single vertex v requires O(d(v)) time. Therefore all the vertex deletions used in the algorithm require at most O(n) time in total, since $\Sigma_{v \in V} d(v) \leq 6n$. Hence we should implement the algorithm so that all the vertex-identifications require O(n) time in total. One can easily execute the single identification of vertices u and v in O(d(u)+d(v)) time, that is, one can modify the adjacency lists of G in that amount of time so that the resulting lists represent a new graph obtained from G by identifying u and v. However the same vertex may appear in identifications O(n) times, so a direct implementation of the algorithm would require $O(n^2)$ time. As we describe the detailes in the following section, the algorithm runs in several stages, in each of which we do the recursive reductions as far as any vertex would not be involved in more than two of identifications, so that the stage requires at most O(n) time. An argument in Section 4 will show that the resulting graph G' at the end of a stage has a positive fraction of vertices at the beginning of the stage. From these facts it will be shown that the algorithm requires O(n) time in total.

Remark We have given a simple "on-line" algorithm to execute any sequence of vertex-identifications of a graph G=(V,E) in O(|E|log|V|) time, by using adjacency lists together with an adjacency matrix [2]. It yields an alternative simple O(nlogn) 5-coloring algorithm of planar graphs.

3. 5-coloring algorithm

In this section we present the linear algorithm for coloring planar graphs with at most five colors. We first have the following lemmas.

LEMMA 1. Let a planar graph G=(V,E) contain a vertex v of degree 5 with $N(v)=\{v_1,v_2,v_3,v_4,v_5\}$. Then, for any specified $v_i \in N(v)$, there exists a pair of nonadjacent vertices v_j and v_k, $j,k \neq i$. Furthermore one can find such a pair in $O(\mathrm{MIN}_{v \in N(v)-v_i} d(v))$ time if the planar embedding of G is given.

Proof. We can assume without loss of generality that $v_i = v_1$, and that the vertices v_1, v_2, v_3, v_4 and v_5 in $N(v)$ are labeled clockwise about v in the plane embedding of G. Consider the case in which $d(v_2)$ is minimum among $d(v_2)$, $d(v_3)$, $d(v_4)$ and $d(v_5)$. Scanning all the elements in the adjacency list for v_2, one can know whether $(v_2, v_4) \in E$ or not. If $(v_2, v_4) \in E$, then $(v_3, v_5) \notin E$. Thus one can find a pair of nonadjacent vertices in $O(d(v_2))$ time. The proof for all the remaining cases is similar to above. Q.E.D.

Lemma 1 implies that for a vertex v of degree 5 one can always find a pair of nonadjacent vertices v_j and v_k in N(v) both of which have not been involved in vertex-identifications even if N(v) contains a vertex v_i involved in a vertex-identification so far.

LEMMA 2. Let a planar graph G=(V,E) contain a vertex v of degree 6 with $N(v) = \{v_1, v_2, \ldots, v_6\}$. Then N(v) contains either

(i) three pairwise nonadjacent vertices,

or (ii) two pairs of nonadjacent vertices v_i, v_j and v_k, v_ℓ such that the identification $\langle v_i, v_j \rangle$ together with $\langle v_k, v_\ell \rangle$ does not destroy the planarity of G-v.

Furthermore one can find these vertices in $O(\mathrm{MIN}_{1 \leq s < t \leq 5}[d(v_s)+d(v_t)])$ time if the planar embedding of G is given.

Proof. Assume that the vertices $v_1, v_2, \ldots, v_6$ in N(v) are labeled clockwise about v in the plane embedding of G. The identifications of two "cross-over" pairs of vertices in N(v), such as v_2, v_5 and v_3, v_6, may destroy the planarity of G-v, since v_3 and v_6 possibly donot lie on the boundary of a common face when v_2 is identified with v_5 in G-v. However the identifications of two "parallel" pairs, such as v_2, v_6 and v_3, v_5, necessarily preserve the planarity of G-v. We establish our claim only for the case in which $d(v_1)+d(v_2)$ is minimum among all the sums of degrees of two vertices in N(v), since the proof for all the remaining cases is similar. Scanning all the elements of the adjacency lists for v_1 and for v_2, one can know whether the edges (v_1, v_5) and (v_2, v_4) exist or not. If exactly one of them, say (v_1, v_5), exists, then v_2, v_4 and v_6 are the required three pairwise nonadjacent vertices. Otherwise, v_2, v_6 and v_3, v_5 (if both (v_1, v_5) and (v_2, v_4) exist) or v_2, v_4 and v_1, v_5 (if neither exists) are the required two "parallel" pairs of nonadjacent vertices in N(v). Thus one can find the required vertices in $O(d(v_1)+d(v_2))$ time. Q.E.D.

As a data structure to represent a graph G, we use an adjacency list L(v) for each $v \in V$. Each adjacency list is doubly linked. The two copies of each edge (u,v), one in L(u) and the other in L(v), are also doubly linked. In addition to L, we use four arrays FLAG, COUNT, DEG and DP together with three queues Q(i), $4 \le i \le 6$. An element DEG(v) of array DEG contains the value of d(v), $v \in V$. FLAG(v) has an initial value "false" at the beginning of each stage of the algorithm, and will be set to "true" when v is identified with another vertex. COUNT(v) contains the number of vertices $w \in N(v)$ with FLAG(w)=true, that is, the number of vertices in N(v) involved in vertex-identifications in the current stage so far. The queue Q(i), $4 \le i \le 6$, contains all the vertices which are available for the recursive reduction of the stage, defined as follows:

$Q(4)=\{v \mid DEG(v) \le 4\}$;

$Q(5)=\{v \mid DEG(v)=5, COUNT(v) \le 1\}$; and

$Q(6)=\{v \mid DEG(v)=6, COUNT(v)=0\}$.

That is, Q(4) is the set of all the vertices of degree 4 or less, Q(5) the set of all the vertices of degree 5 with at most one neighbor involved in an identification in the stage, and Q(6) the set of all the vertices of degree 6 with no neighbors involved in any identification in the stage. DP(v) has a pointer to an element "v" in Q(i) if v is contained in Q(i). We are now ready to present the algorithm.

```
procedure FIVE;
    comment The procedures DELETE and IDENTIFY are for the
    vertex-deletion and the vertex-identification, respectively;
    procedure COLOR(G);
      begin
         if |V|≤5 then assign |V| colors to |V| vertices
         else
          begin
           if Q(4)≠∅
              then begin
                     take a top entry v from Q(4);
                     DELETE(v);
                     let G' be the reduced graph
                   end
              else
                if Q(5)≠∅
                   then begin
```

```
                    take a top entry v from Q(5);
                    choose two nonadjacent vertices
                    x,y∈N(v) such that
                    FLAG(x)=FLAG(y)=false;
                    DELETE(v);
                    IDENTIFY(x,y);
                    let G' be the reduced graph
                  end
              else
               if Q(6)≠∅
                 then
                  begin
                   take a top entry v from Q(6);
                   comment By Lemma 2 either
                   case (i) or case (ii) holds;
                   for case (i) do
                     begin
                       let x,y and z be the three pairwise
                       nonadjacent vertices in N(v);
                       DELETE(v);
                       IDENTIFY(y,x);
                       IDENTIFY(z,x)
                     end;
                   for case (ii) do
                     begin
                       let v_i,v_j and v_k,v_ℓ be the two
                       "parallel" pairs of nonadjacent vertices
                       in N(v);
                       DELETE(v);
                       IDENTIFY(v_i,v_j);
                       IDENTIFY(v_k,v_ℓ)
                     end;
                   let G' be the reduced graph
                  end
                else
                  begin
                    comment Current stage is over. Reset FLAG
                            and COUNT;
                    for v∈V do begin FLAG(v):=false;
                                     COUNT(v):=0 end;
                    COLOR(G)
                  end;
          COLOR(G');
          assign to v a color not used in the coloring of N(v),
          and to each identified vertex of G the color of the
          vertex substituting for it in G';
          comment Note that the number of colors used in the
          coloring of N(v) is at most 4
      end
   end

   begin
     embed a given planar graph G in the plane;
     for v∈V do
       begin
         calculate DEG(v);
         FLAG(v):=false;
         COUNT(v):=0
       end;
     COLOR(G)
   end
```

```
procedure DELETE(v);
 begin
  for w∈L(v) do
       begin
         delete w from L(v);
         delete v from L(w);
         DEG(w):=DEG(w)-1;
         if FLAG(v)=true
            then COUNT(w):=COUNT(w)-1;
       end;
  delete L(v) from the adjacency lists and "v" from Q(i), i=4,5 or
  6, if any, and update appropriately the elements in Q(i)
  according to the modifications of DEG and COUNT above
 end


procedure IDENTIFY(u,v);
  comment This procedure executes the identification <u,v> of two
  nonadjacent vertices u and v such that either FLAG(u) or FLAG(v)
  is "false". We assume FLAG(u)=false without loss of generality.
  The vertex v will act as a new vertex substituting for u and old
  v;
  begin
   if FLAG(v)=false
           then begin
                  FLAG(v):=true;
                  for w∈L(v) do COUNT(w):=COUNT(w)+1
                end;
   for w∈L(v) do mark w with "v";
   for w∈L(u) do
           begin
             delete w from L(u); delete u from L(w);
             if w has no mark "v"
                then begin
                       comment w is adjacent to u, but not to
                       v;
                       add w to L(v); add v to L(w);
                       DEG(v):=DEG(v)+1;
                       COUNT(w):=COUNT(w)+1;
                       if FLAG(w)=true
                          then COUNT(v):=COUNT(v)+1
                     end
                else begin
                       comment w is adjacent to both u and v;
                       DEG(w):=DEG(w)-1
                     end
           end;
      delete L(u) from the adjacency lists and "u" from Q(i),
      i=4,5 or 6, if any, and update appropriately the elements in
      Q(i), i=4,5,6, according to the above modifications of DEG
      and COUNT
  end
```

In the algorithm above we omit the detail of the method for obtaining the planar embedding of G' from that of G, since clearly the time required for the purpose is propotional to that for the vertex-deletions and identifications.

4. Time complexity

In this section, we establish the following theorem.

THEOREM. The procedure FIVE colors a planar graph $G=(V,E)$ with at most five colors in $O(n)$ time, where $n=|V|$.

We first present the following lemma before establishing the Theorem. The lemma implies that at the end of each stage of the algorithm a positive fraction, say 1/12, of the remaining vertices have been involved in vertex-identifications.

LEMMA 3. Let $G=(V,E)$ be a planar graph with minimum degree 5, and let S be a subset of V. If every vertex of degree 5 is adjacent to at least two vertices in S, and every vertex of degree 6 is adjacent to at least one vertex in S, then $|S| \geq n/12$.

Proof. Define $V_5=\{v|d(v)=5, v\in V\}$, $V_6=\{v|d(v)=6, v\in V\}$, and $V_*=\{v|d(v)\geq 7, v\in V\}$ so that $V=V_5\cup V_6\cup V_*$, and let $p_5=|V_5|$, $p_6=|V_6|$, and $p_*=|V_*|$. Define $S_5=S\cap V_5$, $S_6=S\cap V_6$ and $S_*=S\cap V_*$ so that $S=S_5\cup S_6\cup S_*$, and let $r_5=|S_5|$, $r_6=|S_6|$, and $r_*=|S_*|$.

By Euler's formula $|E| \leq 3n$, we have

$$5p_5+6p_6+\Sigma_{v\in V_*}d(v) \leq 6(p_5+p_6+p_*).$$

Hence we have

$$p_5 \geq \Sigma_{v\in V_*}(d(v)-6) \geq p_*. \tag{1}$$

Since $n=p_5+p_6+p_*$, we have from (1)

$$p_5+p_6 \geq n/2. \tag{2}$$

We furthermore have from (1)

$$p_5 \geq \Sigma_{v\in S_*}d(v)-6r_*. \tag{3}$$

Since every vertex of degree 5 is adjacent to at least two vertices in S, and every vertex of degree 6 is adjacent to at least one vertex in S, we have

$$\Sigma_{v\in S}d(v) \geq 2p_5+p_6. \tag{4}$$

On the other hand we have

$$\Sigma_{v\in S}d(v) \leq 6(r_5+r_6)+\Sigma_{v\in S_*}d(v). \tag{5}$$

Combining (4) and (5), we have

$$2p_5+p_6 \le 6(r_5+r_6)+\Sigma_{v\in S_*}d(v). \qquad (6)$$

By (3) and (6),

$$2p_5+p_6 \le 6(r_5+r_6)+p_5+6r_*=6|S|+p_5,$$

and hence

$$|S| \ge (p_5+p_6)/6.$$

Therefore we have $|S| \ge n/12$ by (2), as desired. Q.E.D.

We are now ready to prove the Theorem.

Proof of the Theorem. Noting that the reduced graph G' of a planar graph G is a planar simple graph smaller than G, we can easily prove by induction on the number of vertices of a graph that the algorithm correctly colors a planar graph G with at most 5 colors. Hence we shall show that the algorithm runs in O(n) time.

We first show that the first stage of the algorithm requires at most O(n) time. One can easily verify that the procedure DELETE executes the deletion of a vertex v in O(d(v)) time, and that the procedure IDENTIFY does the identification of two nonadjacent vertices u and w in O(d(u)+d(w)) time since it simply scans the elements of L(u) and L(w). The algorithm calls DELETE for a vertex in each reduction. Since every vertex appears in at most one vertex-deletion, all the vertex-deletions in the stage require O(n) time in total. Consider a reduction around a vertex v of degree 5 or 6, in which IDENTIFY is called in addition to DELETE. If v is in Q(5), the algorithm finds two neighbors v_i and v_j of v with $FLAG(v_i)=FLAG(v_j)=false$, and then calls $IDENTIFY(v_i,v_j)$. The identification requires $O(d(v_i)+d(v_j))$ time. Lemma 1 implies that one can find v_i and v_j in that amount of time. If v is in Q(6), the algorithm finds either three pairwise nonadjacent vertices x,y and z or two pairs of nonadjacent vertices v_i,v_j and v_k,v_ℓ, and then calls IDENTIFY(y,x) and IDENTIFY(z,x) or $IDENTIFY(v_i,v_j)$ and $IDENTIFY(v_k,v_\ell)$, respectively. These two identifications together require O(d(x)+d(y)+d(z)) or $O(d(v_i)+d(v_j)+d(v_k)+d(v_\ell))$ time, respectively. Lemma 2 implies that one can find these vertices in that amount of time. Of course, FLAG's for these vertices are all "false", since COUNT(v)=0. That is, all these vertices have not been involved in any vertex-identification in the stage. Thus every vertex is involved in at most two identifications in the stage. (The vertex x above is possibly involved in two identifications.) Therefore all the identifications in the stage require O(n) time in total. Clearly the book-keeping operations required for the four arrays and three queues need O(n) time in total. Note that one can directly access "v" via a pointer in DP(v). Hence we can conclude that the stage requires O(n) time.

We next show that at the end of the first stage the reduced graph $G'=(V',E')$ contains at most $8n/9$ vertices. Suppose that $|V'|=n'\neq 0$. Then the minimum degree of G' is 5, and $COUNT(v) \geq 2$ for every vertex v of degree 5, and $COUNT(v) \geq 1$ for every vertex of degree 6, since Q(4),Q(5) and Q(6) are all empty at the end of the stage. Let $S=\{v|FLAG(v)=true, v\in V'\}$ so that the subset S of V' satisfies the requirement of Lemma 3, then we have $|S| \geq n'/12$. Clearly at least $|S|$ vertices disappear from the graph G by vertex-identifications. Since each reduction produces at most two vertices in S, there must occur at least $|S|/2$ graph reductions around vertices of degree 5 or 6 in the stage. Therefore at least $|S|/2$ vertices are deleted from G by vertex-deletions in the stage. Hence at least $3|S|/2$ vertices disappear from G in the stage. Therefore we have

$$n-n' \geq 3|S|/2$$

Since $|S| \geq n'/12$, we have

$$n' \leq 8n/9.$$

Using the two facts above, we have the following equations on T(n) the number of steps (or time) needed to 5-color a planar graph G of n vertices:

$$\begin{cases} T(n) \leq c_1 & \text{if } n \leq 5; \\ T(n) \leq T(8n/9)+c_2 n & \text{otherwise,} \end{cases}$$

where c_1 and c_2 are constants. Solving these equations, we have $T(n)=O(n)$. Q.E.D.

Acknowledgement. We wish to thank Dr. T. Asano for his valuable suggestions and discussions on the subjects. This work was partly supported by the Grant in Aid for Scientific Research of the Ministry of Education, Science and Culture of Japan under Grant: Cooperative Research (A) 435013 (1980).

REFERENCES

[1] B. Carre, Graphs and Network, Clarendon Press, Oxford, 1979.

[2] N. Chiba, T. Nishizeki and N. Saito, An Approximation Algorithm for the Maximum Independent Set Problem on Planar Graphs, submitted to SIAM J. on Comput., 1980.

[3] M. R. Garey, D. S. Jhonson and L. Stockmeyer, Some simplified NP-complete graph problems, Theor. Comput. Sci. 1, 237-267, 1976.

[4] R. J. Lipton and R. E. Miller, A batching method for coloring planar graphs, Information Processing Letters, 7,4, 185-188, 1978.

ON THE LAYERING PROBLEM OF MULTILAYER PWB WIRING*

S. Tsukiyama†, E. S. Kuh††, and I. Shirakawa†

† Department of Electronic Engineering, Faculty of Engineering
Osaka University, Suita, Osaka 565, Japan

†† Department of Electrical Engineering and Computer Sciences
and Electronics Research Laboratory
University of California, Berkeley, CA 94720, U.S.A.

Abstract: This paper deals with the layering problem of multilayer PWB wiring, associated with single-row routing. The problem to be considered is restricted to the special case of street capacities up to two in each layer, and it is reduced to a problem of the interval graph by relaxing some restrictions in the original problem. Then, a heuristic algorithm is proposed for this problem.

1. Introduction

The single-row routing[1-4], first introduced for the backboard wiring[1], has been one of the fundamental routing methods for the multilayer high density printed wiring boards (PWB's)[5-7], due to "topological fluidity," that is, the capability to defer detailed wire patterns until all connections have been considered[6]. In the single-row routing, it is assumed that the multilayer board has fixed geometries; that is, the positions of pins and vias are restricted on nodes of a rectangular grid. Associated with this single-row routing the following problems are formulated: [Via-Assignment Problem]; to determine which vias are assigned for each net[7-9], [Layering Problem]; to decompose the interconnections on a single-row into the portions of each layer, and [Single-Row, Single-Layer Routing]; to lay out wire pattern on each layer[1-4].

Recent advance in the technology of microelectronics have changed the design rule for PWB's in such a way that the total amount of design for PWB's of four or more signal layers tends to grow rapidly, and hence

* This work was supported in part by the Grant in Aid for Scientific Research of the Ministry of Education, Science, and Culture of Japan under Grant: Cooperative Research (A) 435013 (1980).

the layering problem is of central importance. However, no specific development has been reported on this problem.

To attack the layering problem, we first have to seek a necessary and sufficient condition for a given net list to be realized by the single-row single-layer routing with the prescribed upper and lower street capacities. Concerning this, a specific development has been recently accomplished[3,4], and especially in the case of the upper and lower street capacities up to two, a necessary and sufficient condition is obtained[4], which can be easily checked. Noting that the case in which four etch paths are permitted to be laid out between two consecutive pins of an ordinary dual in line package corresponds to the single-row routing with the upper and lower street capacities both equal to two[7], we may assume that the upper and lower street capacities are up to two in each layer.

Thus, in this paper, we pay our attention to the layering problem such that in each layer the interconnections must be realized by single-row routing with the street capacities equal to two.

2. Difinitions and Formulation

Consider a set $\{v_1,v_2,\cdots,v_r\}$ of r nodes on the real line R, each of which corresponds to a pin or a via. A set of nodes on R to be interconnected is referred to as a net, and a set of nets is designated as a net list.

Given a net list $L=\{N_1,N_2,\cdots,N_n\}$ on R, the interconnection for each net N_i is to be realized by means of a set of paths on a certain number of layers, such that on each layer a path is constructed of horizontal and vertical line segments according to specifications. For example, consider a net list L as shown in Fig. 1 (a), where each net is represented by a horizontal line segment and each node denoted by a circle (note here that there exist nodes which are not used for any net). The interconnections of these nets using one layer are realized as shown in Fig. 1 (b). This way of realization for a given net list L on R is called single-row (in this example, single-layer) routing[1,2], where upward and downward zigzagging is allowed, but not forward and backward zigzagging.

In a realization, the space above the real line R on a layer is designated as the upper street on the layer, and the one below R as the lower street on the layer. The number of horizontal tracks available in the upper (lower) street on a layer is called the upper (lower) street

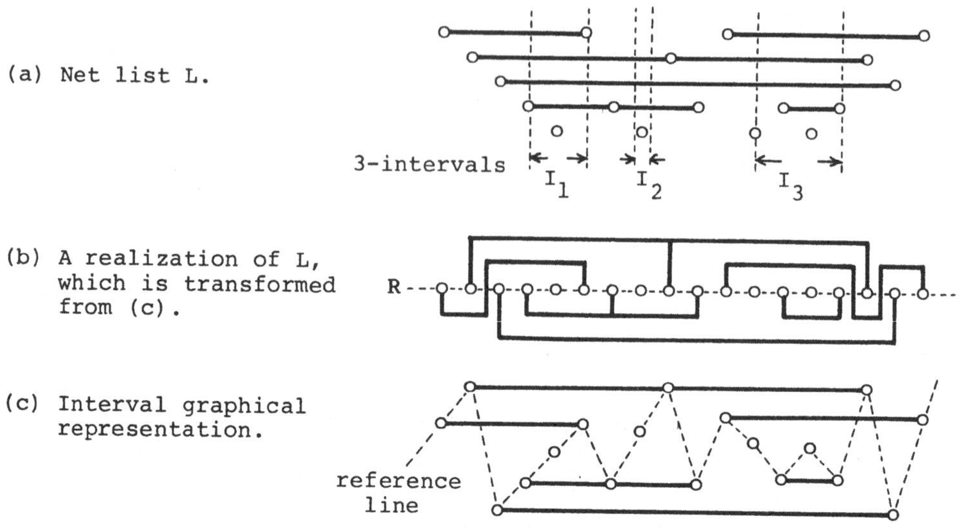

Fig. 1 Single-row single-layer routing.

capacity on the layer. For example, if both the upper and lower street capacities are specified as two, then a net list L of Fig. 1 (a) can be realized on a sigle layer, as shown in Fig. 1 (b).

Using these terms, the problem to be considered in this paper is stated as follows: Given a net list L defined for r nodes on the real line R, and integers K_u and K_w, find a partition of L into the minimum number of subsets $L_1, L_2, \cdots, L_\ell$ such that each L_i $(i=1,2,\cdots,\ell)$ can be realized by single-row single-layer routing with the upper and lower street capacities K_u and K_w, respectively.

2.1 Single-Layer Case

In order to consider the layering problem stated above, we need a necessary and sufficient condition for each such L_i to be realized with prescribed street capacities on a sigle layer. Let us consider this in the following.

The single-row single-layer routing problem can be formulated with the use of the interval graphical representation[3,4]. For example, given a net list L of Fig. 1 (a), consider an ordered sequence s of nets of L and nodes not used for any net, then the interval graphical representation associated with s is dipicted as in Fig. 1 (c), where each horizontal line segment represents the interval covered by a net, and such line segments and nodes not used for any net are arranged according to the order in s.

In an interval graphical representation, let us define the <u>reference line</u>[3] as the continuous line segments which connect the nodes in succession from left to right. For example, in Fig. 1 (c), the reference line is shown by broken lines.

Now, let us stretch out the reference line and map it into the real line R. Associated with this topological mapping, let each interval line be transformed into a path composed of horizontal and vertical line segments so that the portions above and below the refernce line correspond to paths in the upper and lower streets, respectively. Then, this topological mapping yields a realization of a given net list. For example, by this topological transformation for the interval graphical representation of Fig. 1 (c), we obtain a realization as shown in Fig. 1 (b).

Let $I=[v_i,v_j]$ $(i \le j)$ denote a closed interval between nodes v_i and v_j. Given an interval graphical representation, let us draw a vertical line at an inner point on interval $[v_i,v_{i+1}]$, and let us define the <u>density</u> $d(v_i,v_{i+1})$ as the number of interval lines cut by the vertical line[1,2]. Similarly, draw a vertical line at a node v_i, then define the <u>cut number</u> $c(v_i)$ as the number of interval lines cut by the vertical line, ignoring the one to which v_i belongs[2,3].

Let an interval $I=[v_i,v_j]$ such that $c(v_k) \ge h$ for all v_k on I and $c(v_{i-1}) = c(v_{j+1}) = h-1$, be referred to as an <u>h-interval</u>. For an interval $I=[v_i,v_j]$, let $\bar{L}(I)$ denote a set of nets which have no node on I, but have two nodes v_a and v_b such that $a < i$ and $j < b$; and let L(I) represent the union of $\bar{L}(I)$ and a set of nets having nodes on I.

By using the interval graphical representation, we can obtain necessary and sufficient conditions for a given net list to be realized with the upper and lower street capacities K_u and K_w[3,4]. However, only in the case of both K_u and K_w up to two, a simple necessary and sufficient condition is known[4], which is derived on the assumption that

(1) every net of a given net list contains at least two nodes,

(2) every nodes belongs to a net, and

(3) any net does not contain a pair of consecutive nodes v_i and v_{i+1}.

However, in the layering problem, there may possibly exist a node which does not belong to any net of subset L_i. Thus, the assumption of (2) is not satisfied in this case, and hence it should be removed.

Based on the necessary and sufficient condition derived in [4] on the assumption of (1), (2), and (3), we can describe another one when assumption (2) is removed, as follows.

THEOREM: A necessary and sufficient condition for a given net list L to be realized with the upper and lower street capacities K_u and K_w is as follows:

CASE A: $0 \le K_u + K_w \le 2$ $(0 \le K_u, K_w \le 1)$.

The maximum density $d_M \triangleq \max_{1 \le j < r} [\, d(v_j, v_{j+1}) \,]$ is not greater than $K_u + K_w$.

CASE B: $3 \le K_u + K_w \le 4$ $(1 \le K_u, K_w \le 2)$.

i) $d_M \le K_u + K_w$.

ii) For any (K_u+K_w-1)-interval I, $|\bar{L}(I)| \ge K_u + K_w - 2$.

iii) There do not exist two (K_u+K_w-1)-intervals I_1 and I_2 such that

$|\bar{L}(I_1)| = |\bar{L}(I_2)| = K_u + K_w - 2$,

$|L(I_1) \cap L(I_2)| = K_u + K_w - 1$, and

$\bar{L}(I_1) \ne \bar{L}(I_2)$.

Proof: The condition in CASE A can be easily verified, and henceforth we shall consider CASE B. The necessity of the conditions (i), (ii), and (iii) can be proved in a similar way as in [4]. Thus, the sufficiency is to be shown in the follwoing:

Let L be a net list satisfying conditions (i), (ii), and (iii), and let $L_{(2)}$ be a net list obtained from L by applying the following two operations repeatedly as far as possible.

[I] Delete every node not belonging to a net.

[II] Delete any one of two consecutive nodes which are contained in the same net.

Then, we can see that $L_{(2)}$ satisfies the assumption (1), (2), and (3), and also satisfies the necessary and sufficient condition for the realizability derived in [4]. Therefore, $L_{(2)}$ can be realized with the upper and lower street capacities K_u and K_w, respectively. Thus, the remaining task that we have to show is that from any realization of $L_{(2)}$ with the street capacities K_u and K_w, we can construct a realization of L with these street capacities, by adding nodes and nets deleted in the transformation from L to $L_{(2)}$. However, this can be easily done through the use of the condition (i), and the details are ommitted.

q.e.d.

For example, the net list shown in Fig. 1 (a) has three 3-intervals I_1, I_2, and I_3, and satisfies this necessary and sufficient condition. Thus, it has a realization with both the upper and lower street capacities equal to 2, as depicted in Fig. 1 (b).

2.2 Layering Problem

As can be verified from this theorem, it is easy to partition a given net list L into $L_1, L_2, \cdots, L_\ell$ so that each L_i can be realized with the upper and lower street capacities up to one. Thus, we shall pay attention to the layering problem in the case of $K_u = K_w = 2$, as follows.

[Layering Problem]: Given a net list L defined for r nodes on the real line R, find a partition of L into the minimum number of subsets $L_1, L_2, \cdots, L_\ell$ such that each L_i $(i = 1, 2, \cdots, \ell)$ satisfies the following conditions;

C1: the maximum density $d_M^i \le 4$,

C2: for each 3-interval I, $|\overline{L}_i(I)| \ge 2$, and

C3: there do not exist two 3-intervals I_1 and I_2 with $|\overline{L}_i(I_1)| = |\overline{L}_i(I_2)| = 2$, $|L_i(I_1) \cap L_i(I_2)| = 3$, and $\overline{L}_i(I_1) \ne \overline{L}_i(I_2)$,

where $\overline{L}_i(I)$ and $L_i(I)$ are defined for net list L_i similarly to $\overline{L}(I)$ and $L(I)$, respectively.

Note here that the discussion for the case of $K_u = K_w = 2$ can be applied to the case of $K_u = 2$ and $K_w = 1$ with a slight modification, since the realizability condition in both cases are quite similar.

Let d_M be the maximum density of a given net list, then from condition C1, we have $\ell \ge \lceil d_M/4 \rceil$ where $\lceil x \rceil$ denotes an integer not less than x. On the other hand, if we partition a given net list L into subsets L_i such that each L_i has the maximum density equal to or less than 3, then each L_i satisfies C2 and C3 automatically. Thus, we have

$$\lceil d_M/4 \rceil \le \ell \le \lceil d_M/3 \rceil .$$

Namely, at least $\lceil d_M/4 \rceil$ layers are necessary, and at most $\lceil d_M/3 \rceil$ layers are sufficient to realize a net list under the constraint that both the upper and lower street capacities in each layer are equal to 2.

3. Simplifications of the Problem

Since this Layering Problem seems too hard to be solved in its original form, we may have to simplify the problem. In the folowing, we relax conditions C2 and C3 so that the Layering Problem can be reduced to another one in terms of the so-called interval graph[10].

SIMPLIFICATION I: We first transform a given net list L into another L' such that each net of L' contains exactly two nodes, as follows: For each net N_a of L with more than two nodes $v_{a_1}, v_{a_2}, \cdots, v_{a_k}$ ($a_i < a_j$ for $i < j$), split each v_{a_j} $(1 < j < k)$ into two nodes $v_{a_j}^-$ and $v_{a_j}^+$ such that $v_{a_j}^-$ is located at an inner point on $[v_{a_j - 1}, v_{a_j}]$ and $v_{a_j}^+$ is located at an inner point on $[v_{a_j}, v_{a_j+1}]$, and replace N_a by k-1 nets N_{a_1}, $N_{a_2}, \cdots$, $N_{a_{k-1}}$ such that $N_{a_j} = \{ v_{a_j}^-, v_{a_{j+1}}^+ \}$ (let $v_{a_1}^- = v_{a_1}$ and $v_{a_k}^+ = v_{a_k}$).

By this transformation, we can disregard condition C3 in the Layering Problem, since any such L' does not have two 3-intervals I_1 and I_2 such that $|L'(I_1) \cap L'(I_2)| = 3$. Note here that the maximum density d_M' of L' increases by at most one from the maximum density d_M of L, i.e., $d_M' \le d_M + 1$. Moreover, we have the following proposition.

Proposition 1: If a subset L_i' of L' satisfies conditions C1 and C2, then the subset L_i of L, which is obtained from L_i' by merging every pair of splitted nodes v_j^- and v_j^+ into the original node v_j, satisfies conditions C1, C2, and C3.

Proof: To prove the proposition, we have only to show that the subset L_i of L can be realized with the upper and lower street capacities both equal to two. Since a subset L_i' of L' satisfying conditions C1 and C2 satisfies condition C3 automatically, L_i' can be realized with the upper and lower street capacities both equal to two. Therefore, there exists an interval graphical representation of L_i', which yields a realization of L_i' with these street capacities by means of the topological mapping stated in Section 2.1. From this interval graphical representation, we can construct an interval graphical representation of L_i which yields a realization of L_i with the upper and lower street capacities both equal to two, as follows.

[a] In the case of $d(v_j^-, v_j^+) = 2$, the interval graphical representation of L_i' can be divided into two portions as illustrated in Fig. 2 (a). Merge v_j^- and v_j^+, and we can obtain a required interval graphical representation of L_i.

[b] In the case of $d(v_j^-, v_j^+) = 3$, suppose that two nets containing v_j^- and v_j^+ are adjacent in the interval graphical representation of L_i'. Then, merge v_j^- and v_j^+ as illustrated in Fig. 2 (b), and we can obtain a required interval graphical representation of L_i.

[c] In the case of $d(v_j^-, v_j^+) = 3$, suppose that two nets containing v_j^- and v_j^+ are not adjacent in the interval graphical representation of L_i'. Turn upside down the sequence of nets in the right-hand portion and merge v_j^- and v_j^+, as illustrated in Fig. 2 (c). Then, we can obtain a required interval graphical represenation of L_i.

[d] In the case of $d(v_j^-, v_j^+) = 4$, there exists an interval graphical representation of L_i' in which two nets containing v_j^- and v_j^+ are adjacent, as illustrated in Fig. 2 (d). Merge v_j^- and v_j^+, and we can obtain a required interval graphical representation of L_i. q.e.d.

Thus, our problem is to find a partition of L' into subsets L_i' such that each subset L_i' satisfies conditions C1 and C2. Henceforth, unless

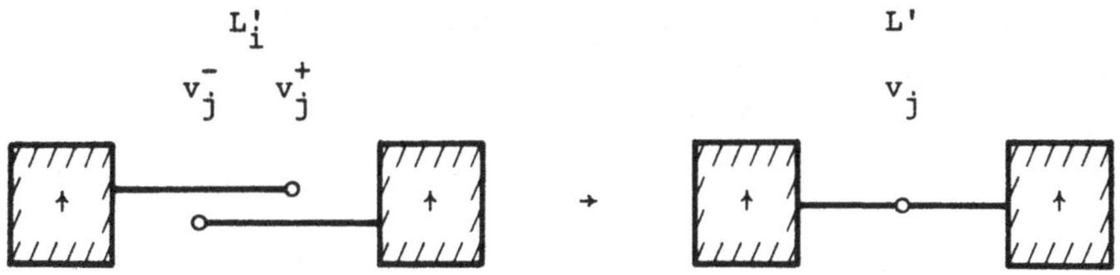

(a) The case of $d(v_j^-,v_j^+) = 2$.

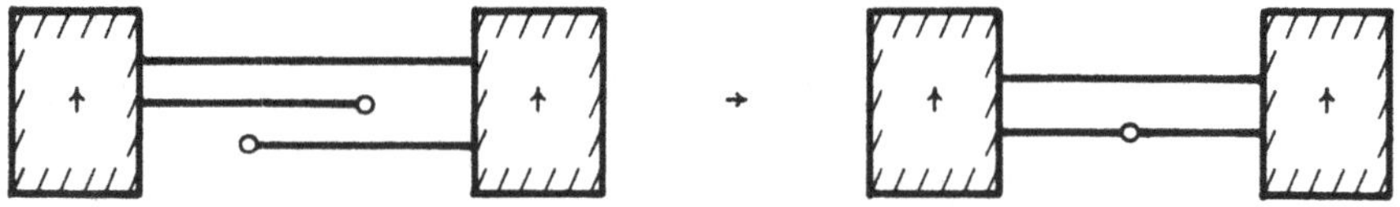

(b) The case of $d(v_j^-,v_j^+) = 3$.

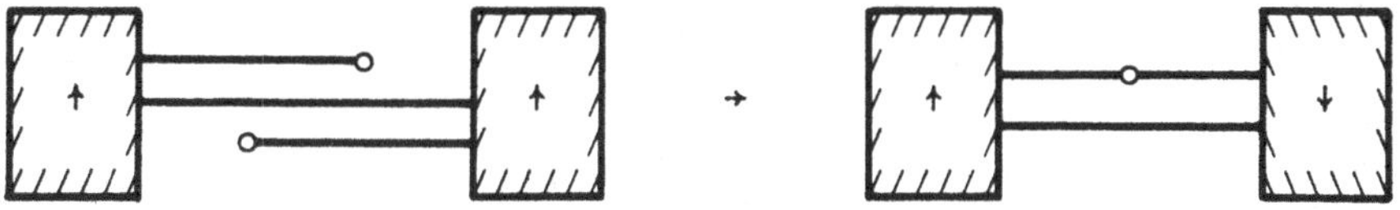

(c) The case of $d(v_j^-,v_j^+) = 3$.

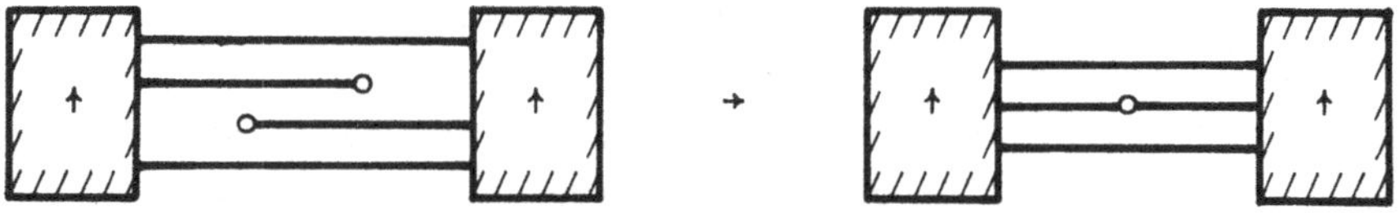

(d) The case of $d(v_j^-,v_j^+) = 4$.

Fig. 2 The transformation from an interval graphical representations of L_i' into that of L_i.

otherwise specified, a given net list L' is assumed to contain only nets with exactly two nodes.

<u>SIMPLIFICATION II</u>: Let us now consider a relaxation of condition C2 as follows: Given a subset L_i' of L', let $\mathcal{J}(L_i')$ be a set of intervals $[v_a,v_b]$ such that v_a and v_b are contained in some nets of L_i'. If $L_i'(I)$ for $I \in \mathcal{J}(L_i')$, where $L_i'(I)$ for I is defined just as L(I) for I, is maximal and I is minimal, i.e., there does not exist an interval $I' \in \mathcal{J}(L_i')$ such that $L_i'(I') \supsetneq L_i'(I)$, or $L_i'(I') = L_i'(I)$ and $I' \subsetneq I$, then interval $I \in \mathcal{J}(L_i')$ is called a <u>zone</u> of L_i'. As can be readily seen from the definition, any two distinct zones do not overlap each other. By using this concept, we can introduce a condition C2' stronger than C2, as follows.

C2': For any two consecutive zones Z_j and Z_{j+1} of L_i',

$$|L_i'(Z_j) \cap L_i'(Z_{j+1})| \le 2.$$

Proposition 2: If a net list L_i' satisfies conditions C1 and C2', then L_i' also satisfies condition C2.

Proof: Let $Z = [v_p, v_q]$ be an arbitrary zone of L_i'.

(i) If $|L_i'(Z)| \leq 2$, then there exists no 3-interval of L_i' which overlapps with zone Z.

(ii) If $|L_i'(Z)| = 3$, then even if there exists a 3-interval I of L_i' which overlapps with Z, we have $I \subset Z$, and moreover each node on I does not belong to any net of L_i'. Therefore, we have $L_i'(I) = L_i'(Z)$, and hence $|L_i'(I)| = 3$.

(iii) In the case of $|L_i'(Z)| = 4$, consider eight nodes belonging to four nets of $L_i'(Z)$, and denote them by v_a, v_b, v_c, v_p, v_q, v_x, v_y, and v_z ($a < b < c < p < q < x < y < z$). Then, we can see from condition C2' that interval $I = [v_{c+1}, v_{x-1}]$ must be a 3-interval of L_i'. Moreover, among three nets which cover node v_{c+1}, at most one net has node v_q on I. Therefore, there holds $|L_i'(I)| \geq 2$. q.e.d.

Thus, through these simplifications I and II stated above, the Layering Problem can be reduced to the following problem.

[Simplified Layering Problem (SLP)]: Given a net list L' such that every net has exactly two nodes, partition L' into the minimum number ℓ' of subsets so that each subset satisfies conditions C1 and C2'.

For example, Fig. 3 shows a partition of a given net list L' into L_1' and L_2' each of which satisfies C1 and C2', where zones of L', L_1', and L_2' are also depicted. It can be seen from the reference lines drawn in the figure that both L_1' and L_2' are realized with the upper and lower street capacities equal to two.

Considering that condition C2' is concerned only with zones, to check whether or not C2' is satisfied, it is sufficient to know how many zones there are and which nets cover each zone. Thus, we define a zone representation, which indicates which nets cover which zones. For example, the zone representations associated with the net lists L', L_1', and L_2' of Fig. 3 are illustrated in Fig. 4.

Now, construct an interval graph G(L') from a given net list L' such that each vertex corresponds to a net and there exists an edge between vertices v and w if and only if the nets corresponding to v and w overlap each other. As can be readily seen, each zone and the maximum density of a given net list L' correspond to a maximal clique and the clique number[10] of G(L'), respectively. Therefore, problem SLP can be restated as a problem of the interval graph.

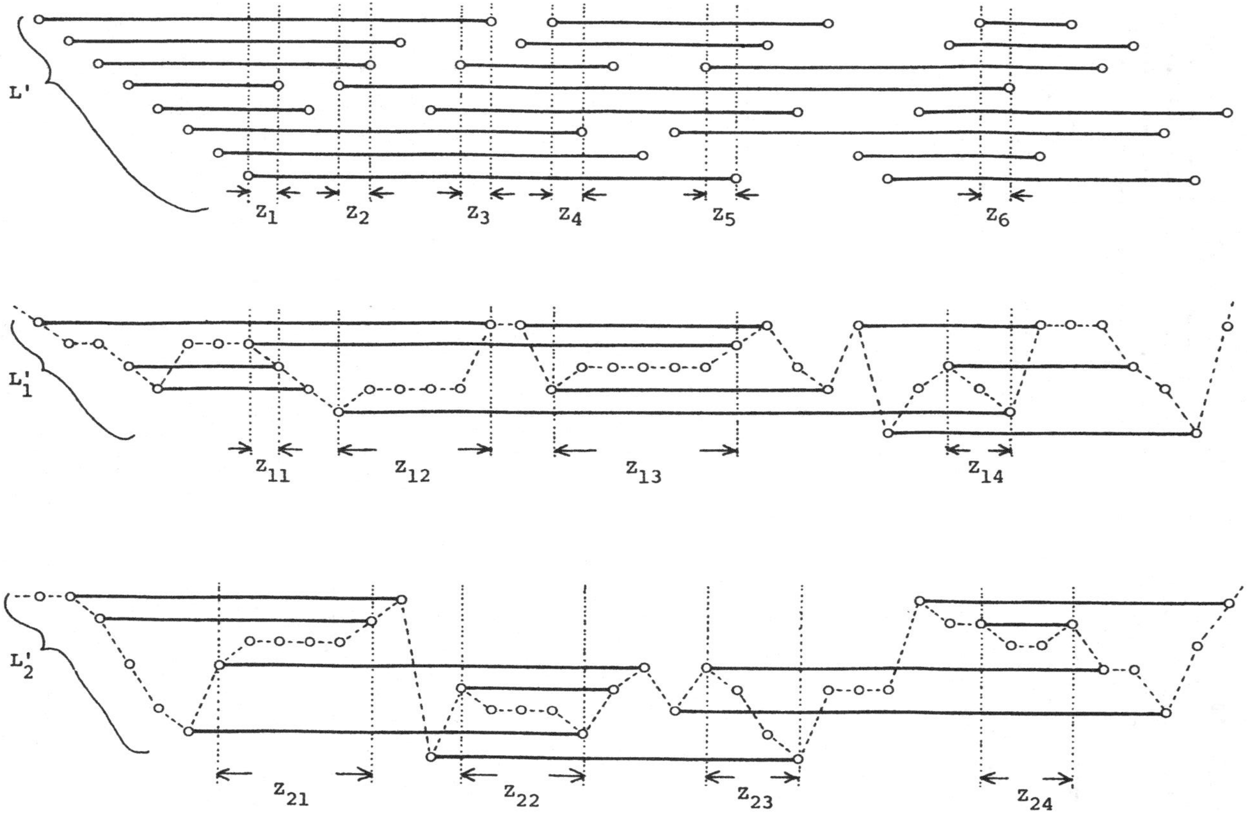

Fig. 3 Net list L' and its subsets L_1' and L_2'.

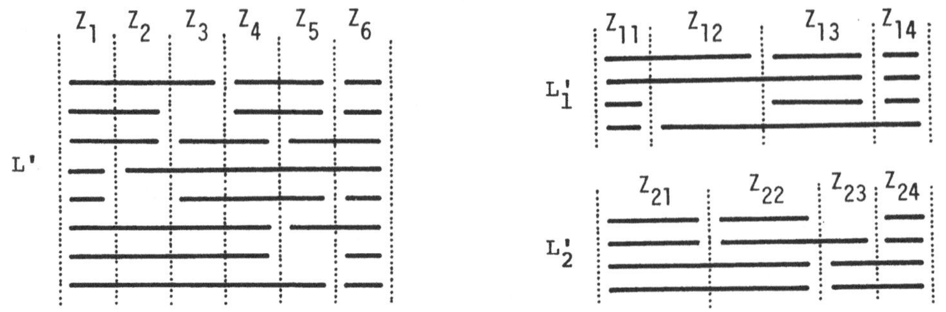

Fig. 4 Zone representations.

4. Lower Bound to the Number of Layers

Now, let us consider a lower bound to the minimum number ℓ' of subsets into which L' is partitioned in problem SLP. Let d'_M be the maximum density of a given net list L', then as can be readily seen from condition C1, we have $\lceil d'_M/4 \rceil$ as a lower bound to ℓ'. Moreover, let q'_M be the maximum number of nets which are common to two consecutive zones Z_j and Z_{j+1}, i.e., $q'_M \triangleq \max_j [\ |L'(Z_j) \cap L'(Z_{j+1})|\ ]$. Then, we have the following proposition.

Proposition 3: There holds the following inequality.

$$\max[\ \lceil d'_M/4 \rceil,\ \lceil (q'_M + 2)/4 \rceil\ ] \le \ell'.$$

Proof: Since $\lceil d'_M/4 \rceil \le \ell'$ can be readily verified, we have only to show $\lceil (q'_M + 2)/4 \rceil \le \ell'$. Let $q'_M \triangleq 4k + \alpha$, where k is a non-negative integer and $\alpha = 0$, 1, 2, or 3.

(i) If $\alpha \le 2$, then from the difinition of q'_M, there holds $d'_M \ge q'_M + 1 = 4k + 1 + \alpha$. Thus, $\ell' \ge \lceil d'_M/4 \rceil = k + 1 = \lceil (q'_M + 2)/4 \rceil$.

(ii) In the case of $\alpha = 3$, let Z_1 and Z_2 be zones of L' such that $q'_M = |L'(Z_1) \cap L'(Z_2)| = 4k + 3$. From the definition of a zone, we can see that $L'(Z_1) - L'(Z_2) \ne \phi$ and $L'(Z_2) - L'(Z_1) \ne \phi$. Therefore, for any partition of L' into k+1 subsets L'_i such that each L'_i satisfies C1, there exists a subset L'_h which has zones Z_1^h and Z_2^h satisfying $|L'(Z_1^h) \cap L'(Z_2^h)| = 3$. Thus, $\ell' \ne k + 1$. Moreover, similarly to (i), we have $\ell' \ge k + 1$. Hence, $\ell' \ge k + 2 = \lceil (q'_M + 2)/4 \rceil$. q.e.d.

Now, to obtain another lower bound, consider the case where the maximum density d'_M is a multiple of four, i.e., $d'_M = 4k$ (k : integer). Let $Z_1^{4k}, Z_2^{4k}, \cdots, Z_m^{4k}$ be zones of a net list L' arranged from left to right in this order such that $|L'(Z_j^{4k})| = 4k$ $(1 \le j \le m)$. For these zones, let us define

$$TR(Z_j^{4k}) \triangleq L'(Z_j^{4k}) - L'(Z_{j+1}^{4k}),$$

$$TL(Z_j^{4k}) \triangleq L'(Z_j^{4k}) - L'(Z_{j-1}^{4k}),$$

where let $L'(Z_0^{4k}) = L'(Z_{m+1}^{4k}) = \phi$.

If a net list L' with $d_M' = 4k$ has a zone Z_j^{4k} such that $|TR(Z_j^{4k})| =$ 2 or 3, then in order to partition L' into subsets $L_1', L_2', \cdots, L_k'$ each of which satisfies conditions C1 and C2', all the nets of $TR(Z_j^{4k})$ have to be contained in a subset L_i'. In other words, if L' has such a zone Z_j^{4k} and can be partitioned into k subsets each of which satisfies C1 and C2', then such a partition contains all the nets of $TR(Z_j^{4k})$ in a single subset. The reason is as follows: Assume that the nets of $TR(Z_j^{4k})$ such that $|TR(Z_j^{4k})| = 2$ or 3 are partitioned into two or more subsets. Then, there exists a subset L_i' which contains exactly one net of $TR(Z_j^{4k})$, say N_h, and hence we have two consecutive zones Z_a $(\supset Z_j^{4k})$ and Z_b $(\supset Z_{j+1}^{4k})$ of L_i' such that $N_h \in L_i'(Z_a)$, $N_h \notin L_i'(Z_b)$, and $|L_i'(Z_a) \cap L_i'(Z_b)| = 3$, which do not satisfy C2'.

Noting this fact, let us introduce a binary relation $\mathcal{R}^*$ into a set L* of nets defined by

$$L^* \triangleq \bigcup_{j=1}^{m} L'(Z_j^{4k}),$$

such that $N_x \mathcal{R}^* N_y$ if and only if nets N_x and N_y in L* have to be contained in the same subset, so that L' can be partitioned into k subsets each of which satisfies conditions C1 and C2'.

In the following, we list up cases in which we can easily find a pair of nets in relation $\mathcal{R}^*$.

<u>1°</u>: If there exist zones Z_j^{4k} and Z_{j+1}^{4k} such that $|TR(Z_j^{4k})| = |TL(Z_{j+1}^{4k})| = 2$ or 3, then as discussed above, we have $N_x \mathcal{R}^* N_y$ for any pair of nets N_x and N_y in $TR(Z_j^{4k}) \cup TL(_{j+1}^{4k})$.

Similarly to 1°, we can find a pair of nets satisfying relation $\mathcal{R}^*$ in the following.

<u>2°</u>: If there exists a zone Z_j^{4k} such that $|TR(Z_j^{4k})| = 4$ and $N_a \mathcal{R}^* N_b$ for N_a and $N_b \in TR(Z_j^{4k})$, then we have $N_x \mathcal{R}^* N_y$ for N_x and $N_y \in TR(Z^{4k}) - \{N_a, N_b\}$.

<u>3°</u>: The case similar to 2° with $TR(Z_j^{4k})$ replaced by $TL(Z_j^{4k})$.

<u>4°</u>: If there exists a zone Z_j^{4k} such that $|TR(Z_j^{4k})| = 5$ and there hold $N_a \mathcal{R}^* N_b$ and $N_b \mathcal{R}^* N_c$ for N_a, N_b, and $N_c \in TR(Z_j^{4k})$, then we have $N_x \mathcal{R}^* N_y$ for N_x and $N_y \in TR(Z_j^{4k}) - \{N_a, N_b, N_c\}$.

<u>5°</u>: The case similar to 4° with $TR(Z_j^{4k})$ replaced by $TL(Z_j^{4k})$.

Let $N \mathcal{R}^* N$ for any net $N \in L^*$, then we can readily see that relation $\mathcal{R}^*$ is an <u>equivalence relation</u>. Thus, we can partition L* into <u>equivalence classes</u> S_i $(i = 1, 2, \cdots)$ by $\mathcal{R}^*$. Using these equivalence classes, we can find other pairs of nets, for which there holds relation $\mathcal{R}^*$, as in the following.

6°: If there exists a zone Z_j^{4k} satisfying the following conditions;

i) there exists exactly one equivalence class S_x such that $|TR(Z_j^{4k}) \cap S_x| = 1$,

ii) there exists exactly one equivalence class S_y other than S_x such that $TR(Z_j^{4k}) \cap S_y \neq \phi$ and $|L'(Z_j^{4k}) \cap S_y| \leq 4 - |L'(Z_j^{4k}) \cap S_x|$, and

iii) for any equivalence class S_i exclusive of S_x and S_y such that $TR(Z_j^{4k}) \cap S_i \neq \phi$, there holds $|L'(Z_j^{4k}) \cap S_i| > 4 - |L'(Z_j^{4k}) \cap S_x|$,

then we have $N_x \mathcal{R}^* N_y$ for any pair of nets $N_x \in S_x$ and $N_y \in S_y$.

7°: The case similar to 6° with $TR(Z_j^{4k})$ replaced by $TL(Z_j^{4k})$.

8°: If there exists a zone Z_j^{4k} satisfying the following conditions;

i) there exist exactly two equivalence classes, say S_x and S_y, such that $|TR(Z_j^{4k}) \cap S_x| = |TR(Z_j^{4k}) \cap S_y| = 1$, and

ii) there do not exist two equivalence classes S_a and S_b other than S_x and S_y such that $TR(Z_j^{4k}) \cap S_a \neq \phi$, $TR(Z_j^{4k}) \cap S_b \neq \phi$, $|L'(Z_j^{4k}) \cap S_a| \leq 4 - |L'(Z_j^{4k}) \cap S_x|$, and $|L'(Z_j^{4k}) \cap S_b| \leq 4 - |L'(Z_j^{4k}) \cap S_y|$,

then we have $N_x \mathcal{R}^* N_y$ for any $N_x \in S_x$ and $N_y \in S_y$.

9°: The case similar to 8° with $TR(Z_j^{4k})$ replaced by $TL(Z_j^{4k})$.

10°: If there exists a zone Z_j^{4k} satisfying the folloiwng conditions;

i) there exist exactly three equivalence classes, say S_x, S_y, and S_z, such that $|TR(Z_j^{4k}) \cap S_x| = |TR(Z_j^{4k}) \cap S_y| = |TR(Z_j^{4k}) \cap S_z| = 1$, and

ii) there does not exist an equivalence class S_i different from S_x, S_y, and S_z such that $TR(Z_j^{4k}) \cap S_i \neq \phi$ and $|L'(Z_j^{4k}) \cap S_i| \leq 4 - A$, where $A \triangleq \min_{h=x,y,z} [\, |L'(Z_j^{4k}) \cap S_h| \,]$,

then we have $N_x \mathcal{R}^* N_y$ and $N_y \mathcal{R}^* N_z$ for any $N_x \in S_x$, $N_y \in S_y$, and $N_z \in S_z$.

11°: The case similar to 10° with $TR(Z_j^{4k})$ replaced by $TL(Z_j^{4k})$.

Now, given a net list L', check whether or not L' satisfies any condition of 1° - 11°, and seek as many pairs of nets in relation $\mathcal{R}^*$ as possible. Let S_i^* $(i = 1, 2, \cdots)$ be equivalence classes thus obtained (namely, S_i^* are the equivalence classes associated with the coarsest partition of L* by $\mathcal{R}^*$ through the use of 1° - 11°). From the definition of $\mathcal{R}^*$, and S_i^*, we can easily verify the following proposition.

Proposition 4: Given a net list L' with $d_M' = 4k$, if there holds one of the following conditions I, II, and III, then we have $\ell' \geq k + 1$.

I: There exist an equivalence class S_i^* and a zone Z (not necessarily $|L'(Z)| = 4k$) such that $|L'(Z) \cap S_i^*| \geq 5$.

II: There exist an equivalence class S_i^* and zones Z (not necessarily $|L'(Z)| = 4k$) and Z_j^{4k} such that $|L'(Z) \cap S_i^*| = 4$ and $|L'(Z) \cap S_i^* \cap L'(Z_j^{4k})| = 3$.

<u>III</u>: There exists a zone Z_j^{4k} such that

i) there exists an equivalence class S_x^* satisfying $|L'(Z_j^{4k}) \cap S_x^*| < 4$, and

ii) for any equivalence class S_i^* with $L'(Z_j^{4k}) \cap S_i^* \neq \phi$ exclusive of S_x^*, there holds $|L'(Z_j^{4k}) \cap S_i^*| > 4 - |L'(Z_j^{4k}) \cap S_x^*|$.

For example, zone representations of net lists which satisfy conditions I, II, and III are shown in Figs. 5 (a), 5 (b), and 5 (c), respectively, and we can see that for these net lists, we have $\ell' \geq k+1 = 3$.

(a)

Condition I.

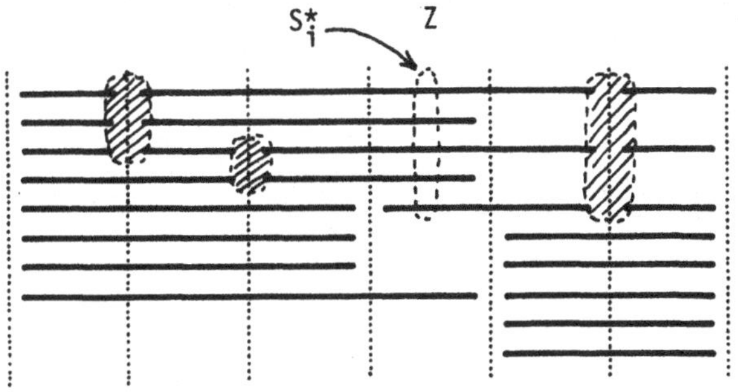

(b)

Condition II.

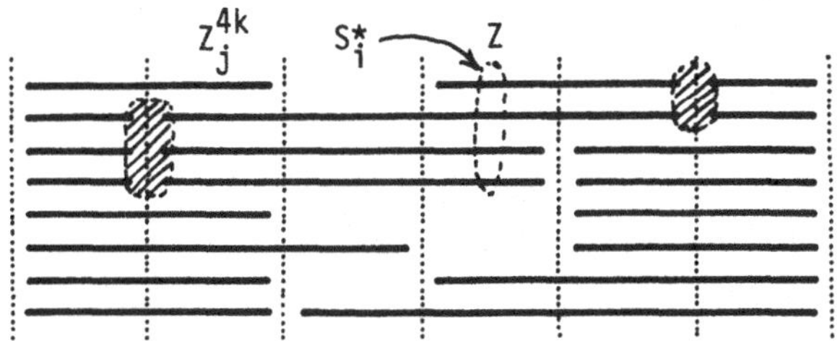

(c)

Condition III.

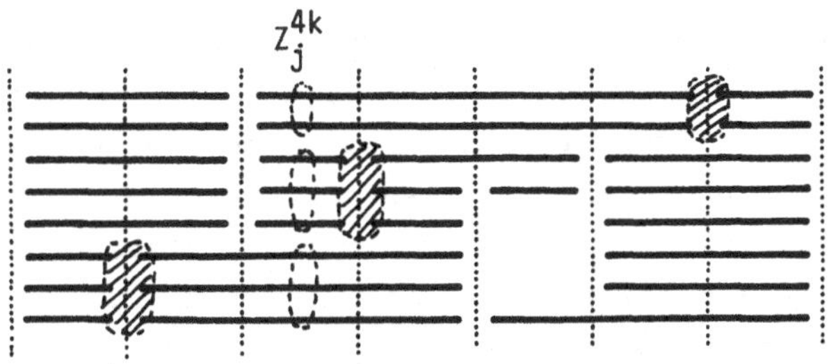

Fig. 5 Examples of net lists with $\ell' > 2$.

5. Outline of Algorithm

In what follows, we describe a heuristic algorithm for problem SLP.

The algorithm tries to seek subsets L_i' of a given net list L' through a number of stages such that at each stage a subset L_i' satisfying C1 and C2', is taken out from L'. In this process, relation $\mathcal{R}^*$ is made use of in such a way that if the current subset L_i' contains any net in an equivalence class S_h^*, then let L_i' contain all the nets in S_h^*; if the union of L_i' and S_h^* does not satisfy condition C1 or C2', then let any net of S_h^* be not added to L_i'.

Before describing the algorithm, let us consider the case in which any pair of nets in relation $\mathcal{R}^*$ have not been found. Then, let us provide p ($\geq d_M'$) tracks, and allocate all nets of L' on these tracks without overlapping. If we can choose four tracks among them such that a set L_0' of nets allocated on these four tracks satisfies condition C2', then this L_0' can be a subset L_i' of L'. Thus, the problem here is how to find such four tracks, on which we touch in the following.

First, construct a <u>directed bipartite graph</u> $G = [T,B;E,D]$ such that

i) each vertex $t_i \in T$ corresponds to a track,

ii) each $b_j^i \in B$ corresponds to a <u>break</u> b_j^i of track t_i, where a break of a track indicates an interval $[v_a,v_b]$ such that there are two nets on the track; one starting at v_a to the left and the other starting at v_b to the right, and there is no net on the track between v_a and v_b,

iii) $E \triangleq \{ (b_j^i,t_i) \}$, where (b_j^i,t_i) denotes an edge incident from b_j^i into t_i, and

iv) there exists an edge $(t_h,b_j^i) \in D$ if and only if on track t_h there does not exist any net passing over break b_j^i.

For a set X of vertices on this graph G, let $\Gamma^+(X) \triangleq \{ v \mid (x,v) \in E \cup D, x \in X \}$ and $\Gamma^-(X) \triangleq \{ v \mid (v,x) \in E \cup D, x \in X \}$. Then, a subset $T_0 \subset T$ such that $|T_0| = 4$ and $\Gamma^-(T_0) \subset \Gamma^+(T_0)$, yields desired four tracks, and hence a set of nets on these four tracks satisfies conditions C1 and C2'.

<<u>ALGORITHM</u>>

<u>Input</u> : A net list L' with the maximum density d_M'.

<u>Output</u> : A subset L_0' of L' satisfying conditions C1 and C2'.

<u>Step 1</u>: Using Propositions 3 and 4, seek a lower bound k to ℓ'. If $d_M' = 4k$, then go to Step 2; else go to Step 4.

<u>Step 2</u>: If there exists an equivalence class containing more than one net, which is generated in Step 1 to find a lower bound by Proposition 4, then go to Step 3; else go to Step 4.

<u>Step 3</u>: Define a weight $w(S_i^*)$ of each equivalence class S_i^* by an ordered pair such that $w(S_i^*) \triangleq (|S_i^*|, \max_Z [|L'(Z) \cap S_i^*|])$, and a weight

$w(N_h)$ of each net N_h in $L' - L^*$ by the length of the interval covered by N_h, i.e., $w(N_h) \triangleq |a-b|$ for $N_h = \{v_a, v_b\}$. Then, let L_0' be an equivalence class with a lexicographically maximum weight. While L_0' satisfies conditions C1 and C2', add to L_0' as many equivalence classes as possible in lexicographically descending order of weight. After this, conduct the similar process for nets in $L' - L^*$ according to the weight $w(N_h)$ of $N_h \in L' - L^*$. Then, go to Step 9.

Step 4: Provide 4k tracks, and assign all the nets in L' to these tracks, so that the nets assigned to a track do not overlap each other. This assignment is done as follows: Pick out a net with the leftmost node among unassigned nets, and assign it to the one among 4k tracks such that the rightmost node of nets on it is located at the leftmost position. In case there exist any tracks to which no net is assigned, choose one of them arbitrarily.

Step 5: Construct a directed bipartite graph $G = [T,B;E,D]$ mentioned above, and define a weight of each vertex $t \in T$ by an ordered pair such that

$$W(t) \triangleq \begin{cases} \left(\min\limits_{b \in \Gamma^-(t)} [\, |\Gamma^-(b)|\,],\ [\sum\limits_{b \in \Gamma^-(t)} |\Gamma^-(b)|]/|\Gamma^-(t)| \right); & \text{if } \Gamma^-(t) \neq \phi, \\ (\infty, \infty);\ \text{otherwise.} \end{cases}$$

Let $t_0 \in T$ be a vertex with a lexicographically minimum weight $W(t_0)$. Then, set $T_0 \leftarrow \{t_0\}$, and add vertices in T to T_0 in lexicographically ascending order of weight, until T_0 satisfies $|T_0| \leq 4$ and $\Gamma^-(T_0) \subset \Gamma^+(T_0)$. If such T_0 can be found, then go to Step 7; else go to Step 6.

Step 6: Choose three vertices of T in ascending order of weight, and let L_0' be a set of nets contained in the corresponding three tracks. Then, go to Step 8.

Step 7: If $|T_0| = 4$, then let L_0' be a set of nets contained in the tracks corresponding to the vertices in T_0, and go to Step 8. Otherwise, try to find a set T_0' such that $T_0 \subset T_0' \subset T$, $|T_0'| \leq 4$, and $\Gamma^-(T_0') \subset \Gamma^+(T_0')$, similarly to Step 5. If $|T_0'| < 4$ and there exists a vertex t of weight (∞, ∞), then add each such vertex to T_0', unless $|T_0'| = 4$.

i) If $|T_0'| = 4$, then let L_0' be a set of nets contained in the tracks corresponding to the vertices in T_0', and go to Step 8.

ii) If $|T_0'| = 3$, then conduct (iv).

iii) If $|T_0'| \leq 2$, then add to T_0' the vertices in $T - T_0'$ with a lexicographically minimum weight, unless $|T_0'| = 3$.

iv) Let L_0' be a set of nets contained in the tracks corresponding to the vertices in T_0', then go to Step 8.

Step 8: Add to L_0' as many nets in L' as possible in descending order of weight defined for nets in $L' - L_0'$ similarly to $w(N_h)$ for $N_h \in L' - L^*$, while L'_0 satisfies conditions C1 and C2'.

Step 9: Terminate by setting $L' \leftarrow L' - L'_0$.

By repeated applications of this algorithm, we can partition a given net list L' into subsets satisfying conditions C1 and C2'. Moreover, it should be noted that we can introduce into Steps 3 and 5 - 7, a procedure to find pairs of nets in relation $\mathcal{R}^*$ by using 6° - 11°, so that the current execution of the algorithm may not decrease the possibility in the next execution that the remaining net list L' may be partitioned into a minimum number of subsets.

6. Concluding Remarks

In this paper, we have described an approach to the layering problem in multilayer PWB wiring. We have paid attention only to the case of $K_u = K_w = 2$, since the discussion on it can be applied to the case of $K_u = 2$ and $K_w = 1$ with a slight modification. However, there still remain a number of problems, among which of primary importance is a necessary and sufficient condition (or non-trivial sufficient condition) for a net list to be realized with a given number of layers.

In what follows, we point out another approach to problem SLP, which is applied only to the case of $K_u = K_w = 2$.

A set of pairwise disjoint pairs of distinct nets is called a matching M of a given net list L'. For two nets $N_1 = \{v_a, v_b\}$ and $N_2 = \{v_c, v_d\}$, the following operation is called a merging of nets N_1 and N_2: Replace two nets N_1 and N_2 by a new net $N_{12} = \{v_x, v_y\}$ defined by $x = \min[a,c]$ and $y = \max[b,d]$. Given a net list L' and a matching M of L', the net list L" obtained from L' by merging every pair of nets in M is denoted by L'[M]. Let ρ be the maximum density of L" = L'[M], and consider a partition of L" into $\lceil \rho/2 \rceil$ subsets $L''_1, L''_2, \cdots, L''_{\lceil \rho/2 \rceil}$ such that each subset L''_i has the maximum density not greater than 2. Based on this partition, we can generate a partition of the original net list L' into subsets L'_i such that each L'_i of L' is obtained from L''_i by decomposing every merged net in L''_i into two original nets. Then, we can readily see that each subset L'_i satisfies conditions C1 and C2', and hence we can use such a partition of L' as an approximate solution to problem SLP. Noting that it is easy to find a partition of L" into $\lceil \rho/2 \rceil$ subsets, in this approach, the following problem has to be solved.

[Matching Problem]: Given a net list L', find a matching M of L' such that the maximum density ρ of L'[M] is minimized.

With respect to this problem, we have the following propositions;

Proposition 5: If there holds $\mathcal{Z}(N_j) = \mathcal{Z}(N_h)$ for two distinct nets N_j and N_h, then there exists an optimum matching M* containing pair $\{ N_j, N_h \}$, where $\mathcal{Z}(N)$ is a set of zones which have net N, i.e.,

$$\mathcal{Z}(N) \triangleq \{ Z \mid N \in L'(Z) \}.$$

Proposition 6: The Matching Problem is polynomially transformable[11] to problem SLP.

REFERENCES

[1] H.C.So, "Some theoretical results on the routing of multilayer printed wiring boards," Proc. IEEE ISCAS, pp. 296-303, 1974.

[2] B.S.Ting, E.S.Kuh, and I.Shirakawa, "The multilayer routing problem: Algorithms and necessary and sufficient conditions for the single-row single-layer case," IEEE Trans. CAS, vol. CAS-23, no. 12, pp. 768-778, 1976.

[3] E.S.Kuh, T.Kashiwabara, and T.Fujisawa, "On optimum single-row routing," IEEE Trans. CAS, vol. CAS-26, no. 6, pp. 361-368, 1979.

[4] S.Tsukiyama, E.S.Kuh, and I.Shirakawa, "An algorithm for single-row routing with prescribed street congestions," IEEE Trans. CAS, vol. CAS-27, no. 9, pp. 765-772, 1980.

[5] B.S.Ting and E.S.Kuh, "An approach to the routing of multilayer printed circuit boards," Proc. IEEE ISCAS, pp. 907-911, 1978.

[6] M.T.Doreau and L.C.Abel, "A topological based nonminimum distance routing algorithm," Proc. 15th Design Automation Conf., pp. 92-99, 1978.

[7] S.Asahara, Y.Ogura, M.Odani, I.Shirakawa, and H.Ozaki, "An automatic layout system based on single-row routing for multilayer printed wiring boards," Monograph CAS 79-74, IECE Japan, pp. 79-86, 1979 (in Japanese), also, Proc. IEEE ICCC, pp. 290-294, 1980.

[8] B.S.Ting, E.S.Kuh, and A.Sangiovanni-Vincentelli, "Vias assignment problem in multilayer printed circuit board," IEEE Trans. CAS, vol. CAS-26, no. 4, pp. 261-272, 1979.

[9] S.Tsukiyama, I.Shirakawa, and S.Asahara, "An algorithm for the via assignment problem in multilayer backboard wiring," IEEE Trans. CAS, vol. CAS-26, no. 6, pp. 369-377, 1979.

[10] M.R.Golumbic, "Algorithmic Graph Theory and Perfect Graphs," Academic Press, N.Y., 1980.

[11] R.M.Karp, "Reducibility among combinatorial problems," Complexity of Computer Computations, R.E.Miller and J.W.Thatcher, Eds., Plenum Press, N.Y., pp. 85-103, 1972.

A STATUS ON THE LINEAR ARBORICITY

J. Akiyama
Department of Mathematics, Nippon Ika University
Kawasaki, Japan 211

Abstract. In a linear forest, each component is a path. The linear arboricity $\Xi(G)$ of a graph G is defined in Harary [8] as the minimum number of linear forests whose union is G. This invariant first arose in a study [10] of information retrieval in file systems. A quite similar covering invariant which is well known to the linear arboricity is the arboricity of a graph, which is defined as the minimum number of forests whose union is G. Nash-Williams [11] determined the arboricity of any graph, however only few results on the linear arboricity are known. We shall present these discoveries and an open problem on this new invariant.

1. Introduction

In a linear forest, each component is a path. The linear arboricity $\Xi(G)$ of a graph G is defined as the minimum number of linear forests whose union is G. All other definitions and terminology employed in this paper can be found in Behzad, Chartrand and Lesniak-Foster [6] or Harary [9]. We now present a few fundamental results for specified families of graphs.

Theorem 1. If T is a tree with maximum degree ΔT, then

(1) $$\Xi(T) = \{\Delta T/2\}.$$

Proof. The lower bound $\Xi(T) \geq \{\Delta T/2\}$ is obvious. Since tree T has maximum degree ΔT, its edge chromatic number $\chi'(T)$ is equal to ΔT. Each subgraph induced by subsets of edges with two colors is a linear forest. Thus we obtain the upper bound:

$$\Xi(T) \leq \{\chi'(T)/2 = \{\Delta T/2\}. \blacksquare$$

The linear arboricity of the complete graph coincides with its path number, which was determined by Stanton, Cowan and James [14].

Theorem 2. (Stanton, Cowan and James) For the complete graph K_p,
$\Xi(K_p) = \{p/2\}$. ∎

We also calculate this for complete bipartite graphs in [2], but we omit the proof since it is rather long.

The notation $\delta(m,n)$ is the conventional Kronecker delta.

Theorem 3. For the complete bipartite graph $K_{m,n}$ with $m \geq n$, the linear arboricity is given by:

(2) $$\Xi(K_{m,n}) = \{(m + \delta(m,n)/2\}.$$ ∎

2. The linear arboricity for cubic graphs

We now turn our attention to cubic graphs G and find that the linear arboricity of G is 2. This result was proved by finding an avoidable set for cubic graphs by Akiyama, Exoo and Harary [2], but the following proof which applies Kempe chain arguments is due to Akiyama and Chvátal [1].

Recall that $\chi'(G)$ stands for the edge chromatic number of G.

Theorem 4. The linear arboricity for a cubic graph G is two;
$\Xi(G) = 2$

Proof. By Vizing's Theorem [16], we have the inequalities;
$$3 = \Delta G \leq \chi'(G) \leq \Delta G + 1 = 4.$$
We first color all the edges of G with 4 distinct colors, say, a, b, c and d, such that no adjacent edges have the same color. We replace the color of the edges as follows:
The edges colored with a or b are replaced with color 1.
The edges colored with c or d are replaced with color 2.
The subgraph G_1 (or G_2) induced by the edges with color 1 (or 2) has degree at most two, i.e., $\Delta G_i \leq 2$, $i = 1, 2$. If neither G_1 or G_2 contains a cycle, the theorem is true. We now assume that G_1 or G_2 contains a cycle. Our purpose is to show the possibility that we can replace the color of some edges on each monochromatic cycle with the other color so that no monochromatic cycles are left. Let C_1 be a cycle induced by the edges with color 1, and take three successive vertices on C_1, say v_1, v_2, v_3. We denote the edges, outside of C_1, incident to v_i by e_i, $i = 1, 2, 3$, respectively as illustrated in Figure 1.

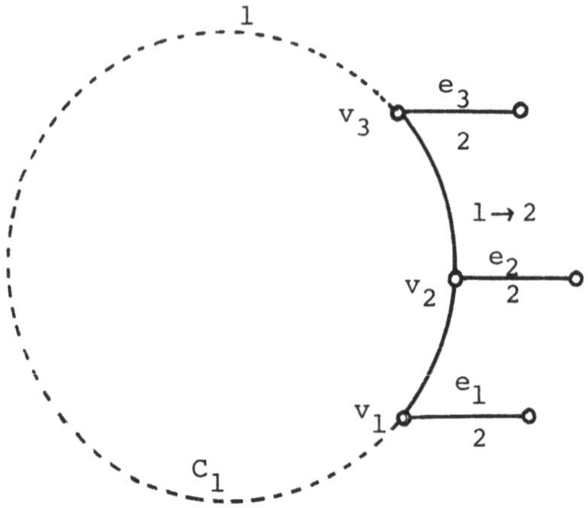

Figure 1. A step in the proof of Theorem 4.

It is obvious that the three edges e_i (i = 1, 2, 3) have color 2, since $\Delta G_i \leqq 2$ for i = 1, 2.

There are two essentially distinct cases:

Case 1. There is no path joining v_2 and v_3, consisting of edges with color 2. In this case, it is possible to replace the color 1 of the edge $\{v_2, v_3\}$ with color 2. As a consequence of the operation, we avoid the monochromatic cycle C_1 and produce no new monochromatic cycles.

Case 2. There is a path P, joining v_2 and v_3, consisting of edges with color 2. In this case, we show that there are no paths, joining v_2 and v_1, consisting of edges with color 2. Suppose that there exists a path P_1 consisting of edges with color 2 joining v_1 and v_2, see Figure 2.

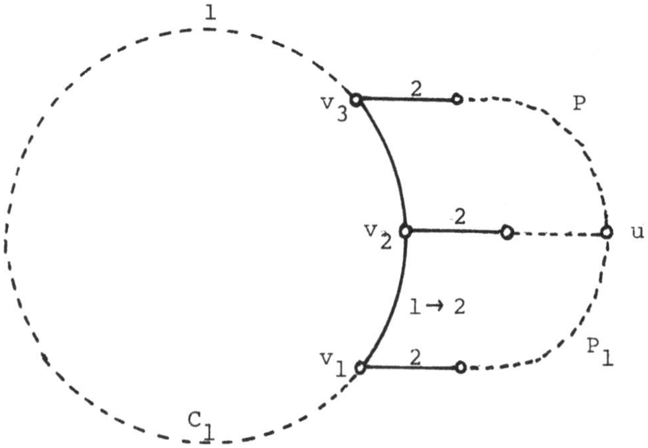

Figure 2. A step in the proof of Theorem 4.

Then there must be a vertex u on both P and P_1, which contradicts the fact that deg u $\leq$ 2 in G_2. Thus we can replace the color 1 of the edge $\{v_1, v_2\}$ with color 2 so that no new monochromatic cycles are produced and the monochromatic cycle C_1 is broken. Repeating the operation above until no monochromatic cycle is left, we complete the proof.∎

3. 4-regular graphs

In the determination of the linear arboricity for 4-regular graphs, we found it impossible to apply either proof techniques applied in the proofs [1], [2], that is, to find an avoidable set for 4-regular graphs or to apply Kempe chain arguments. However, it was proved that every 4-regular graph has the linear arboricity 3 in [3] (later, independently by Enomoto [7] and Peroche [12]) by applying the classical results of Petersen [13] on the factorizations of regular graphs of even degree.

Theorem 5. The linear arboricity of every 4-regular graph is 3.

Proof. Let G be a 4-regular graph. Then Petersen showed that G has a 2-factorization. Let $C(1,1),\ldots, C(1,m_1)$ and $C(2,1),\ldots, C(2,m_2)$ be the cycles of two 2-factors of G comprising a 2-factorization.

We shall describe a edge-coloring of G, using the colors red, white and blue, such that each maximal monochromatic subgraph is a linear forest. This is done in three steps.

Step 1. Select one edge $e(1,i)$ from each cycle $C(1,i)$ in the first 2-factor. Color these edges blue and color all the other edges of the first 2-factor red.

Step 2. Select one edge $e(2,i)$ from each $C(2,i)$ of the cycles in the 2nd 2-factor. We will color these edges in Step 3. Now color the remaining $q/2 - m_2$ edges of the second 2-factor white.

Before developing Step 3, we note that the edges already colored form three monochromatic linear forests. It remains to color the edges $e(2,i)$, $i = 1$ to m_2. It is convenient to denote the path formed from $C(k,i)$ upon deletion of edge $e(k,i)$ by $P(k,i)$.

Step 3. We color the edges $e(2,1), e(2,2),\ldots$ blue so long as the blue subgraph remains a linear forest. Suppose $e(2,j)$ is the first edge, if any, which cannot be colored blue because its addition to the blue subgraph forms a cycle, as we now see.

Since the edges $e(1,i)$ are independent, as are the edges $e(2,i)$, coloring e(2,j) blue cannot create a vertex of degree 3 in the blue subgraph. Thus so coloring e(2,j) must complete a blue cycle. This means that two blue edges $e(1,j_1)$ and $e(1,j_2)$ must be adjacent to e(2,j). So we color e(2,j) red, thereby making one red path out of the paths $P(1,j_1)$, $P(1,j_2)$ and the edge e(2,j).

We follow this pattern in coloring the remainder of the edges e(2,i). That is, we color them blue so long as this leaves the blue subgraph a linear forest. And when any e(2,i) cannot be colored blue, we color it red.

We now show that the red subgraph is a linear forest. If coloring any e(2,k) blue creates a blue cycle, then there must be edges $e(1,k_1)$ and $e(1,k_2)$ adjacent to e(2,k). Further, each of $e(1,k_1)$ and $e(1,k_2)$ is adjacent to a blue edge of the form e(2,i) since coloring e(2,k) blue would have completed a blue cycle, and $e(1,k_1)$ and $e(1,k_2)$ are independent. Thus the other endvertices of the paths $P(1,k_1)$ and $P(1,k_2)$ are incident with blue edges e(2,i). This observation means that each path P(1,i) has at most one endvertices incident with a red e(2,k), and of course as observed above, no interior vertex of such a path is incident with any red e(2,k). So coloring edges e(2,k) red as needed leaves the red subgraph a linear forest.∎

4. The linear arboricity of 5-regular and 6-regular graphs

We heard very recently that B. Peroche [12] proved that the linear arboricity for 5-regular graphs (or 6-regular graphs) is 3 (or 4) respectively. We state these results without proofs, since it is rather long.

Theorem 6. The linear arboricity of 5-regular graph is 3.∎

Theorem 7. The linear arboricity of 6-regular graph is 4.∎

5. Bounds on the linear arboricity of a graph

In [3], the bounds of the linear arboricity for a graph G with maximum degree Δ is given as follows:

$$\{\Delta/2\} \leq \Xi(G) \leq \{3\{\Delta/2\}/2\}.$$

However, Peroche [12] obtained the better bounds of the linear arboricity for a graph G with maximum degree Δ by applying Theorem 7 recursively, which is stated as follows.

<u>Theorem 8.</u> If G is a graph with maximum degree Δ, then

$$\{\Delta/2\} \leq \Xi(G) \leq \{2\Delta/3\} \text{ if } \Delta \text{ is even,}$$

$$\{\Delta/2\} \leq \Xi(G) \leq \{(2\Delta + 1)/3\} \text{ if } \Delta \text{ is odd.} \blacksquare$$

6. Unsolved problem

We proved in [4] that the arboricity $\Upsilon(G) = \{(r + 1)/2\}$ for any r-regular graph G. It was conjectured in [2] that for r-regular graphs $\Xi(G) = \Upsilon(G) = \{(r + 1)/2\}$ and this equation was proved for $0 \leq r \leq 6$ as seen in the previous sections.

We do not know any graph G which is r-regular for which $\Xi(G) > \{(r + 1)/2\} = \Upsilon(G)$. Thus the conjecture of equality is still open.

<u>Appendix.</u> The linear arboricity for multigraphs has been studied in [5].

<u>Acknowledgement.</u> It is a pleasure to thank Claude Berge, Vasek Chvátal, Geoffrey Exoo and Frank Harary for valuable comments.

References

[1] J.Akiyama and V.Chvátal, Another proof of the linear arboricity for cubic graphs, to appear.

[2] J.Akiyama, G.Exoo and F.Harary, Covering and packing in graphs III: Cyclic and acyclic invariants. <u>Math. Slovaca</u> 29(1980)

[3] J.Akiyama, G.Exoo and F.Harary, Covering and packing in graphs IV: Linear arboricity. <u>Networks</u> 11(1981)

[4] J.Akiyama and T.Hamada, The decompositions of line graphs, middle graphs and total graphs of complete graphs into forests. <u>Discrete Math.</u> 26(1979)203-208.

[5] J.Akiyama and I.Sato, A comment on the linear arboricity for regular multigraphs, to appear.

[6] M.Behzad, G.Chartrand and L.Lesniak-Foster, <u>Graphs and Digraphs</u>, Prindle, Weber & schmidt, Boston (1979)

[7] H.Enomoto, The linear arboricity of cubic graphs and 4-regular graphs, Private communication.

[8] F.Harary, Covering and packing I, <u>Ann. N.Y.Acad. Sci.</u> 175(1970) 198-205.

[9] F.Harary, Graph Theory, Addison-Wesley, Mass. (1969)

[10] F.Harary and D.Hsiao, A formal system for information retrieval files, Comm.A.C.M., 13(1970)67-73.

[11] C.Nash-Williams, Decomposition of finite graphs into forests. J. London Math Soc. 39(1964)12.

[12] B.Peroche, On partition of graphs into linear forests and dissections, Rapport de recherche, Centre National de la recherche scientifique

[13] J.Petersen, Die Theorie der regularen Graphen, Acta Math. 15(1891) 193-200.

[14] R.Stanton, D.Cowan and L.James, Some results on path numbers, Proc. Louisiana Conf. Combinatorics, Graph Theory and Computing, Baton. Rouge (1970)112-135.

[15] W.Tutte, The subgraph problem, Advances in Graph Theory (B.Bollbás, ed.) North-Holland, Amsterdam (1978)289-295.

[16] V.Vizing, On an estimate of the chromatic class of p-graph, Diskret. Analiz. 3(1964)25-30.

ON CENTRALITY FUNCTIONS OF A GRAPH

G. Kishi

Graduate School of Coordinated Science
Tokyo Institute of Technology
Nagatsuta-cho 4259, Midori-ku, Yokohama, Japan

Abstract: For a connected nondirected graph, a centrality function is a real valued function of the vertices defined as a linear combination of the numbers of the vertices classified according to the distance from a given vertex. Some fundamental properties of the centrality functions and the set of central vertices are summarized. Inserting an edge between a center and a vertex, the stability of the set of central vertices are investigated.

For a weakly connected directed graph, we can prove similar theorems with respect to a generalized centrality function based on a new definition of the modified distance from a vertex to another vertex.

1. Introduction

In many practical applications, it is often necessary to find the best location of facilities in networks or graphs. In this context, a real number f(G,v) is associated with every vertex v of the graph G for the criterion of deciding what vertex is best. The criterion of optimality may be taken to be the minimization of the function f(G,v) with respect to v.

One of the most important problems is to determine what kind of functions is suitable for the measure of centrality of vertices in a graph. It is well-known that the transmission number is an example of such functions. In this survey, the centrality function, a generalized form of the transmission number, is defined as a linear combination with real coefficients of the numbers of vertices classified according to the distance from a given vertex in a connected nondirected graph.

As a fundamental theorem, a necessary and sufficient condition for the function to satisfy the centrality axioms is stated in terms of the coefficients.

Inserting an edge between a center and a vertex, the sets of central vertices settled before and after the edge inserting are generally different. Some stability theorems of the sets of central vertices are presented for a connected nondirected graph.

However the situation often arises where a nondirected graph will not be able to meet various requirements and what is then needed is to introduce a centrality function for a directed graph. For a weakly connected directed graph, a modified distance from a vertex to another vertex is defined as a two-dimensional vector of integer components showing the numbers of forward and backward edges contained in the shortest path with respect to a newly defined order relation. It is shown that the major results for a nondirected graph can be extended similarly to a directed graph with respect to a generalized centrality function based on the modified distance.

2. Transmission Number

Let G be a connected nondirected graph with the set of vertices V. A distance d(u,v) between a pair of vertices u and v in G is defined as the minimum number of edges in a path connecting u and v. We now define $c_0(G,v)$ for every vertex v in G as follows :

$$c_0(G,v) = \sum_{w \in V} d(v,w) \tag{1}$$

The number $c_0(G,v)$ is often refered to as the transmission number[1]. A central vertex v_0 for which

$$c_0(G,v_0) = \min_{v \in V} c_0(G,v) \tag{2}$$

is called a median[1] of the graph G.

3. Centrality Function

Let c(G,v) be a real valued function of vertices of G. Then the function is said to be a centrality function if c(G,v) satisfies the following centrality axioms[2].

Centrality Axioms : If there exist no edges between a pair of vertices p and q in a connected nondirected graph G, the insertion of an edge between p and q yields the graph G_{pq} and the difference

$$\Delta_{pq}(v) = c(G,v) - c(G_{pq},v) \tag{3}$$

for any vertex v in G.

Now the function c(G,v) is called a centrality function if and only if

(i) $\Delta_{pq}(p) > 0$ (4)

(ii) $\Delta_{pq}(p) \geqq \Delta_{pq}(v)$ for any v satisfying

$d(v,p) \leqq d(v,q)$ (5)

for any pair of vertices p and q which are not adjacent. (End)

As a generalized form of the transmission number, we deal with a real valued function c(G,v) as follows :

$$c(G,v) = \sum_{k=1}^{\infty} a_k n_k(v) \qquad (6)$$

where $n_k(v)$ stands for the number of vertices whose distances from v are k, and a_k's are real constants.

For the function defined by (6), the following theorem can be proved[3].

Theorem 1 : The function c(G,v) defined by (6) is a centrality function for any graph G if and only if a_k's satisfy

(i) $a_1 < a_2 \leqq a_3 \leqq a_4 \leqq \cdots$ (7)

(ii) $2a_k \geqq a_{k-1} + a_{k+1}$, $(k \geqq 2)$ (8)

(End)

As an illustrative example, suppose

$$a_k = k, \quad (k = 1,2,3, \ldots). \qquad (9)$$

It is easily shown that

$$\sum_{k=1}^{\infty} k\, n_k(v) = \sum_{w \in V} d(v,w) = c_0(G,v) \qquad (10)$$

and a_k's given by (9) satisfy (7) and (8). Thus we can conclude that the transmission number is a centrality function.

Let c(G,v) defined by (6) be a centrality function for any connected nondirected graph G. A vertex v_0 for which

$$c(G,v_0) = \min_{v \in V} c(G,v) \qquad (11)$$

is called a center of G with respect to c(G,v) or shortly a c-center. Let $S_c(G)$ be the set of all the c-centers of G.

4. Stability Theorems

If a c-center p and a vertex q in G are not adjacent, the insertion of an edge between p and q yields the graph G_{pq} with its set of all the c-centers $S_c(G_{pq})$. Then two cases can occur, either

Case A : $S_c(G_{pq}) \subseteqq S_c(G) \cup \{q\}$ (12)

or

Case B : $S_c(G_{pq}) \not\subseteqq S_c(G) \cup \{q\}$ (13)

for any vertex p in $S_c(G)$ and q in V. A graph for which case B occurs is said to be unstable with respect to c(G,v).

Case A can be classified into two cases,

Case A-1 : $S_c(G_{pq}) \subseteqq S_c(G)$ and $p \in S_c(G_{pq})$ (14)

and

Case A-2 : $S_c(G_{pq}) \not\subseteqq S_c(G)$ or $p \notin S_c(G_{pq})$ (15)

for any vertex p in $S_c(G)$ and q in V.

A graph G is said to be stable if case A-1 occurs. A quasi-stable graph is a graph for which case A-2 occurs.

We can then prove the following theorem[4].

Theorem 2 : For any centrality function c(G,v) satisfying $a_2 < a_3$, there exist a quasi-stable graph. (End)

A quasi-stable graph with respect to the transmission number is shown in Fig. 1[4].

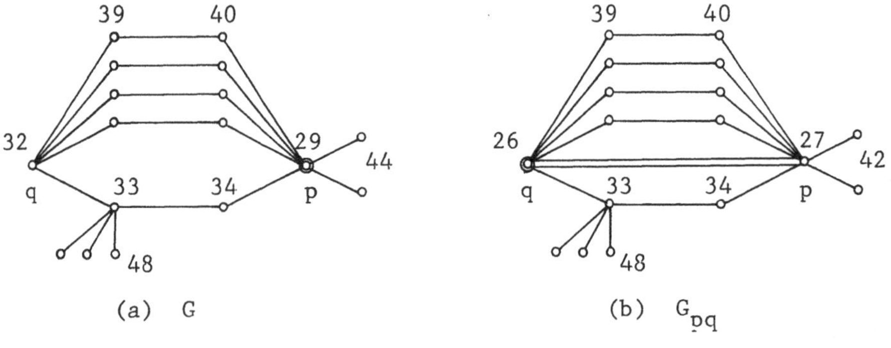

Fig. 1. Quasi-stable graph.

Theorem 3 : For any centrality function c(G,v) satisfying $a_2 = a_3$, all the connected nondirected graphs are stable. (End)

Theorem 4 : Any connected nondirected graph is stable if and only if the centrality function c(G,v) given by (6) satisfies $a_2 = a_3$. (End)

Theorem 5 : For any centrality function c(G,v) satisfying $a_3 < a_4$, there exists an unstable graph. (End)

An unstable graph with respect to the transmission number is shown in Fig. 2[3].

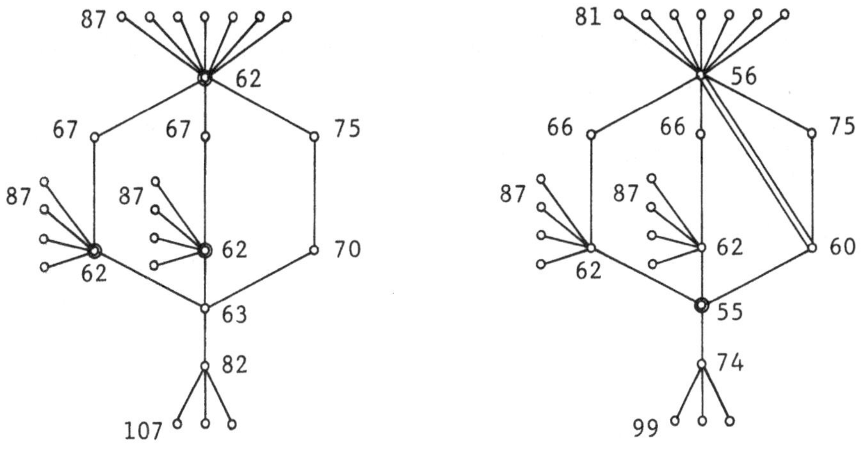

(a) G (b) G_{pq}

Fig. 2. Unstable graph.

Theorem 6 : For any centrality function satisfying $a_3 = a_4$ all the connected nondirected graphs are quasi-stable or stable. (End)

Theorem 7 : Any connected nondirected graph is not unstable if and only if the centrality function given by (6) satisfies $a_3 = a_4$. (End)

5. Stable Graphs

The theorems in the preceding section show that a centrality function with which all the graphs are stable or quasi-stable is rather trivial one. Characterizing stable or quasi-stable graphs with respect to a given centrality function is an important problem to be solved. The following theorem[2] is basic with respect to the centrality function specified as the transmission number.

Theorem 8 : If a graph G forms a tree, then G is stable with respect to the transmission number. (End)

Let H_k ($k = 0,1,2, \ldots$) be the collection of all the connected graphs of nullity k. Then Theorem 8 shows that any graph of H_0 is stable. Since H_2 contains an unstable graph shown in Fig. 2, we may ask if there exists an unstable or a quasi-stable graphs in H_1. Counting the number m of edges in the only loop contained in any graph of H_1, we can define a subset $H_1(m)$ as the collection of graphs containing the single loop of length m.

Recent results with respect to the transmission number include the following two theorems[5].

Theorem 9 : For any $m \leq 4$, all the graphs of $H_1(m)$ are stable. For any $m \geq 5$, $H_1(m)$ contains a quasi-stable graph. (End)

Theorem 10 : For $m = 7$, $H_1(m)$ contains an unstable graph. For $m \leq 6$, $H_1(m)$ contains no unstable graphs. (End)

The graph shown in Fig. 3 is an example of unstable graph of m=7.

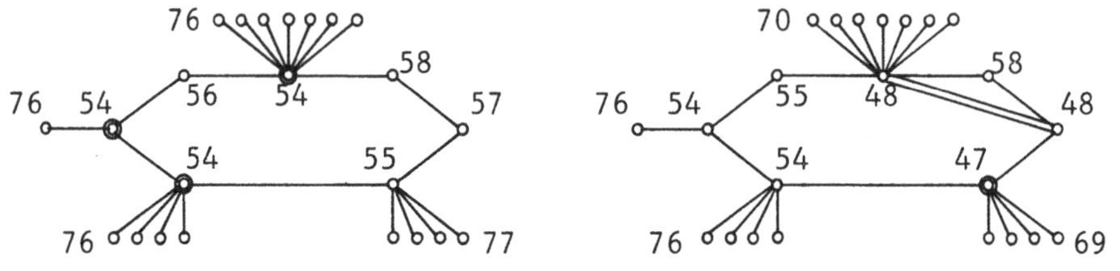

(a) G (b) G_{pq}

Fig. 3. Unstable graph.

6. Centrality Functions for A Directed Graph

The definitions and the theorems discussed so far can be extended for a directed graph[6]. Let us begin with some preliminary definitions.

Let R^2 be the two dimensional real space defined by

$$R^2 = \{(x,y) \mid x,y \in R\} \tag{16}$$

where R is the set of real numbers. For the simplicity, a vector $(x,y) \in R^2$ is expressed by $x+y\omega \in R^2$, where ω is the symbol specifying the second component.

A natural order and the vector addition can be defined in R^2 as follows.

$$\text{(i)} \quad x+y\omega > 0 \quad \text{if and only if} \quad y > 0 \quad \text{or} \quad y = 0 \text{ and } x > 0 \tag{17}$$

$$\text{(ii)} \quad (x+y\omega)+(x'+y'\omega) = (x+x')+(y+y')\omega \quad \text{where} \quad 0 = 0 + 0\omega \tag{18}$$

Let N^2 be the subset of R^2 similarly defined with the set of non-negative integer N. It is obvious that R^2 is an ordered abelian group, while N^2 is an ordered semigroup contained in R^2.

Let a directed graph G be weakly connected. A path P between two vertices u and v may be oriented as from u to v. We can then define a vector (a_p,b_p) of integer component associated with the path P where

a_p and b_p are the number of coincide and opposite edges in the path P, respectively. Since (a_p, b_p) can be interpreted as an element $a_p + b_p\omega$ in N^2, we can define a generalized length of the path P such that

$$L_{uv}(P) = a_p + b_p\omega \tag{19}$$

The modified distance from vertex u to vertex v in a weakly connected graph is given by

$$D(u,v) = \min_P L_{uv}(p) \tag{20}$$

where P is an arbitrary path connecting u and v.

Naturally D(u,v) does not fulfil the reflective law, but still satisfies

$$D(u,v) \leqq D(u,w) + D(w,v) \tag{21}$$

Similar to the centrality axioms for a nondirected graph, a centrality function C(G,v) whose values are in R^2 can be defined in terms of the modified distance.

Centrality Axioms : If there exist no edges between a pair of vertices p and q in a weakly connected directed graph G, the insertion of edges from p to q and from q to p yields two graphs G'_{pq} and G''_{pq}, respectively. Let us define

$$\left.\begin{aligned} \Delta'_{pq}(v) &= C(G,v) - C(G'_{pq},v) \\ \Delta''_{pq}(v) &= C(G,v) - C(G''_{pq},v) \end{aligned}\right\} \tag{22}$$

for any vertex v in G.

Now the function C(G,v) is called a centrality function if and only if

$$\text{(i)} \quad \Delta'_{pq}(p) > 0, \quad \Delta''_{pq}(p) \geqq 0 \tag{23}$$

$$\text{(ii)} \quad \Delta'_{pq}(p) \geqq \Delta'_{pq}(v) \quad \text{and} \quad \Delta''_{pq}(p) \geqq \Delta''_{pq}(v)$$

for any v satisfying

$$D(v,p) \leqq D(v,p) \tag{24}$$

for any pair of vertices p and q which are not adjacent. (End)

We will deal with the function defined by

$$C(G,v) = \sum_{1<\mu\varepsilon N^2} \alpha_\mu n_\mu(v) \tag{25}$$

where $\alpha_\mu (\varepsilon\ R^2)$ does not depend on G and $n_\mu(v)$ denotes the number of vertices whose modified distance from v are $\mu (\varepsilon\ N^2)$.

Corresponding to Theorem 1, we now obtain the following theorem.

Theorem 11 : The function defined by (25) is a centrality function if α_μ's satisfy

$$\text{(i)} \quad \alpha_1 < \alpha_2, \quad \alpha_{\mu_1} \leqq \alpha_{\mu_2} \tag{26}$$

$$\text{(ii)} \quad \alpha_{\mu_2} - \alpha_{\mu_1} \geqq \alpha_{\mu_2+\delta} - \alpha_{\mu_1+\delta} \tag{27}$$

where $1 \leqq \mu_1 < \mu_2$ and $1 \leqq \delta$. (End)

For a directed graph, we can also prove some stability theorems corresponding to those for a nondirected graph.

7. Conclusion

It has been supposed to be true that any connected nondirected graph is stable with respect to the transmission number [2]. The theorems given here show that the conjecture is false.

Theorem 4 and 6 show that centrality functions with which all the nondirected graphs are stable or quasi-stable are rather trivial. Characterizing stable or quasi-stable graphs with respect to a given centrality function is an interesting problem.

The definitions and theorems of centrality functions for a nondirected graph can be extended for a directed graph, employing the concept of modified distance which seems to be useful in the theory of directed graphs.

References

[1] Christofides, N. : "Graph theory, an algorithmic approach", Academic Press, London, 1975

[2] Sabidussi, G. : "The centrality index of a graph", Theory of graphs, International Symposium, Rome, pp. 369-372, 1966

[3] Kajitani, Y. and Maruyama, T. : "Functional extention of centrality in a graph", Trans. IECE Japan, vol. 59, pp. 531-538, July 1976 (in Japanese)

[4] Kishi, G. and Takeuchi, M. : "On centrality functions of a nondirected graph", Proc. of the 6th Colloq. on Microwave Comm., Budapest, Aug. 1978

[5] Kajitani, Y. : "Centrality of vertices in a graph", Proc. 1979 International Colloq. on Circuits & Systems, Taipei, July 1979

[6] Kishi, G. and Takeuchi, M. : "Centrality functions of directed graphs", Tech. Rep. CST 77-106, Technical Group on Circuit and System Theory, IECE Japan, Dec. 1977 (in Japanese)

CANONICAL DECOMPOSITIONS OF SYMMETRIC SUBMODULAR SYSTEMS

S. Fujishige
Institute of Socio-Economic Planning
University of Tsukuba
Sakura, Ibaraki, Japan 305

Abstract. Let E be a finite set, R the set of real numbers and $f: 2^E \to R$ a symmetric submodular function. The pair (E,f) is called a symmetric submodular system. We examine the structures of symmetric submodular systems and provide a decomposition theory of symmetric submodular systems. The theory is a generalization of the decomposition theory of 2-connected graphs developed by W. T. Tutte.

1. Introduction

A decomposition theory of graphs is developed by W. T. Tutte [9]. A connected graph G is decomposed into a set of 2-connected subgraphs of G and the incidence relation of these 2-connected subgraphs is represented by a tree. Moreover, a 2-connected graph G is decomposed into a set of 3-connected graphs, bonds and polygons, and their structural relation is represented by a tree. Also R. E. Gomory and T. C. Hu [7] derived a tree structure of the set of minimum cuts of a capacitated undirected (or symmetric) multi-terminal network. In extracting these tree structures, symmetric submodular functions play a crucial role. Related tree representation of a collection of sets was examined by J. Edmonds and R. Giles [4].

Let E be a finite set and $f: 2^E \to R$ a symmetric submodular function, whose precise definition will be given in Section 2. The pair (E,f) is called a symmetric submodular system. We shall consider symmetric submodular systems and provide a theory of decomposition of symmetric submodular systems, which is a generalization of the decomposition theory of 2-connected graphs by Tutte [9]. The decomposition theory can be applied to any systems with submodular functions such as graphs [9], capacitated networks [7], matroids [10], communication networks [5] etc., where if necessary the underlying submodular functions should be symmetrized (see Section 5).

2. Definitions and Assumptions

Let E be a finite set, R the set of real numbers and $f: 2^E \to R$ a submodular function, i.e.,

$$f(A) + f(B) \geqq f(A \cup B) + f(A \cap B) \tag{2.1}$$

for any $A, B \subseteqq E$. The pair (E,f) is called a <u>submodular system</u> [6] and if the submodular function f is <u>symmetric</u>, i.e.,

$$f(A) = f(E-A) \tag{2.2}$$

for any $A \subseteqq E$, then (E,f) is called a <u>symmetric submodular system</u>.

If $C \subseteqq E$ satisfies $|C| \geqq k$ and $|E-C| \geqq k$ for a positive integer k, we call C a <u>k-cut</u> of (E,f). Let $e_A \notin E$ be a new element corresponding to a nonempty subset A of E and define

$$E' = (E-A) \cup \{e_A\}, \tag{2.3}$$

$$f'(B) = f(B) \qquad \text{if} \quad e_A \notin B \subseteqq E', \tag{2.4a}$$

$$\quad = f((B-\{e_A\}) \cup A) \qquad \text{if} \quad e_A \in B \subseteqq E'. \tag{2.4b}$$

Then we call the submodular system (E',f') an <u>aggregation of</u> (E,f) <u>by</u> A and we denote it by $(E,f)//A$. Let $P = \{A_0, A_1, \cdots, A_k\}$ be a partition of E, i.e., $A_i \neq \emptyset$ $(i=0,1,\cdots,k)$, $A_i \cap A_j = \emptyset$ $(i \neq j; i,j=0,1,\cdots,k)$ and $A_0 \cup A_1 \cup \cdots \cup A_k = E$. For the partition P, let us define

$$(E,f)//P = (\cdots(((E,f)//A_0)//A_1)\cdots)//A_k. \tag{2.5}$$

Note that $(E,f)//P$ does not depend on the order of the A_i's in (2.5). If subsets C_1 and C_2 of E satisfy $C_1 \cup C_2 \neq E$, $C_1 \cap C_2 \neq \emptyset$, $C_1 - C_2 \neq \emptyset$ and $C_2 - C_1 \neq \emptyset$, then we say C_1 and C_2 <u>cross</u>. We define a partial order $\leqq$ on the set of partitions of E as follows. For partitions P and P' of E, $P \leqq P'$ if and only if for each $A \in P$ there is an element $A' \in P'$ such that $A \subseteqq A'$.

Throughout the present paper, we assume that (E,f) is a symmetric submodular system and

$$\min\{f(C) \mid C \text{ is a 1-cut of } (E,f)\} = \lambda^*. \tag{2.6}$$

We denote by $\mathcal{C}_f$ the set of 2-cuts C such that $f(C) = \lambda^*$. We shall examine the structure of the set $\mathcal{C}_f$ and decompose (E,f) based on $\mathcal{C}_f$. It should be noted that $\mathcal{C}_f$ is complemented, i.e., if $C \in \mathcal{C}_f$ then $E-C \in \mathcal{C}_f$.

3. Main Theorems

The following lemma is fundamental for the symmetric submodular system (E,f) satisfying (2.6).

Lemma 1: Suppose that subsets C_1 and C_2 of E cross and satisfy

$$f(C_1) = f(C_2) = \lambda^*. \tag{3.1}$$

Then we have

$$f(C_1 \cup C_2) = f(C_1 \cap C_2) = f(C_1 - C_2) = f(C_2 - C_1) = \lambda^*. \tag{3.2}$$

(Proof) Since

$$f(C_1) + F(C_2) \geqq f(C_1 \cup C_2) + f(C_1 \cap C_2) \tag{3.3}$$

and C_1 and C_2 cross, we have from (2.6)

$$f(C_1 \cup C_2) = f(C_1 \cap C_2) = \lambda^*. \tag{3.4}$$

Because of the symmetry of f, Lemma 1 follows from (3.4). Q.E.D.

Lemma 2: Let e_1, e_2, e_3 and e_4 be four distinct elements of E. If $\{e_1,e_2\}$, $\{e_1,e_3\}$, $\{e_1,e_4\} \varepsilon\, C_f$, then $\{e_2,e_3\}$, $\{e_2,e_4\}$, $\{e_3,e_4\} \varepsilon\, C_f$.

(Proof) Since $\{e_1,e_2\}$ and $\{e_1,e_3\}$ in C_f cross, we have from Lemma 1

$$f(\{e_1,e_2,e_3\}) = \lambda^*. \tag{3.5}$$

If $E = \{e_1,e_2,e_3,e_4\}$, then $\{e_2,e_3\} = E - \{e_1,e_4\} \varepsilon\, C_f$. Therefore, suppose $E \neq \{e_1,e_2,e_3,e_4\}$. Then, since $\{e_1,e_2,e_3\}$ and $\{e_1,e_4\}$ cross, we have from (3.5) and Lemma 1

$$\{e_2,e_3\} = \{e_1,e_2,e_3\} - \{e_1,e_4\} \varepsilon\, C_f. \tag{3.6}$$

Because of the symmetry among the elements e_2, e_3 and e_4, this completes the proof of Lemma 2. Q.E.D.

Now, let R_f be a collection of two-element subsets of E defined by

$$R_f = \{C \mid C \varepsilon\, C_f, |C|=2\}. \tag{3.7}$$

Theorem 1: Let $G = (E,R_f)$ be a graph with the vertex set E and the edge set R_f defined by (3.7). If G is connected, then G is a complete graph or an elementary closed path.

(Proof) By definition, connectedness of G implies that $|E| = 1$ or $|E| \geqq 4$ and thus we assume $|E| \geqq 4$. It follows from Lemma 2 that G can be a complete graph, an elementary closed path or an elementary nonclosed path. Therefore, let us assume that $E = \{e_1,e_2,\cdots,e_n\}$ $(n \geqq 4)$ and that $\{e_i,e_{i+1}\} \varepsilon\, C_f$ $(i=1,2,\cdots,n-1)$. Then $\{e_1,e_n\}$ must be in C_f because from Lemma 1 we have $\{e_2,e_3,\cdots,e_{n-1}\} \varepsilon\, C_f$. Consequently, G cannot be an elementary nonclosed path. Q.E.D.

Suppose that the graph $G = (E,R_f)$ has at least four vertices. If G is a complete graph or an elemenary closed path, then we say (E,f) is of bond type or of polygon type, respectively. We call (E,f) irreducible if C_f is empty or (E,f) is of bond type or of polygon type. In particular, if C_f is empty, we call (E,f) absolutely irreducible.

Suppose that, for $e^* \in E$, a partition $P(e^*) = \{\{e^*\},A_1,A_2,\cdots,A_k\}$ of E satisfies

(i) $(E,f)//P(e^*)$ is irreducible,

(ii) for each $i = 1, 2, \cdots, k$, if $|A_i| \geqq 2$, then $A_i \in C_f$.

Then $P(e^*)$ is called an irreducibility partition associated with $e^* \in E$. Let us denote by $\mathcal{P}(e^*)$ the set of all irreducibility partitions associated with $e^* \in E$. Note that $\mathcal{P}(e^*)$ is nonempty for every $e^* \in E$.

For partitions P and P' of E given by $P = \{A_0,A_1,\cdots,A_k\}$ and $P' = \{A_0',A_1',\cdots,A_h'\}$, let us define a partition $P\wedge P'$ of E by

$$P\wedge P' = \{A_i \cap A_j' \mid i=0,1,\cdots,k;j=0,1,\cdots,h;A_i \cap A_j' \neq \emptyset\}. \tag{3.8}$$

We shall show Theorems 2 - 5 from which follows the fact that, for every $e^* \in E$, $\mathcal{P}(e^*)$ is closed with respect to the operation $\wedge$ (Theorem 6). We need some preliminary lemmas.

Lemma 3: Suppose $P \equiv \{A_0,A_1,\cdots,A_k\}$ $(k \geqq 4)$ is a partition of E and define

$$A_\ell^* = \bigcup\{A_j \mid j=\ell,\ell+1,\cdots,k\} \tag{3.9}$$

and

$$P' = \{A_0,A_1,\cdots,A_{\ell-1},A_\ell^*\}, \tag{3.10}$$

where $3 \leqq \ell < k$. Then the following (i) and (ii) hold.

(i) If $(E,f)//P$ is of polygon type and $f(A_i \cup A_{i+1}) = \lambda^*$ $(i=0,1,\cdots,k)$, where $A_{k+1} = A_0$, then $(E,f)//P'$ is also of polygon type and $f(A_{\ell-1} \cup A_\ell^*) = f(A_\ell^* \cup A_0) = \lambda^*$.

(ii) If $(E,f)//P$ is of bond type, then $(E,f)//P'$ is also of bond type.

(Proof) From Lemma 1 we have $f(A_\ell^*) = \lambda^*$ and $f(A_{\ell-1} \cup A_\ell^*) = f(A_\ell^* \cup A_0) = \lambda^*$. Because of the assumption and Theorem 1 this implies that $(E,f)//P'$ is of polygon type or of bond type according as $(E,f)//P$ is of polygon type or of bond type. Q.E.D.

Lemma 4: Suppose $P \equiv \{A_0,A_1,\cdots,A_k\}$ $(k \geqq 3)$ is a partition of E such that $(E',f') \equiv (E,f)//P$ is of polygon type and that $f(A_i \cup A_{i+1}) = \lambda^*$ $(i=0,1,\cdots,k)$, where $A_{k+1} = A_0$. Also suppose $B \in C_f$ and $A_0 \cap B = \emptyset$ and define

$$J = \{j \mid j=1,2,\cdots,k;A_j \cap B \neq \emptyset\}. \tag{3.11}$$

Then, for any integer i^* such that $\min J < i^* < \max J$, we have $A_{i^*} \subsetneqq B$, where $\min J$ and $\max J$ denote the minimum integer and the maximum integer in J, respectively.

(Proof) Suppose there were an integer i^* such that $\min J < i^* < \max J$ and $A_{i^*} - B \neq \emptyset$. Put

$$J_1 = \{j \mid j \in J, j < i^*\}, \tag{3.12}$$
$$J_2 = \{j \mid j \in J, j > i^*\}. \tag{3.13}$$

Also define

$$A_1^* = \bigcup\{A_j \mid \min J_1 \leqq j \leqq \max J_1\}, \tag{3.14}$$
$$A_2^* = \bigcup\{A_j \mid \min J_2 \leqq j \leqq \max J_2\}, \tag{3.15}$$
$$P' = (P - \{A_j \mid A_j \subsetneqq A_1^* \cup A_2^*;\ j=1,2,\cdots,k\}) \cup \{A_1^*, A_2^*\}. \tag{3.16}$$

It follows from Lemma 3 that the aggregation $(E'',f'') \equiv (E,f)//P'$ is of polygon type. Furthermore, put $B^* = B - A_{i^*}$. Then $f(B^*) = \lambda^*$ and we have from Lemma 1 and the definition of A_1^* and A_2^*

$$f(A_1^* \cup A_2^*) = f((A_1^* \cup B^*) \cup (A_2^* \cup B^*)) = \lambda^*. \tag{3.17}$$

This contradicts the assertion that (E'',f'') is of polygon type. Q.E.D.

<u>Lemma 5</u>: Under the assumption of Lemma 4, if B and A_{j^*} with $j^* = \min J$ cross, then $(E,f)//P'$ is of polygon type, where

$$P' = \{A_0, A_1, \cdots, A_{j^*-1}, A_{j^*}-B, A_{j^*} \cap B, A_{j^*+1}, \cdots, A_k\}. \tag{3.18}$$

Furthermore, we have

$$f(A_{j^*-1} \cup (A_{j^*}-B)) = f((A_{j^*} \cap B) \cup A_{j^*+1}) = \lambda^*. \tag{3.19}$$

(Proof) Since $A_{j^*-1} \cap B = \emptyset$ and either $A_{j^*-1} \cup A_{j^*} \cup B = E$ or $A_{j^*-1} \cup A_{j^*}$ and B cross, we have $f(A_{j^*-1} \cup (A_{j^*}-B)) = f(A_{j^*} \cap B) = \lambda^*$. Therefore, from the assumption and Theorem 1 $(E,f)//P'$ must be of polygon type and the remaining part follows. Q.E.D.

<u>Theorem 2</u>: Suppose $P, P' \in \mathcal{P}(e^*)$ and $|P| \geqq 4$. If $(E,f)//P$ is of polygon type, then $(E,f)//P \wedge P'$ is of polygon type and, therefore, $P \wedge P' \in \mathcal{P}(e^*)$. Moreover, if $|P'| \geqq 4$, $(E,f)//P'$ is also of polygon type.

(Proof) Suppose $P = \{\{e^*\}=A_0, A_1, \cdots, A_k\}$ $(k \geqq 3)$ and $P' = \{\{e^*\}=A_0', A_1', \cdots, A_h'\}$. If $A_i \in P$ and $A_j' \in P'$ cross, then for the partition P_1 obtained from P by dividing A_i into $A_i - A_j'$ and $A_i \cap A_j'$, $(E,f)//P_1$ is irreducible and of polygon type due to Lemma 5. By repeating this process we obtain a partition $P^* = \{\{e^*\}=A_0^*, A_1^*, \cdots, A_{k^*}^*\}$ which is minimal, with respect to the partial order $\precsim$, with the property: " $P^* \precsim P$ and A_i^* and A_j' do not cross for any $A_i^* \in P^*$ and $A_j' \in P'$." The obtained $(E,f)//P^*$ is of polygon type.

If there is no A_i^* in P^* such that A_i^* contains at least two

A_j' 's, then $P^* = P \wedge P'$ and this completes the proof. Therefore, suppose that some $A_{i_0}^*$ is expressed as $A_{i_0}^* = \bigcup \{A_j' \mid j = t_1, t_2, \cdots, t_p\}$ $(p \geq 2)$. Since $(E,f)//P^*$ is of polygon type, $f(A_{i_0}^*) = \lambda^*$. It follows that $(E,f)//P'$ must be of polygon type or of bond type. In either case, from Theorem 1, for some $j^* \in \{t_1, t_2, \cdots, t_p\}$ and some $j' \in \{0, 1, \cdots, h\} - \{t_1, t_2, \cdots, t_p\}$ there holds $f(A_{j^*}' \cup A_{j'}') = \lambda^*$. Therefore, since $A_{i_0}^*$ and $A_{j^*}' \cup A_{j'}'$ cross, we see from Lemma 5 that $(E,f)//P_1^*$ is of polygon type, where P_1^* is the partition of E obtained from P^* by dividing $A_{i_0}^*$ into $A_{i_0}^* \cap (A_{j^*}' \cup A_{j'}') = A_{j^*}'$ and $A_{i_0}^* - (A_{j^*}' \cup A_{j'}') = A_{i_0}^* - A_{j^*}'$. By repeating this process we reach the partition $P \wedge P'$ for which $(E,f)//P \wedge P'$ is of polygon type.

Moreover, since $P \wedge P' \precneqq P'$, if $|P'| \geq 4$, then $(E,f)//P'$ is of polygon type due to Lemma 3. Q.E.D.

Lemma 6: Suppose $P \equiv \{A_0, A_1, \cdots, A_k\}$ $(k \geq 3)$ is a partition of E and $(E',f') \equiv (E,f)//P$ is of bond type. Also suppose $B \in \mathcal{C}_f$ and $A_{j^*} \in P$ cross and $A_0 \cap B = \emptyset$. Then $(E,f)//P'$ is of bond type, where $P' = \{A_0, A_1, \cdots, A_{j^*-1}, A_{j^*}-B, A_{j^*} \cap B, A_{j^*+1}, \cdots, A_k\}$.

(Proof) Since B and A_{j^*} cross, there is an $A_{i^*} \in P$ such that $A_{i^*} \cap B \neq \emptyset$ and $i^* \neq 0, j^*$. Put $B^* = A_{i^*} \cup B$. Then we have $f(B^*) = \lambda^*$. Since B and A_{j^*} cross and B^* and $A_{i^*} \cup A_{j^*}$ cross, we get

$$f(A_{j^*} \cap B) = f(A_{j^*} - B) = f(A_{i^*} \cup (A_{j^*} \cap B)) = \lambda^*. \tag{3.20}$$

From (3.20) and Theorem 1 we see that $(E,f)//P'$ is of bond type. Q.E.D.

Theorem 3: Suppose $P, P' \in \mathcal{P}(e^*)$ and $|P| \geq 4$. If $(E,f)//P$ is of bond type, then $(E,f)//P \wedge P'$ is of bond type and, therefore, $P \wedge P' \in \mathcal{P}(e^*)$. Moreover, if $|P'| \geq 4$, $(E,f)//P'$ is also of bond type.

(Proof) Theorem 3 can be shown by using Lemmas 3 and 6 and Theorem 1 in a way similar to the proof of Theorem 2. Q.E.D.

Theorem 4: Suppose $e^* \in E$, $P = \{\{e^*\}, A_1, A_2\} \in \mathcal{P}(e^*)$ and $P' = \{\{e^*\}, A_1', A_2'\} \in \mathcal{P}(e^*)$. Then $P \wedge P' \in \mathcal{P}(e^*)$. If $|P| = 3$ for any $P \in \mathcal{P}(e^*)$, then $|\mathcal{P}(e^*)| = 1$.

(Proof) Suppose $P \neq P'$.

First, suppose $A_1 \subsetneqq A_1'$. Then $|A_2| \geq 2$ and $f(\{e^*\} \cup A_1) = f(E - A_2) = \lambda^*$. Therefore, for the partition $P \wedge P' \equiv \{\{e^*\}, A_1, A_2 \cap A_1', A_2 - A_1'\}$, $(E,f)//P \wedge P'$ is of bond type or of polygon type and $P \wedge P' \in \mathcal{P}(e^*)$.

Next, suppose A_1 and A_1' cross and A_2 and A_1' cross. Then $f(\{e^*\} \cup (A_1 - A_1')) = f(A_1 \cap A_1') = f(A_2 \cap A_1') = f(A_2 - A_1') = \lambda^*$. It follows that, for $P \wedge P' \equiv \{\{e^*\}, A_1 - A_1', A_1 \cap A_1', A_2 \cap A_1', A_2 - A_1'\}$, $(E,f)//P \wedge P'$ is of bond type or of polygon type and $P \wedge P' \in \mathcal{P}(e^*)$.

The remaining part of the theorem follows from the fact that, if

$P, P' \in \mathcal{P}(e^*)$, $P \neq P'$ and $|P| = |P'| = 3$, then $P \wedge P' \in \mathcal{P}(e^*)$ and $|P \wedge P'| \geqq 4$. Q.E.D.

Lemma 7: Suppose that $P \equiv \{A_0, A_1, \cdots, A_k\}$ $(k \geqq 3)$ is a partition of E and that $(E,f)//P$ is absolutely irreducible. Then, for any $B \in \mathcal{C}_f$ such that $A_0 \cap B = \emptyset$, B and any of $A_1, \cdots, A_k$ do not cross.
(Proof) Suppose B and A_1 cross. Let us define

$$I = \{i \mid A_i \cap B \neq \emptyset,\ i=1,2,\cdots,k\}. \tag{3.21}$$

Then $|I| \geqq 2$ and, from Lemma 1, $A^* \equiv \bigcup\{A_i \mid i \in I\}$ satisfies $f(A^*) = \lambda^*$. It follows that $I = \{1,2,\cdots,k\}$, since $(E,f)//P$ is absolutely irreducible. Put

$$B^* = (B \cup (\bigcup\{A_i \mid i=2,\cdots,k\})) - A_1. \tag{3.22}$$

From Lemma 1 we have $f(B^*) = \lambda^*$. Consequently, $f(A_0 \cup A_1) = \lambda^*$, since $B^* = E - (A_0 \cup A_1)$. This contradicts the absolute irreducibility of $(E,f)//P$. Q.E.D.

Theorem 5: Suppose that, for some $P \in \mathcal{P}(e^*)$ such that $|P| \geqq 4$, $(E,f)//P$ is absolutely irreducible. Then $|\mathcal{P}(e^*)| = 1$.
(Proof) Suppose $P = \{\{e^*\}, A_1, \cdots, A_k\}$ and there is another $P' = \{\{e^*\}, A_1', \cdots, A_h'\}$ in $\mathcal{P}(e^*)$. It follows from Lemma 7 and the absolute irreducibility of $(E,f)//P$ that each $A_j' \in P'$ is included in some $A_i \in P$. Suppose that, for some distinct indices $j_1, j_2 \in \{1,2,\cdots,h\}$, $A_{j_1}' \cup A_{j_2}'$ is included in some A_i. Then $(E,f)//P'$ must be of polygon type or of bond type. This contradicts Theorem 2 or 3. Therefore, $P = P'$. Q.E.D.

It should be noted that, if $|E| \leqq 3$, (E,f) is absolutely irreducible. Therefore, from Theorems 2 - 5 we have the following.

Theorem 6: For any $e^* \in E$, there is a unique minimal element of the partially ordered set $(\mathcal{P}(e^*), \preceq)$.

Because of Theorem 6, for each $e^* \in E$, we call the unique minimal element of $\mathcal{P}(e^*)$ the minimal irreducibility partition of E associated with e^* and denote it by $\hat{P}(e^*)$. Moreover, we call $A \in \hat{P}(e^*)$ a minimal irreducibility component of (E,f) associated with e^*.

Lemma 8: For $e^*, e \in E$, if the set $\{e\}$ is a minimal irreducibility component of (E,f) associated with e^*, then $\hat{P}(e^*) = \hat{P}(e)$.
(Proof) From the assumption, $\hat{P}(e^*) \in \mathcal{P}(e)$. Therefore, $\hat{P}(e) \preceq \hat{P}(e^*)$ and $\hat{P}(e) \in \mathcal{P}(e^*)$. By the minimality of $\hat{P}(e^*)$, this means $\hat{P}(e^*) = \hat{P}(e)$. Q.E.D.

Theorem 7: Suppose a set $D \subsetneqq E$ is a minimal irreducibility component of (E,f) associated with $e^* \in E$ such that $|D| \geqq 2$. Then, for any $e \in D$, $E - D$ is included in a minimal irreducibility component of (E,f) associated with e.

(Proof) Let $\hat{P}(e^*) = \{\{e^*\}=A_0, A_1, \cdots, A_k\}$ and $\hat{P}(e) = \{\{e\}=A_0', A_1', \cdots, A_h'\}$, where $e \in A_1 = D$ and $e^* \in A_1'$. Suppose that $A_1 \cup A_1' \neq E$. Then, since from Lemma 8 we have $\{e^*\} \subsetneqq A_1'$ and since from Lemmas 5, 6 and 7 for each $A_j' \in \hat{P}(e)$ A_j' and any of $A_1, \cdots, A_k$ do not cross, both A_1' and $E - A_1'$ are unions of at last two A_i's of $\hat{P}(e^*)$. Therefore, $(E,f)//\hat{P}(e^*)$ is of bond type or of polygon type, and, by the same argument, $(E,f)//\hat{P}(e)$ is also of bond type or of polygon type. Similarly as the proof of Theorem 2, this contradicts the minimality of $\hat{P}(e)$ and $\hat{P}(e^*)$. Therefore, $A_1 \cup A_1' = E$. Q.E.D.

4. Canonical Decomposition

Let us define an equivalence relation $\hat{R} \subseteqq E \times E$ as follows: For $e^*, e \in E$, $(e^*, e) \in \hat{R}$ if and only if $\hat{P}(e^*) = \hat{P}(e)$. Let $\Pi \equiv \{S_1, S_2, \cdots, S_p\}$ be the partition of E composed of the equivalence classes of E relative to $\hat{R}$. The partition Π is called the _canonical 2-cut partition, of level 1, of_ E. For any $S_j \in \Pi$, define

$$\hat{P}(S_j) = \hat{P}(e) \tag{4.1}$$

for any $e \in S_j$, where note that $\hat{P}(e) = \hat{P}(e')$ for any $e, e' \in S_j$. Each $A \in \hat{P}(S_j)$ with $|A| \geqq 2$ is called a _minimal irreducibility component of_ (E,f) _associated with_ S_j.

Suppose that, for each $i = 1, 2, \cdots, k$ $(k \geqq 3)$, A_i is a minimal irreducibility component of (E,f) associated with $S_{j(i)} \in \Pi$ and that $P^* \equiv \{E-A_1, E-A_2, \cdots, E-A_k\}$ is a partition of E. Then we call the partition P^* a _2-cut aggregation partition, of level 1, of_ E. Denote by $\mathcal{A}$ the set of all 2-cut aggregation partitions, of level 1, of E. Moreover, we call the aggregation $(E,f)//P^*$ $(P^* \in \mathcal{A})$ a _2-cut aggregation, of level 1, of_ (E,f) _by_ P^*.

Let $G_1^* = (V_1^*, E_1^*)$ be a graph with a vertex set V_1^* and an edge set E_1^* defined as follows:

$$V_1^* = V_\Pi \cup V_{\mathcal{A}}, \tag{4.2}$$

where $V_\Pi = \{v_S \mid S \in \Pi\}$ and $V_{\mathcal{A}} = \{v_P \mid P \in \mathcal{A}\}$, and

$$E_1^* = A_1^* \cup B_1^*, \tag{4.3}$$

where

(i) $a \in A_1^*$ if and only if $a = \{v_S, v_{S'}\}$ such that $S, S' \in \Pi$

and $E - A = A'$ for minimal irreducibility components A and A' associated with S and S', respectively,

and

(ii) $a \in B_1^*$ if and only if $a = \{v_S, v_P\}$ such that $S \in \Pi$, $P \in A$ and $E - A = B$ for a minimal irreducibility component A associated with S and a component B of the 2-cut aggregation partition P.

We can easily see from Theorem 7 that the graph $G_1^* = (V_1^*, E_1^*)$ is a tree. We call the tree G_1^* the <u>canonical decomposition tree, of level 1, of</u> (E,f). It should be noted that for each vertex v of G_1^*, if v corresponds to an $S_j \in \Pi$, then the vertex v is associated with $(E,f)//P(S_j)$ and, if v corresponds to a 2-cut aggregation partition P^*, then v is associated with the 2-cut aggregation $(E,f)//P^*$. Also note that there may be more than one 2-cut aggregation partitions of E of (E,f).

If a 2-cut aggregation $(E,f)//P^*$ of (E,f) is reducible, then further construct the canonical decomposition tree, of level 1, of $(E,f)//P^*$ and repeat this decomposition process until the constructed canonical decomposition tree does not contain any vertex which corresponds to a reducible 2-cut aggregation. If a canonical decomposition tree is obtained after k-1 repeated 2-cut aggregations, then we call the tree the canonical decomposition tree, <u>of level k</u>, of (E,f).

In this way we can decompose (E,f) into irreducible aggregations of (E,f) and extract the tree structures of these aggregations of all levels and, at the same time, the hierarchical structure of the reducible 2-cut aggregations.

A canonical decomposition tree of level $k+1$ can be embedded into a canonical decomposition tree of level k as follows. Let G_{k+1}^* and G_k^* be canonical decomposition trees, of level 1, of $(E^{(k)}, f^{(k)})$ and $(E^{(k-1)}, f^{(k-1)})$, respectively, and

$$(E^{(k)}, f^{(k)}) = (E^{(k-1)}, f^{(k-1)})//P^{(k-1)}, \qquad (4.4)$$

where $P^{(k-1)}$ is a 2-cut aggregation partition of $E^{(k-1)}$ of $(E^{(k-1)}, f^{(k-1)})$. Note that $E^{(k)} = \{e_A \mid A \in P^{(k-1)}\}$. Let v^* be the vertex in G_k^* which corresponds to $P^{(k-1)}$. Also let $v_S^{(k)}$ be the vertex in G_k^* which corresponds to a component S of the canonical 2-cut partition of $E^{(k-1)}$ such that $v_S^{(k)}$ is adjacent to v^* and $E - A = B$ for a minimal irreducibility component A associated with S and a component B of $P^{(k-1)}$. Furthermore, let S^* be a component of the canonical 2-cut partition of $E^{(k)}$ containing the element e_B. Then replace the edge $\{v_S^{(k)}, v^*\}$ by $\{v_S^{(k)}, v_{S^*}^{(k+1)}\}$, where $v_{S^*}^{(k+1)}$ is the vertex in G_{k+1}^* which corresponds to S^*. In this way we replace all the edges, in G_k^*, incident to v^* and then delete v^*, which yields a tree composed of G_k^* and G_{k+1}^*.

All the canonical decomposition trees can thus be embedded into the canonical decomposition tree, of level 1, of (E,f) by repeatedly embedding canonical decomposition trees into canonical decomposition trees of lower levels. We call the tree composed of all the canonical decomposition trees the <u>total decomposition tree of</u> (E,f).

5. Examples of Symmetric Submodular Systems and Their Decompositions

Now, let us show some examples.

<u>Example 1</u>: Let $G = (V,E)$ be a connected but not 2-connected graph and define

$$f(A) = |V(A)| + |V(E-A)| - |V| \tag{5.1}$$

for any $A \subseteq E$, where for $B \subseteq E$ $V(B)$ is the set of end-vertices of edges in B. Then (E,f) is a symmetric submodular system and satisfies (2.6) with $\lambda^* = 1$. Any 2-cut aggregations, of level 1, of (E,f) are of bond type if the ground sets have the cardinality not less than 4, so that (E,f) is decomposed up to level 1.

The canonical decomposition tree, of level 1, of (E,f) is different from, but essentially the same as, the tree representing the incidence relation of 2-connected subgraphs of G which is described in [9]. See Figure 1.

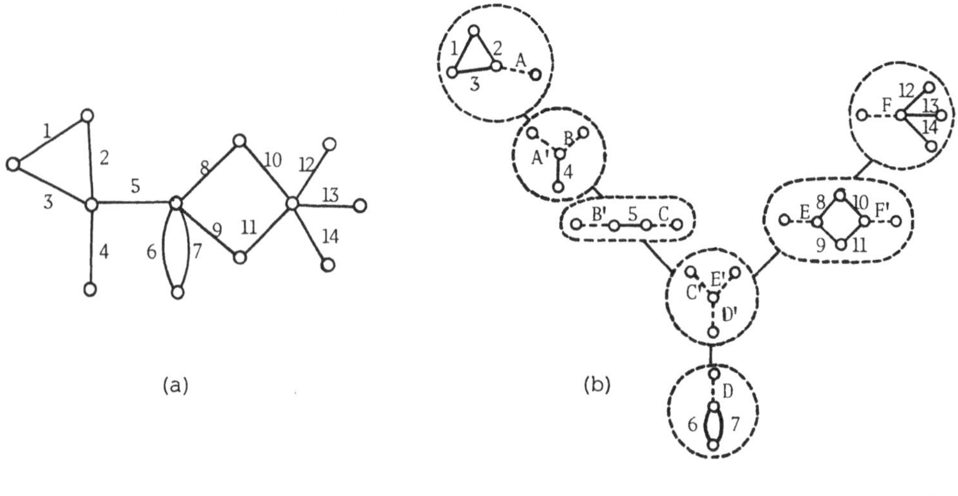

Figure 1. (a) A graph G; and (b) the canonical decomposition tree of (E,f) defined by (5.1).

Remark 1: The decomposition of a connected graph into 2-connected subgraphs [9] is determined by the structure of minimum 1-cuts of the symmetric submodular system (E,f) defined by (5.1). We can develop a decomposition theory based on the structure of minimum 1-cuts of symmetric submodular systems, which is similar to the theory, by Gomory and Hu [7] for representing the structure of the set of minimum cuts in a symmetric network by a tree.

Example 2: Let $G = (V,E)$ be a 2-connected graph and define $f: 2^E \to R$ by (5.1). Then (E,f) is a symmetric submodular system and satisfies (2.6) with $\lambda^* = 2$. The total decomposition tree of (E,f) is the same as the tree representing the structure of the set of two-terminal subgraphs of G described by Tutte [9], where the hierarchical structure of the set of two-terminal subgraphs is implicit.

Example 3: Let $M = (E,\rho)$ be a 2-connected matroid with a rank function ρ. Let us define

$$f(A) = \rho(A) + \rho(E-A) - \rho(E) + 1 \qquad (5.2)$$

for any $A \subsetneqq E$. Then (E,f) is a symmetric submodular system and satisfies (2.6) with $\lambda^* = 2$ (cf. [10], [11]). Therefore, we can obtain the canonical decomposition trees of (E,f). Note that f defined by (5.2) is a symmetrization of the rank function ρ. It may also be noted that, if E with $|E| \geqq 4$ is a circuit of the matroid (E,ρ), the corresponding (E,f) is not of polygon type but of bond type. Related works on matroid decompositions were made by R. E. Bixby [1] and W. H. Cunningham [3].

Remark 2: We have not discussed the algorithmic aspects of decompositions of symmetric submodular systems. Whether or not there exists an efficient algorithm for decomposing a symmetric submodular system depends on how the submodular system is represented. See [8] for decompositions of 2-connected graphs and [2] and [3] for decompositions of 2-connected matroids.

Acknowledgement

The author is deeply indebted to Professor Masao Iri of the University of Tokyo for his valuable discussions on the present paper.

References

[1] R.E. Bixby: Composition and Decomposition of Matroids and Related Topics. Ph.D. Thesis, Cornell University, 1972.
[2] R.E. Bixby and W.H. Cunningham: Matroids, graphs and 3-connectivity. Graph Theory and Related Topics (J.A. Bondy and U.S.R. Murty, eds.,

Academic Press, New York, 1979), pp. 91-103.
[3] W.H. Cunningham: _A Combinatorial Decomposition Theory_. Ph.D. Thesis, University of Waterloo, 1973; also W.H. Cunningham and J. Edmonds: A combinatorial decomposition theory. _Canadian Journal of Mathematics_, Vol. 32 (1980), pp. 734-765.
[4] J. Edmonds and R. Giles: A min-max relation for submodular functions on graphs. _Annals of Discrete Mathematics_, Vol. 1 (1977), pp. 185-204.
[5] S. Fujishige: Polymatroidal dependence structure of a set of random variables. _Information and Control_, Vol. 39 (1978), pp. 55-72.
[6] S. Fujishige: Principal structures of submodular systems. _Discrete Applied Mathematics_, Vol. 2 (1980), pp. 77-79.
[7] R.E. Gomory and T.C. Hu: Multi-terminal network flows. _J. SIAM_, Vol. 9 (1961), pp. 551-570.
[8] J.E. Hopcroft and R.E. Tarjan: Dividing a graph into triconnected components. _SIAM Journal on Computing_, Vol. 2 (1973), pp. 135-158.
[9] W.T. Tutte: _Connectivity in Graphs_. University of Toronto Press, Toronto, 1966.
[10] W.T. Tutte: Connectivity in matroids. _Canadian Journal of Mathematics_, Vol. 18 (1966), pp. 1301-1324.
[11] D.J.A. Welsh: _Matroid Theory_. Academic Press, London, 1976.

THE SUBGRAPH HOMEOMORPHISM PROBLEM ON REDUCIBLE FLOW GRAPHS

T. Hirata and M. Kimura
Dept. of Information Science
Faculty of Engineering, Tohoku University
Sendai, Japan 980

Abstract We investigate the subgraph homeomorphism problem in which one would like to determine whether a fixed pattern graph is homeomorphic to a subgraph of an input graph. We show that for every fixed pattern graph, there is a polynomial-time algorithm to solve the problem if the input graphs are restricted to reducible flow graphs.

1. Introduction

For a fixed pattern graph H, the subgraph homeomorphism problem (SHP) with respect to H asks to determine whether H is homeomorphic to a subgraph of an input graph G. The graphs G and H are either both directed or both undirected.

There are many graph properties for which the recognition problems can be reduced to the SHPs. For example, the recognition problem of planar graphs can be reduced to the SHP with respect to K_5 and $K_{3,3}$, and that of series-parallel graphs can be reduced to the SHP with respect to K_4 [2]. The SHP arises also in the study of program schema. In fact, many schema properties are characterized by the presence or reachability of certain substructures [7].

"Homeomorphism" between H and a subgraph of G is defined in terms of two mappings h_1 and h_2: h_1 from vertices of H to vertices of G, and h_2 from edges of H to pairwise disjoint paths in G. If we are concerned with only homeomorphisms with h_1 specified a priori, then we refer to the SHP as the fixed SHP. This restricted problem can be viewed as the problem of deciding whether there is a set of disjoint paths connecting the specified vertices of G. In the case of undirected graphs, A. S. LaPaugh and R. L. Rivest have shown that there exists a linear time algorithm to solve the fixed SHP if the pattern graph consists of exactly one triangle [8]. Y. Shiloach has given a polynomial-time algorithm for the fixed SHP with a pattern graph consisting of two disjoint edges [10]. When it comes to directed graphs, however, the fixed SHP is known to be NP-complete even if the pattern graph consists of exactly two disjoint edges [3]. This implies that the fixed SHP is NP-complete if a pattern graph contains at least two disjoint edges [3].

In this paper we first present a polynomial-time algorithm for reducible flow graphs to solve the fixed SHP with respect to the pattern graph consisting of only two edges. Extending the algorithm, we next give a polynomial-time algorithm to solve the (fixed) SHP with respect to any pattern graph H for reducible flow graphs.

2. Definitions

Let $G=(V,E)$ be a directed graph, where V is a finite set of vertices and E is a subset of $V\times V$, each member of which is called an edge. For an edge (x,y), vertex x is called its initial endpoint and y its terminal endpoint. Edge (x,y) is said to leave vertex x and enter vertex y. We say that x is a predecessor of y, and y is a successor of x. A path P of length k-1 from x_1 to x_k is a sequence of vertices $(x_1,\ldots,x_k)$ with $(x_i,x_{i+1}) \in E$ for $1 \le i \le k-1$. If a path consists of a single vertex, the length is 0. P is called a cycle if $x_1=x_k$ and $x_i \ne x_j$ for $1 \le i < j \le k-1$. A cycle of length 1 is called a loop. P is said to be simple if no two vertices in P are identical. Two simple paths are disjoint if they have no vertices in commom except for their endpoints. A graph $G'=(V',E')$ is called a subgraph of G if $V' \subset V$ and $E' \subset E$. Furthermore G' is an induced subgraph of G if $E'=E \cap (V' \times V')$. A flow graph, denoted by a triple $F=(V,E,s)$, is a directed graph (V,E) such that there is a path from the initial vertex $s \in V$ to each vertex in G. In a flow graph, vertex x dominates vertex y if every path from the initial vertex to y passes through x.

Given directed graphs G and H, we say that H is homeomorphic to a subgraph of G if there exist two one-to-one mappings h_1 and h_2, h_1 from the set of vertices of H into the set of vertices of G, and h_2 from the set of edges of H onto a set of pairwise disjoint paths in G, such that for every edge (x,y) of H the path $h_2(x,y)$ starts from $h_1(x)$ and ends at $h_1(y)$. For a fixed pattern graph H, the subgraph homeomorphism problem with respect to H asks to determine whether H is homeomorphic to a subgraph of an input graph G. (A pattern graph might be allowed to have multi edges.) If we concerned only homeomorphisms with h_1 specified a priori, then we refer to this restricted problem as the fixed subgraph homeomorphism problem. The k disjoint paths problem is to determine, given a directed graph G and k pairs of vertices $(s_1,t_1),(s_2,t_2),\ldots,(s_k,t_k)$ of G, whether there is a set of k disjoint paths $P_1,\ldots,P_k$ in G with each P_i running from s_i to t_i, $1 \leq i \leq k$.

3. Reduction of a flow graph

M. S. Hecht and J. D. Ullman defined reducible flow graphs in terms of the following two transformations T_1 and T_2 on flow graphs [5]. Let $F=(V,E,s)$ be a flow graph. Transformation from F to a new flow graph by removing a loop is called the transformation of type T_1. (We refer to this transformation as T_1 henceforce for simplicity.) Let x and y be vertices in F such that x is the unique predecessor of y, and y is not the initial vertex s. The transformation from F to a new flow graph F' by replacing vertices x,y and edge (x,y) with a new vertex, say $z \notin V$, is called the transformation of type T_2 (We refer to this transformation as T_2 henceforce); predecessors of x become those of z in the new flow graph; and successors of x and y become those of z. F' has a loop (z,z) if and only if F has an edge (y,x) or (x,x). We illustrate these two transformations in Fig. 1.

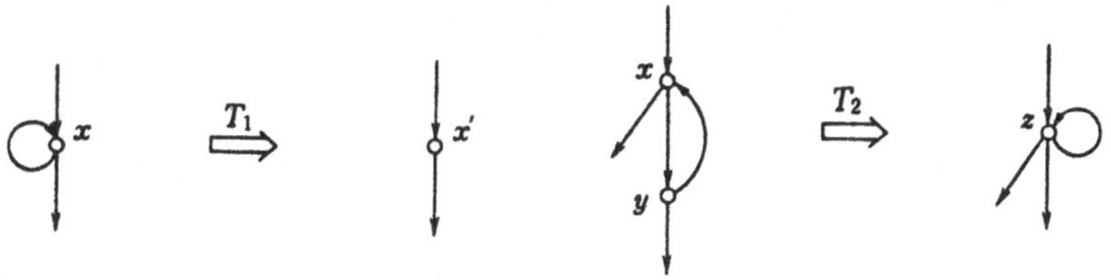

Fig. 1 - Transformations T_1 and T_2.

A given flow graph F is transformed to a flow graph F_ℓ if T_1 and T_2 are applied in any order to F until they can no longer be applied; the resulting flow graph F_ℓ is called the limit graph of F. It is known that the limit graph F_ℓ of F is unique, independent of the sequence of applications of T_1 and T_2 actually chosen [5].

If F_ℓ consists of a single vertex, the original flow graph F is said to be reducible. The class of reducible flow graphs defined above is identical with the class defined by F. E. Allen and J. Cock in terms of "intervals" [5].

As we proceed to apply T_1 and T_2 to a flow graph F, each vertex of an intermediate graph can be viewed to represent a subgraph, called a region, of the original flow graph F, and each edge to represent a set of edges of F, which are defined as follows.

(i) In the original flow graph, every vertex v represents region $(\{v\},\emptyset)$, and every edge e represents singleton set $\{e\}$.

(ii) If T_1 is applied to vertex n with the loop (n,n) and they are replaced by a new vertex n', then n' represents region $(V',E'\cup E'')$, where (V',E') is the region represented by n, and E" is the edge set represented by (n,n).

(iii) If T_2 is applied to n_1 and n_2 with edge (n_1,n_2) and they are replaced by a new vertex n, then n represents region $(V_1\cup V_2,E_1\cup E_2\cup E_3)$, where (V_1,E_1) is the region represented by n_1, and (V_2,E_2) the region represented by n_2, and E_3 is the edge set represented by (n_1,n_2). If two edges (n_1,n') and (n_2,n') are replaced by edge (n,n'), then (n,n') represents the union of the two sets represented by (n_1,n') and by (n_2,n').

The following lemma is implicit in [6].

Lemma 1. Let F=(V,E,s) be a flow graph. Let F' be a flow graph formed at some stage of the reduction of F.

(i) Let n be a vertex of F'. If n represents (V',E'), and (n_1,n_2) E', then $n_1\in V'$ and $n_2\in V'$ (that is, (V',E') is a graph).

(ii) Let n_1 and n_2 be (not necessarily distinct) vertices of F' and (n_1,n_2) an edge of F'. If n_1 and n_2 represent (V',E') and (V",E") respectively and (n_3,n_4) belongs to the set represented by (n_1,n_2), then $n_3\in V'$ and $n_4\in V''$.

(iii) The family of the vertex sets of all the regions represented by vertices of F' is a partition of the set of vertices of F.

(iv) The family of all edge sets represented by edges of F' is a partition of the set of all edges of G with two ends in distinct regions.

A parse of a reducible flow graph F is a sequence of T_1 and T_2 which are applied to F until the limit graph results. Formally it is defined to be a sequence of four-tuples (T_1,u,v,S) and five-tuples (T_2,u,v,w,S) as follows, where u,v, and w are vertices of F, and S is a set of edges of F.

(i) The parse of a flow graph consisting of a single vertex is an empty sequence.

(ii) If F' is reduced to F" by an application of T_1 to vertex u with loop (u,u), and u is replaced with a vertex v in F", then (T_1,u,v,S) followed by a parse of F" is a parse of F', where S is the set of edges represented by edge (u,u) eliminated from F'.

(iii) If F' is reduced to F" by applying T_2 to edge (u,v), and u and v are replaced with a new vertex w, then (T_2,u,v,w,S) followed by a parse of F" is a parse of F', where S is the set of edges represented by edge (u,v) of F'.

Generally the parse of a flow graph is not unique. Fig. 2 illustrates a parsing of a flow graph, and Fig. 3 illustrates the regions of the graph.

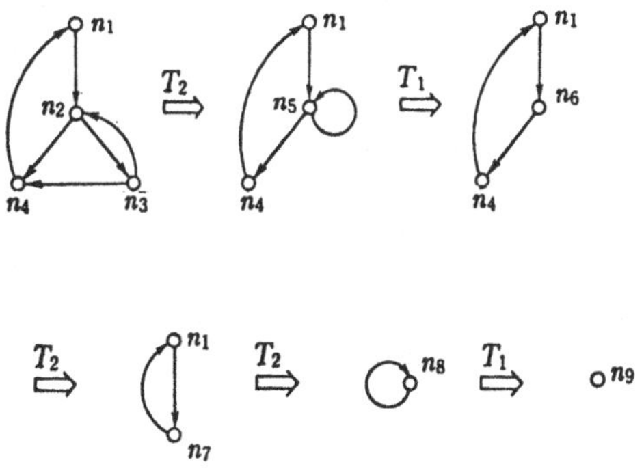

Fig. 2 - Example of a parsing.

The parse in Fig. 2 is:

$$\Pi_F = (T_2, n_2, n_3, n_5, \{(n_2, n_3)\}),$$
$$(T_1, n_5, n_6, \{(n_3, n_2)\}),$$
$$(T_2, n_6, n_4, n_7, \{(n_3, n_4), (n_2, n_4)\}),$$
$$(T_2, n_1, n_7, n_8, \{(n_1, n_2)\}),$$
$$(T_1, n_8, n_9, \{(n_4, n_1)\})$$

According to Π_F one can form larger and larger regions by combining smaller regions as illustrated in Fig. 3 .

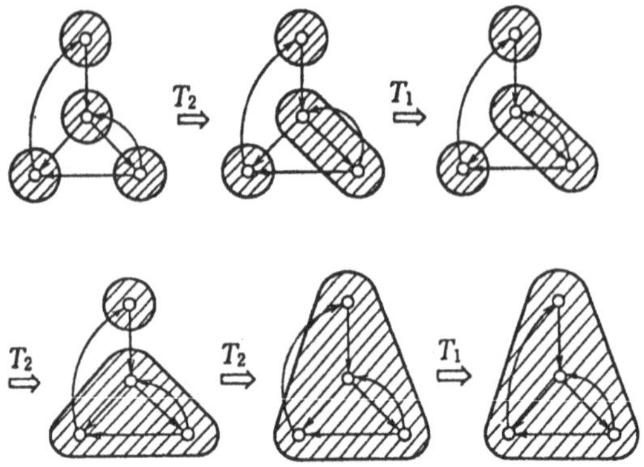

Fig. 3 - Formation of regions.

The following lemma illustrates how regions are combined and how edges are incorporated to regions. The proof can be found in [6].

Lemma 2. Let F be a flow graph and R a region of F. There exists a vertex h in R such that (a) any edge not contained in R but entering some vertex of R has necessarily h as its terminal endpoint, and (b) h dominates every vertex of R. Hence, if R' is R plus all the edges that leave vertices of R and enter h of R, then R' is an induced subgraph of F.

It is clear from the lemma above that every path from a vertex outside a region R to some vertex of R must pass through h of R. Since there is a path in R from h to every vertex of R, R is itself a flow graph with initial vertex h. We call h the header of R.

Suppose that there is a vertex n_1 with edge (n_1,n_1) in some intermediate graph of the reduction of a flow graph F. If n_1 represents a region $R'=(V_1,E_1,h_1)$ of F, each edge in the set represented by (n_1,n_1) has its initial and terminal endpoints in R' by (ii) of Lemma 1, and in particular the terminal endpoint is h_1 by Lemma 2. Fig. 4 shows how a region is expanded by T_1, where R is the region represented by the new vertex n. We say that R is formed by applying T_1 to R', or R' is expanded to R.

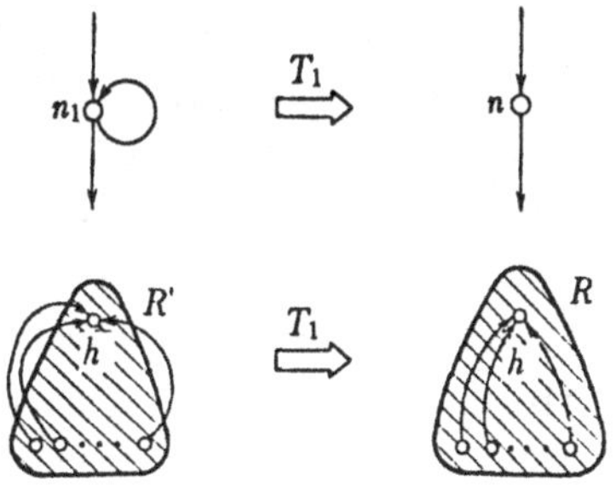

Fig. 4 - Expansion of a region.

Suppose that there are vertices n_1 and n_2 with edge (n_1,n_2) in some intermediate graph of the reduction of F. If n_1 and n_2 represent regions $R'=(V_1,E_1,h_1)$ and $R''=(V_2,E_2,h_2)$ respectively, then each edge in the set represented by (n_1,n_2) has its initial endpoint in R' and its terminal endpoint h_2 in R" by Lemmas 1 (ii) and 2. Fig. 5 illustrates the combination of two regions by T_2, where R is the region represented by the new vertex n. We say that R is formed by applying T_2 to R' and R" , or R' and R" are combined to be R.

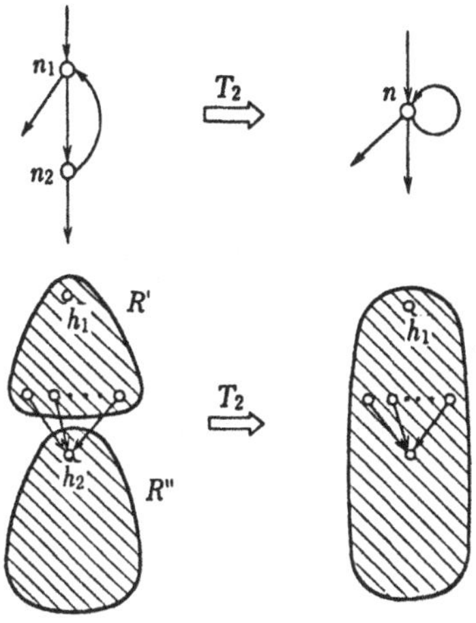

Fig. 5 - Union of regions.

4. An algorithm to solve the two disjoint paths problem

The fixed SHP with a pattern graph consisting of two edges is reduced to the two disjoint paths problem. In this section we give an algorithm to solve the two disjoint paths problem for reducible flow graphs. To begin with, we define three propositional functions $A^1_R(n_1,n_2)$, $A^2_R(n_1,n_2,n_3,n_4)$ and $B^2_R(n_1,n_2,n_3,n_4,n_5)$ for region R, where n_1,n_2,n_3,n_4, and n_5 range over all the vertices of R.

Definition 1. Let F be a flow graph, $R=(V_1,E_1,h)$ a region of F.

(a) $A^1_R(n_1,n_2)$=TRUE iff there is a path in R from n_1 to n_2.

(b) $A^2_R(n_1,n_2,n_3,n_4)$=TRUE iff there are two disjoint paths in R such that one runs from n_1 to n_2 and the other from n_3 to n_4.

(c) $B^2_R(n_1,n_2,n_3,n_4,n_5)$=TRUE iff there are three pairwise disjoint paths in R such that one runs from n_1 to n_2, another from n_3 to n_4, and the other from h to n_5.

In terms of $A^2_R(n_1,n_2,n_3,n_4)$, our aim is to compute the value of $A^2_R(s_1,t_1,s_2,t_2)$ for a given flow graph F with specified vertices s_1, t_1, s_2, and t_2. Our algorithm computes the values of these functions recursively for larger and larger regions, using Lemmas 3 and 4. Note that $A^1_R(n,n)=A^2_R(n,n,n,n)=B^2_R(n,n,n,n,n)$=TRUE if region R consists of a single vertex.

Lemma 3. Let $R=(V,E,h)$ be a region formed by an application of T_1 from region $R'=(V,E_1,h)$. (See Fig.4.) Then,

$$A^1_R(n_1,n_2)=A^1_{R'}(n_1,n_2)+\sum_{n'\in M} A^2_{R'}(h_1,n_2,n_1,n'), \qquad \text{----(1)}$$

$$\begin{aligned}
&A^2_R(n_1,n_2,n_3,n_4)\\
&\quad =A^2_{R'}(n_1,n_2,n_3,n_4)\\
&\quad +\sum_{n'\in M} B^2_{R'}(n_1,n_2,n_3,n',n_4)\times((n'=n_3)+(n'\neq n_3)\times(n'\neq n_1)\times(n'\neq n_2))\\
&\qquad\qquad \times((h=n_4)+(h\neq n_4)\times(h\neq n_1)\times(h\neq n_2))\\
&\quad +\sum_{n'\in M} B^2_{R'}(n_3,n_4,n_1,n',n_2)\times((n'=n_1)+(n'\neq n_1)\times(n'\neq n_3)\times(n'\neq n_4))\\
&\qquad\qquad \times((h=n_2)+(h\neq n_2)\times(h\neq n_3)\times(h\neq n_4))\\
&\quad +\sum_{n',n''\in M} A^2_{R'}(n_1,n',n_3,n'')\times(n_2=n_4)\\
&\qquad\qquad \times((n'=n_1)+(n'\neq n_1)\times(n'\neq n_3)\times(n'\neq n''))\\
&\qquad\qquad \times((n''=n_3)+(n''\neq n_3)\times(n''\neq n_1)\times(n'\neq n'')), \text{ and}
\end{aligned} \qquad \text{---(2)}$$

$$B^2_R(n_1,n_2,n_3,n_4,n_5)=B^2_{R'}(n_1,n_2,n_3,n_4,n_5), \qquad \text{----(3)}$$

where $n_i, 1\leq i\leq 5$, range over all vertices in V, + and Σ denote logical OR, $\times$ denotes logical AND, and M is the set of initial endpoints of all the edges in $E-E_1$.

Proof. We first establish the formula (1). Suppose that the left-hand side of (1) is TRUE, that is, there is a simple path from n_1 to n_2 in R. Then there are two cases : (i) the path is also in R', and (ii) it is not in R'. In the former case, the first term of the right-hand side of (1) is TRUE. In the latter case, the path must contain an edge in $E-E_1$. Therefore there are two disjoint paths in R', one running from n_1 to one of initial endpoints of the edges in $E-E_1$, and the other from the header of R' to n_2. In this case, the second term becomes TRUE. It is obvious that if the right-hand side of (1) is TRUE, then the left-hand side is TRUE. Thus the formula (1) holds.

We next verify the formula (2). Suppose that the left-hand side of (2) is TRUE, that is, there are two disjoint paths in R, one running from n_1 to n_2 and the other from n_3 to n_4. Then we have four cases : (i) these paths are also in R', (ii) the path from n_3 to n_4 contains an edge in $E-E_1$ and the other does not, (iii) the path from n_1 to n_2 contains an edge in $E-E_1$ and the other does not, (iv) both of the two paths contain edges in $E-E_1$. In the case (i), the first term of the right-hand side of (2) is TRUE. In the case (ii), there must be three pairwise disjoint paths in R' such that one runs from n_1 to n_2, another from n_3 to a vertex n' that is an initial endpoint of an edge in $E-E_1$, and the other from the header of R' to n_4. Furthermore, if $n' \neq n_3$, then n' can be neither n_1 nor n_2, and if $h \neq n_4$, then h can be neither n_1 nor n_2. In this case, the second term of (2) is TRUE. By an argument similar to above, the third term is TRUE for the case (iii) and the fourth term for the case (iv). It is obvious that if the right-hand side of (2) is TRUE, then the left-hand side is TRUE. Thus the formula (2) holds.

Finally, we can easily verify the formula (3) from the fact that h is the terminal endpoint of each edge in $E-E_1$.

Q.E.D.

<u>Lemma 4</u>. Let $R=(V,E,h_1)$ be a region formed by applying T_2 to two regions $R'=(V_1,E_1,h_1)$ and $R''=(V_2,E_2,h_2)$. (See Fig. 5.) (We abbreviate $A^1_R(n_1,n_2)$, $A^2_R(n_1,n_2,n_3,n_4)$ and $B^2_R(n_1,n_2,n_3,n_4,n_5)$ to A^1_R, A^2_R and B^2_R, respectively.) Let n_i ,$1 \leq i \leq 5$, be verticies in V , and M the set of initial endpoints of the edges in $E-E_1-E_2$. Then,

(a) A^1_R is computed from $A^1_{R'}$ and $A^1_{R''}$ as follows.

Case 1: $n_1, n_2 \in V_1$.

$$A_R^1(n_1,n_2)=A_{R'}^1(n_1,n_2). \qquad (4)$$

Case 2: $n_1, n_2 \in V_2$.

$$A_R^1(n_1,n_2)=A_{R''}^1(n_1,n_2). \qquad (5)$$

Case 3: $n_1 \in V_1$ and $n_2 \in V_2$.

$$A_R^1(n_1,n_2)=(\sum_{n' \in M} A_{R'}^1(n_1,n')). \qquad (6)$$

Case 4: $n_2 \in V_1$ and $n_1 \in V_2$.

$$A_R^1(n_1,n_2)=\text{FALSE}. \qquad (7)$$

(b) A_R^2 is computed as follows.

Case 1: $n_1, n_2, n_3, n_4 \in V_1$.

$$A_R^2=A_{R'}^2(n_1,n_2,n_3,n_4). \qquad (8)$$

Case 2: $n_1, n_2, n_3, n_4 \in V_2$.

$$A_R^2=A_{R''}^2(n_1,n_2,n_3,n_4). \qquad (9)$$

Case 3: $n_1, n_2, n_3 \in V_1$ and $n_4 \in V_2$.

$$A_R^2=\sum_{n' \in M} A_{R'}^2(n_1,n_2,n_3,n') \times((n'=n_3)+(n' \neq n_3) \times(n' \neq n_1)\times(n' \neq n_2)). \qquad (10)$$

Case 4: $n_1, n_3, n_4 \in V_1$ and $n_2 \in V_2$. Similar to Case 3.

Case 5: $n_1, n_2 \in V_1$ and $n_3, n_4 \in V_2$.

$$A_R^2=A_{R'}^1(n_1,n_2)\times A_{R''}^1(n_3,n_4), \qquad (11)$$

Case 6: $n_3, n_4 \in V_1$ and $n_1, n_2 \in V_2$. Similar to Case 5.

Case 7: $n_1 \in V_1$ and $n_2, n_3, n_4 \in V_2$.

$$A_R^2=(\sum_{n' \in M} A_{R'}^1(n_1,n'))\times A_{R''}^2(h_2,n_2,n_3,n_4) \times((h_2=n_2)+(h_2 \neq n_2)\times(h_2 \neq n_3)\times(h_2 \neq n_4)). \qquad (12)$$

Case 8: $n_3 \in V_1$ and $n_1, n_2, n_4 \in V_2$. Similar to Case 7.

Case 9: $n_1, n_3 \in V_1$ and $n_2, n_4 \in V_2$.

$$A_R^2=\sum_{n', n'' \in M} A_{R'}^2(n_1,n',n_3,n'')\times(n_2=n_4=h_2) \times((n'=n_1)+(n' \neq n_1)\times(n' \neq n_3)\times(n' \neq n'')) \times((n''=n_3)+(n'' \neq n_3)\times(n'' \neq n_1)\times(n' \neq n'')). \qquad (13)$$

Case 10: otherwise.

$$A_R^2=\text{FALSE}. \qquad (14)$$

(c) B_R^2 is computed as follows.

Case 1: $n_1, n_2, n_3, n_4, n_5 \in V_1$.

$$B_R^2=B_{R'}^2(n_1,n_2,n_3,n_4,n_5). \qquad (15)$$

Case 2: $n_1, n_2, n_3, n_4, n_5 \in V_2$.

$$B_R^2=B_{R''}^2(n_1,n_2,n_3,n_4,n_5) \times((h_2=n_5)+(h_2 \neq n_5)\times(h_2 \neq n_1)\times(h_2 \neq n_2)\times(h_2 \neq n_3)\times(h_2 \neq n_4)). \qquad (16)$$

Case 3: $n_1,n_3,n_4,n_5 \in V_1$ and $n_2 \in V_2$.

$$B_R^2 = \sum_{n' \in M} B_{R'}^2(n_1,n',n_3,n_4,n_5) \times ((n'=n_1)+(n' \neq n_1)\times(n' \neq h_1)\times(n' \neq n_3)\times(n' \neq n_4)\times(n' \neq n_5)). \quad (17)$$

Case 4: $n_1,n_2,n_3,n_5 \in V_1$ and $n_4 \in V_2$. Similar to Case 3.

Case 5: $n_1,n_2,n_3,n_4 \in V_1$ and $n_5 \in V_2$. Similar to Case 3.

Case 6: $n_3,n_4,n_5 \in V_1$ and $n_1,n_2 \in V_2$.

$$B_R^2 = A_{R'}^2(h_1,n_5,n_3,n_4) \times A_{R''}^1(n_1,n_2). \quad (18)$$

Case 7: $n_1,n_2,n_5 \in V_1$ and $n_3,n_4 \in V_2$. Similar to Case 6.

Case 8: $n_1,n_3,n_5 \in V_1$ and $n_2,n_4 \in V_2$.

$$B_R^2 = \sum_{n',n'' \in M} B_{R'}^2(n_1,n',n_3,n'',n_5) \times (n_2=n_4=h_2)$$
$$\times((n'=n_1)+(n' \neq n_1)\times(n' \neq h_1)\times(n' \neq n_3)\times(n' \neq n_5)\times(n' \neq n''))$$
$$\times((n''=n_3)+(n'' \neq n_3)\times(n'' \neq h_1)\times(n'' \neq n_1)\times(n'' \neq n_5)\times(n' \neq n'')). \quad (19)$$

Case 9: $n_1,n_3,n_4 \in V_1$ and $n_2,n_5 \in V_2$. Similar to Case 8.

Case 10: $n_1,n_2,n_3 \in V_1$ and $n_4,n_5 \in V_2$. Similar to Case 8.

Case 11: $n_3,n_4 \in V_1$ and $n_1,n_2,n_5 \in V_2$.

$$B_R^2 = \sum_{n' \in M} A_{R'}^2(h_1,n',n_3,n_4) \times ((n'=h_1)+(n' \neq h_1)\times(n' \neq n_3)\times(n' \neq n_4))$$
$$\times A_{R''}^2(n_1,n_2,h_2,n_5)$$
$$\times((h_2=n_5)+(h_2 \neq n_5)\times(h_2 \neq n_1)\times(h_2 \neq n_2)). \quad (20)$$

Case 12: $n_1,n_2 \in V_1$ and $n_3,n_4,n_5 \in V_2$. Similar to Case 11.

Case 13: $n_3,n_5 \in V_1$ and $n_1,n_2,n_4 \in V_2$. Similar to Case 11.

Case 14: $n_1,n_5 \in V_1$ and $n_2,n_3,n_4 \in V_2$. Similar to Case 11.

Case 15: $n_1,n_3 \in V_1$ and $n_2,n_4,n_5 \in V_2$.

$$B_R^2 = \sum_{n',n'',n''' \in M} B_{R'}^2(n_1,n',n_3,n'',n''') \times (n_2=n_4=n_5=h_2)$$
$$\times((n'=n_1)+(n' \neq n_1)\times(n' \neq h_1)\times(n' \neq n_3)\times(n' \neq n'')\times(n' \neq n'''))$$
$$\times((n''=n_3)+(n'' \neq n_3)\times(n'' \neq h_1)\times(n'' \neq n_1)\times(n'' \neq n')\times(n'' \neq n'''))$$
$$\times((n'''=h_1)+(n''' \neq h_1)\times(n''' \neq n_1)\times(n''' \neq n_2)\times(n''' \neq n')\times(n'' \neq n''')). \quad (21)$$

Case 16: $n_5 \in V_1$ and $n_1,n_2,n_3,n_4 \in V_2$.

$$B_R^2 = A_{R''}^2(n_1,n_2,n_3,n_4). \quad (22)$$

Case 17: otherwise.

$$B_R^2 = \text{FALSE}. \quad (23)$$

Proof. Omitted.

Now we proceed to construct an algorithm to solve the two disjoint paths problem. We employ a 2-dimensional array $A^1(n_1, n_2)$, a 4-dimensional array $A^2(n_1,n_2,n_3,n_4)$ and a 5-dimensional array $B^2(n_1,n_2,n_3,n_4,n_5)$, and each element of these arrays has a value of $A_R^1(n_1,n_2)$, $A_R^2(n_1,n_2,n_3,n_4)$ or $B_R^2(n_1,n_2,n_3,n_4,n_5)$ with respect to a current region R.

ALGORITHM A^2

Input: A reducible flow graph $F=(V,E,s)$ with specified vertices $s_1,t_1,s_2,t_2 \in V$, and its parse Π_F.

Output: If there are two disjoint paths such that one runs from s_1 to t_1 and the other from s_2 to t_2, then "YES", otherwise "NO".

Method:

Step 1. $\Pi \longleftarrow \Pi_F$. For each vertex $n \in V$, $A^2(n,n,n,n) \longleftarrow$ TRUE, $B^2(n,n,n,n,n) \longleftarrow$ TRUE, $A^1(n,n) \longleftarrow$ TRUE.

Step 2. If the sequence in Π is empty, go to Step 5. Let T_Π be the top of the current sequence in Π. Delete T_Π from the sequence in Π. If T_Π is a four-tuple, that is , a transformation T_1, then go to Step 3. If T_Π is a five-tuple, that is, a transformation T_2, then go to Step 4.

Step 3. Compute the values of $A^1(n_1,n_2)$, $A^2(n_1,n_2,n_3,n_4)$ and $B^2(n_1,n_2,n_3,n_4,n_5)$ for the region newly formed by the transformation T_1 using the formulas in Lemma 3, where n_i, $1 \le i \le 5$, are vertices of the region. Go to Step 2.

Step 4. Compute the values of $A^1(n_1,n_2)$, $A^2(n_1,n_2,n_3,n_4)$ and $B^2(n_1,n_2,n_3,n_4,n_5)$ for the region newly formed by the transformation T_2 using the formulas in Lemma 4, where n_i, $1 \le i \le 5$, are vertices of the region. Go to Step 2.

Step 5. If $A^2(s_1,t_1,s_2,t_2)$=TRUE, then output "YES", otherwise, output "NO". Halt.

Theorem 1. There exists an algorithm of time complexity $O(n^5 e)$ to solve the two disjoint paths problem for reducible flow graphs, where n is the number of vertices and e is the number of edges in a flow graph.

Proof. It is known that there is an algorithm of O(e log e) for finding a parse of a reducible flow graph [11], and it is easy to show that the time complexity of algorithm A^2 is $O(n^5 e)$.

5. Algorithms to solve the SHP and the fixed SHP

In this section we construct an algorithm A^k to solve the k disjoint paths problem. As stated in the Introduction, the fixed SHP for any pattern graph with k edges can be reduced to this problem. Since one can easily extend the algorithm A^2 to the case for the problem above, we give only the outline and omit the details.

We define k+1 propositional functions as follows: for each j $(1 \leq j \leq k)$, $A_R^j(n_1, n_2, \ldots, n_{2j})$=TRUE iff there are j disjoint paths in R such that each path runs from n_{2i-1} to n_{2i} for all i $(1 \leq i \leq j)$; and $B_R^k(n_1, n_2, \ldots, n_{2k+1})$=TRUE iff there are k+1 disjoint paths in R such that one runs from the header of R to n_{2k+1} and each of the others runs from n_{2i-1} to n_{2i} for all i $(1 \leq i \leq k)$. Then clearly, $B_R^k(n_1, \ldots, n_{2k+1})$=TRUE and $A_R^j(n_1, \ldots, n_{2j})$=TRUE for all j if region R consists of a single vertex. We can compute these values for larger and larger regions recursively in the same manner as in algorithm A^2, and finally we compute $A_F^k(n_1, \ldots, n_{2k})$ for a given flow graph F. Thus we have algorithm A^k. Clearly the time complexity is $O(n^{2k+1}e)$.

In order to solve the fixed SHP, it is enough to consult $A_F^k(s_1, t_1, \ldots, s_k, t_k)$, where s_i and t_i are vertices of F mapped from two endpoints of the ith edge of the pattern graph H, and k is the number of edges of H.

If we are concerned with the SHP, then it is sufficient to know whether there is a one-to-one mapping h_1 from vertices of H to vertices of F such that $A_F^k(h_1(s_1'), h_1(t_1'), \ldots, h_1(s_k'), h_1(t_k'))$=TRUE, where s_i' and t_i' are two endpoints of the ith edge of H. Since there exist at most $O(n^k)$ such mappings, this can be done within $O(n^k)$ time. Thus we obtain the following theorem.

Theorem 2. For any pattern graph H, there exists an algorithm of time complexity $O(n^{2k+1}e)$ to solve the (fixed) SHP for reducible flow graphs, where k is the number of edges of H.

ACKNOWLEDGEMENTS We would like to thank Prof. T. Nishizeki for his careful reading of the manuscript and valuable comments.

References

[1] Aho, A., Hopcroft, J., and Ullman, J., The Design and Analysis of Computer Algorithms, Addison-Wesley, Reading, Mass. (1974).

[2] Duffin, R. J.,"Topology of series parallel networks", J. Math. and appli., 10(1965), 303-318.

[3] Fortune, S.,Hopcroft, J., and Wyllie, J.,"The directed subgraph homeomorphism problem", Theor. Comput. Sci.,10(1980), 111-121.

[4] Harary, F., Graph Theory, Addison-Wesley, Reading, Mass. (1969).

[5] Hecht, M. S., and Ullman, J. D.,"Flow graph reducibility", SIAM J. Computing 1,2(1972), 188-202.

[6] Hecht, M. S., and Ullman, J. D.,"Characterization of reducible flow graphs", J. ACM 21, 3(1974), 367-375.

[7] Hunt, H. B., and Szymansky, T. G.,"Dichotomization, reachability and the forbidden subgraph problem", Proc. Eighth Annual ACM Symposium on Theory of Computing, Hershey, PA (1976), 126-134.

[8] LaPaugh, A. S., and Rivest, R. L.,"The subgraph homeomorphism problem", Proc. Tenth Annual ACM Symposium on Theory of Computing, San Diego, CA (1978), 40-50.

[9] Perl, T., and Shiloach, Y.,"Finding two disjoint paths between two paires of vertices in a graph",J. ACM 24, 1(1978), 1-9.

[10] Shiloach, Y.,"A polinomial solution to the undirected two paths problem", J. ACM 27, 3(1980), 445-456.

[11] Tarjan, R. E.,"Testing flow graph reducibility", J. Comput. and Syst. Sci., 9(1974) 355-365.

COMBINATORIAL PROBLEMS ON SERIES-PARALLEL GRAPHS

K. Takamizawa
Central Research Labs., Nippon Electric Co. Ltd.
Kawasaki, Japan 213

T. Nishizeki and N. Saito
Department of Electrical Communications
Faculty of Engineering, Tohoku University
Sendai, Japan 980

Abstract. We show, in a unified manner, that there exist linear time algorithms for many combinatorial problems defined on the class of series-parallel graphs. These include (i) the decision problem, and (ii) the minimum edge (vertex) deletion problem both with respect to a property characterized by a finite number of forbidden graphs, and (iii) the generalized matching problem.

1. Introduction

A large number of combinatorial problems defined on graphs are NP-complete, and hence there is probably no polynomial-time algorithm for any of them [1]. A number of such problems can be formulated as a "minimum edge (vertex) deletion problem" with respect to some graph property $\mathbb{Q}$. The problem asks a minimum number of edges (vertices) of a given graph whose deletion results in a graph satisfying $\mathbb{Q}$. Various other problems can be formulated as a "generalized matching problem", in which one would like to find a maximum number of vertex-disjoint copies of a fixed graph B contained in an input graph. Some systematic approaches have been achieved to these problems. Krishnamoorthy et al. have shown that the minimum vertex deletion problem is NP-complete whenever property $\mathbb{Q}$ is nontrivial and hereditary [12,15,23]. They have also shown that several minimum edge deletion problems are NP-complete. It should be noted that a hereditary property $\mathbb{Q}$ can be characterized by (possibly an infinite number of) "forbidden (induced) subgraphs", that is, a graph G satisfies $\mathbb{Q}$ if and only if G contains none of the forbidden graphs as an (induced) subgraph [3,11,15]. On the other hand Kirkpatrick and Hell [13] have shown that any generalized matching problem is NP-complete if the graph B has a component with at least three vertices.

Some of the combinatorial problems which are NP-complete for general graphs remains so even for a restricted class of graphs [7]. However it has been shown by ad hoc methods that polynomial-time algorithms are available for some combinatorial problems on special classes of graphs, such as planar graphs, regular graphs, bipartite graphs, or series-parallel graphs. An example is the maximum cut problem, which is NP-complete for nonplanar graphs, but there exists a polynomial-time algorithm for planar graphs, as shown by Hadlock [9].

In this paper we consider a special class of graphs, called "series-parallel graphs", which can be constructed by recursively applying "series" and "parallel" connections. The class of such graphs, which is a well known model of series-parallel electrical networks, is a restricted class of planar graphs. It has been known that many practical problems defined on such graphs can be efficiently solved, for example, "resistance of electrical networks", "reliability of systems", and "scheduling" [4,16,17]. The following question naturally arises: do there exist polynomial-time algorithms for <u>all</u> combinatorial problems defined on such a class of graphs? One can easily observe that not every combinatorial problem is polynomial-time computable even if restricted to series-parallel graphs. However we show, in a unified manner, that a number of combinatorial problems are linear time computable for series-parallel graphs. Such a rather broad class of problems includes:

(i) the decision (i.e. yes-no) problem with respect to any property $\mathbb{Q}$ characterized by a finite number of "forbidden (induced or homeomorphic) subgraphs", in which one would like to decide whether an input graph satisfies $\mathbb{Q}$;

(ii) the minimum edge (vertex) deletion problem with respect to the same property as above; and

(iii) the generalized matching problem. (The proof for this problem is omitted.)

Hence the following problems among others prove to be linear time computable for the class of series-parallel graphs :

(1) the minimum vertex cover problem (equivalently the maximum independent vertex set problem);

(2) the maximum (induced) line-subgraph problem;

(3) the minimum edge (vertex) deletion problem with respect to property "without cycles (or paths) of specified length n or any lengh $\leq$ n";

(4) the maximum outerplanar (induced) subgraph problem;

(5) the minimum feedback vertex set problem;

(6) the maximum ladder (induced) subgraph problem ($K_{2,3}$ and its dual are the forbidden homeomorphic subgraphs of a ladder graph [20]);

(7) the minimum path cover problem (in which one would like to find a minimum number of disjoint paths which contain all the vertices of a given graph);

(8) the maximum matching problem; and

(9) the maximum disjoint triangle problem.

Some of these problems have individually been shown to be polynomial-time computable for the class of series-parallel graphs or some larger class containing all such graphs [2,5,6,9,22].

2. Preliminary

A <u>multigraph</u> G=(V,E) consists of a finite set V of <u>vertices</u> and a finite multiset E of <u>edges</u>, each of which is a pair of distinct vertices [10]. Throughout this paper we simply call them <u>graphs</u> since we consider only multigraphs. A graph G'=(V',E') is a <u>subgraph</u> of another G=(V,E) if V' is a subset of V and E' is a subset of E. If V'=V, G' is denoted by $G'=G-E_s$ where $E_s=E-E'$. We write $G'\subseteq G$ if G' is a subgraph of G. For any subset W of the vertices of a graph G, the <u>induced subgraph</u> on W is the maximal subgraph of G with vertex set W, and is denoted by $G-V_s$ where $V_s=V-W$.

Two edges of a graph are <u>series</u> if they are incident to a vertex of degree 2, and are <u>parallel</u> if they join the same pair of distict vertices. A <u>series-parallel graph</u> is defined recursively as follows [4]:

<u>Definition 1.</u> A graph consisting of two vertices joined by two parallel edges is series-parallel. If G is a series-parallel graph, then a graph obtained from G by replacing any edge of G by series or parallel edges is series-parallel.

<u>Definition 2.</u> A graph G=(V,E) is called a <u>2-terminal graph</u> when

two distinct vertices of V are distinguished from the other vertices and also from each other, and are called the first terminal and the second terminal, respectively. We write $G=(V,E,x,y)$ if x is the first terminal of G and y the second.

A 2-terminal graph may have one or two virtual terminals, called dummy i (i=1,2), which are necessarily isolated, and distinguished from a usual terminal. They will play a special role in the "connections" or "separations" of the succeeding sections. When we wish to discriminate a non-virtual vertex from virtual one, we call it a real vertex. An underlying graph of a 2-terminal graph G is a graph consisting of all edges and all real vertices of G.

We will introduce a "2-terminal series-parallel graph", which is slightly different from a series-parallel graph. We define two kinds of connections of 2-terminal graphs, which are used to construct 2-terminal series-parallel graphs, as follows.

Definition 3. Let two 2-terminal graphs $H=(V_H,E_H,a,b)$ and $K=(V_K,E_K,c,d)$ have no vertex in common: $V_H \cap V_K=\emptyset$.

(a) H and K are series-connectable (in type I) if both the second terminal b of H and the first terminal c of K are real. By a series connection (of type I) of 2-terminal graphs H and K, we mean the 2-terminal graph G_s obtained from H and K by identifying b of H with c of K. Note that the resultant graph G_s is regarded as a 2-terminal graph with terminals a and d.

(b) H and K are parallel connectable if both a and c are either real or virtual, and both b and d are also either real or virtual. By a parallel connection of H and K, we mean the 2-terminal graph G_p obtained from H and K by identifying a with c and b with d; the terminal vertices of H are also the terminal vertices of the composite graph.

If a 2-terminal graph G_s (or G_p) is obtained from two 2-terminal graphs H and K by a series connection of type I (or parallel connection), we write $G_s=H*K$ (or $G_p=H//K$), and say that H and K are series separations of type I of G_s (or parallel separations of G_p).

A two-terminal series-parallel (TTSP) graph is recursively defined as follows :

Definition 4. [Two-Terminal Series-Parallel Graphs]

(i) A two-terminal graph consisting of two vertices joined by a single edge is TTSP, and is called a minimum series-parallel graph denoted by G_{min}.

(ii) If H and K are TTSP graphs, the two terminal graphs H*K and H//K are TTSP.

It is known that every series-parallel graph is TTSP if one designates appropriate vertices, for example, two ends of an edge, as the terminals [4].

3. Decision Problems on TTSP Graphs

In this section we consider a decision (i.e. yes-no) problem with respect to property $\mathbb{Q}$ for TTSP graphs, in which one would like to determine whether a given TTSP graph satisfies $\mathbb{Q}$ or not. We will show that whenever $\mathbb{Q}$ can be characterized by a finite number of forbidden (induced) subgraphs, the decision problem is linear time computable.

Throughout this paper we often denote by $\mathbb{Q}$ itself the set of all (2-terminal) graphs satisfying property $\mathbb{Q}$, so that $G \in \mathbb{Q}$ if and only if G satisfies property $\mathbb{Q}$. We employ "divide-and-conquer" [1] based on the recursive definition of a TTSP graph to solve our problems on TTSP graphs. The requirements for the success and efficiency of the method is formulated as follows.

LEMMA 1. Let $\mathbb{Q}$ be a property defined on 2-terminal graphs. The decision problem with respect to $\mathbb{Q}$ is linear time computable for TTSP graphs if there exists a finite set of properties $\mathbb{P}=\{\mathbb{Q}_1,\mathbb{Q}_2,\dots\mathbb{Q}_k\}$ such that

(i) $\mathbb{Q}\in\mathbb{P}$;

(ii) it is decidable whether $G_{min}\in\mathbb{Q}_r$ or not for each property $\mathbb{Q}_r\in\mathbb{P}$; and

(iii) for each property $\mathbb{Q}_r\in\mathbb{P}$, there exist two sets of properties $\{\mathbb{Q}_{h1},\mathbb{Q}_{h2},\dots,\mathbb{Q}_{ht}\}\subset\mathbb{P}$ and $\{\mathbb{Q}_{k1},\mathbb{Q}_{k2},\dots,\mathbb{Q}_{kt}\}\subset\mathbb{P}$ such that

$$G_T\in\mathbb{Q}_r \text{ iff } \bigvee_{i=1}^{t} ((H\in\mathbb{Q}_{hi}) \wedge (K\in\mathbb{Q}_{ki})) ,$$

for any 2-terminal graph G_T satisfying G_T=H*K (or H//K), where * denotes a series connection of type I, $\wedge$ denotes "and", and $\vee$ "or".

Proof. Let G=(V,E,x,y) be a given TTSP graph. Consider an extended decision problem in which one would like to determine for every $\mathbb{Q}_r \in \mathbb{P}$ whether $G \in \mathbb{Q}_r$ or not. Since $\mathbb{Q} \in \mathbb{P}$ by (i), the new problem includes the original one. Therefore it is sufficient to verify that the extended decision problem is linear time computable. We will show that the recursive algorithm shown below solves this problem in linear time of the number of edges of G.

<u>procedure</u> TEST(G):
<u>if</u> $G=G_{min}$ <u>then</u> determine $G_{min} \in \mathbb{Q}_r$ for each $\mathbb{Q}_r \in \mathbb{P}$
<u>else</u> <u>if</u> G=H*K for H and K both having fewer edges than G
<u>then</u> TEST(H) and TEST(K), and determine $G \in \mathbb{Q}_r$ for each $\mathbb{Q}_r \in \mathbb{P}$ by using the solutions to H and K and condition (iii) of Lemma 1
<u>else</u> let G=H//K for H and K both having fewer edges than G; TEST(H), TEST(K), and determine $G \in \mathbb{Q}_r$ for each $\mathbb{Q}_r \in \mathbb{P}$ by using the solutions to H and K and condition (iii) of Lemma 1

First it should be noted that any TTSP graph G with $e=|E|$ edges can be constructed from e copies of the minimum series-parallel graph G_{min} by a sequence of series and parallel connections, and that such a sequence can be determined by constructing a binary decomposion tree of G in O(e) time [8,19,21]. That is, the total amount of time required for series and parallel separations is O(e). Hence we shall verify that the other operations require at most O(e) time. Let T(e) denote the total amount of time required for these operations to solve the extended decision problem on G with e edges. By induction on e we prove that $T(e) \leq c_1 e - c_2$ for some constants c_1 and c_2. If e=1, that is, $G=G_{min}$, then condition (ii) implies that one can determine in a constant time whether $G \in \mathbb{Q}_r$ for r=1,2,...,k. Thus $T(1) \leq c_1 \cdot 1 - c_2$ for appropriate constants c_1 and c_2. If $e \geq 2$, then G=H*K or H//K for two TTSP graphs H and K both with fewer edges than G. Condition (iii) implies that the solution to G can be obtained by combining the solutions to H and K in a constant time. Note that both k and t are constants independent of the size e of the problem instance. Thus, if H has e_H edges and K e_K edges, then

$$T(e) \leq T(e_H) + T(e_K) + kt,$$

where $e_H, e_K \geq 1$ and $e=e_H+e_K$. The inductive hypothesis implies

$$T(e_H) \leq c_1 e_H - c_2 \quad \text{and} \quad T(e_K) \leq c_1 e_K - c_2.$$

Therefore, by appropriately selecting c_1 and c_2, we have $T(e) \le c_1 e - c_2$, which completes the proof. □

We need some more definitions.

Definition 5. Let $G=(V,E)$ be a graph, and let x and y be distinct vertices of V. A 2-terminal graph G_T is a terminal-attached graph of G if G_T is one of the following:

(i) $G_T=(V,E,x,y)$;

(ii) $G_T=(V\cup\{\text{dummy } 1\},E,\text{dummy } 1,y)$;

(iii) $G_T=(V\cup\{\text{dummy } 2\},E,x,\text{dummy } 2)$; and

(iv) $G_T=(V\cup\{\text{dummy } 1,\text{dummy } 2\},E,\text{dummy } 1,\text{dummy } 2)$,

where dummy 1 and dummy 2 are virtual vertices.

Let $G_T=(V,E,x,y)$ and $G_T'=(V',E',x',y')$ be any two 2-terminal graphs. G_T' is a 2-terminal subgraph of G_T if (i) the underlying graph of G_T' is a subgraph of the underlying graph of G_T, (ii) $x'=x$ if $x\in V'$, otherwise x' is an isolated virtual terminal dummy 1, and (iii) $y'=y$ if $y\in V'$, otherwise y' is an isolated virtual terminal dummy 2. If $V'=V$, then we write $G_T'=G_T-E_s$ with $E_s=E-E'$. If E' contains all the edges of E with both ends in V', G_T' is a 2-terminal induced subgraph of G_T. If $V_s\subset V$, then G_T-V_s denotes the induced subgraph G_T' with vertex set V' consisting of all vertices in $V-V_s$ together with dummy i (i=1 or 2) if x(or y)$\in V_s$. We write again $G_T'\subset G_T$ if G_T' is a 2-terminal subgraph of G_T.

Definition 6. Let $H=(V_H,E_H,a,b)$ and $K=(V_K,E_K,c,d)$ be two 2-terminal graphs having no vertex in common: $V_H\cap V_K=\emptyset$. H and K are series-connectable in type II if both b and c are virtual. By a series connection of type II we mean the 2-terminal graph G_s obtained from the union of H and K by deleting b and c. That is,

$G_s=(V_H\cup V_K-\{b,c\},E_H+E_K,a,d)$.

H and K are called series separations of type II of G_s.

If G_s is a series connection of H and K, then we write, from now on, $G_s=H*K$ regardless of type I or II.

Suppose that property $\mathbb{Q}$ is defined on graphs by a finite set of forbidden subgraphs $\mathbb{B}=\{B_1,B_2,\dots,B_q\}$. Thus $G\in\mathbb{Q}$ if and only if G contains no members of $\mathbb{B}$ as a subgraph. Since the algorithm in Lemma 1 works only on TTSP graphs, we shall first reduce the decision problem defined on graphs to one on 2-terminal graphs. We define a set $\mathbb{B}_T$ of forbidden 2-terminal subgraphs as the set of all terminal-attached graphs of a graph in $\mathbb{B}$. It should be noted that the set $\mathbb{B}_T$ is finite since the set $\mathbb{B}$ is finite. Associated with property $\mathbb{Q}$ on graphs, we define property $\mathbb{Q}_T$ on 2-terminal graphs by $\mathbb{B}_T$: $\mathbb{Q}_T$ is the set of all the 2-terminal graphs that contain no member of $\mathbb{B}_T$ as a 2-terminal subgraph.

<u>LEMMA 2.</u> Let G_T be any terminal-attached graph of a graph G. Then $G \in \mathbb{Q}$ if and only if $G_T \in \mathbb{Q}_T$.

According to Lemma 2, it is sufficient to verify that the property $\mathbb{Q}_T$ on 2-terminal graphs satisfies the requirements of Lemma 1. Let a set $\mathbb{S}$ consist of all 2-terminal graphs that belong to $\mathbb{B}_T$ or can be obtained from a 2-terminal graph in $\mathbb{B}_T$ by a sequence of series (of type I and type II) and parallel separations. Note that set $\mathbb{B}_T$ is finite and that any separation graph has not more vertices than the original 2-terminal graph. It hence follows that set $\mathbb{S}$ is finite. We will show intuitively that the set of all the properties defined by a subset of $\mathbb{S}$ satisfies the requirements of Lemma 1. In what follows we will write $\mathbb{S}=\{S_1,S_2,\ldots,S_\ell\}$. Furthermore we define $S[I]$, $\sigma_I(i)$, $\mu_I(i)$, $\sigma_I(J)$, and $\mu_I(J)$ for $i=1,2,\ldots,\ell$, and $I,J\subseteq\{1,2,\ldots,\ell\}$ as follows:

$S[I]=\{S_j : j\in I\}$;

$\sigma_I(i)=\{j : S_j\in S \text{ and } S_i{*}S_j\in S[I]\}$;

$\mu_I(i)=\{j : S_j\in S \text{ and } S_i//S_j\in S[I]\}$;

$\sigma_I(J)=\bigcup_{j\in J}\sigma_I(j)$; and $\mu_I(J)=\bigcup_{j\in J}\mu_I(j)$.

We need some more lemmas.

<u>LEMMA 3.</u> Let G_T be a 2-terminal graph such that $G_T=H{*}K$ (or $H//K$) for some 2-terminal graphs H and K, and let G_T' be a 2-terminal graph. Then $G_T'\subset G_T$ if and only if there exist 2-terminal graphs H' and K' such that $H'\subset H$, $K'\subset K$, and $G_T'=H'{*}K'$ (or $H'//K'$).

<u>LEMMA 4.</u> Let $G_T=H{*}K$ (or $H//K$), and $S_r\in\mathbb{S}$. Then $S_r\subset G_T$ if and only if there exist $S_f,S_g\in\mathbb{S}$ such that $S_r=S_f{*}S_g$ (or $S_f//S_g$), and $S_f\subset H$, $S_g\subset K$.

Let G_T be a 2-terminal graph, and $I \subseteq \{1,2,\ldots,\ell\}$. We denote by $S[I] \subset G_T$ the proposition that G_T contains at least one member of set $S[I]$ as a 2-terminal subgraph, and denote by $S[I] \not\subset G_T$ the proposition that G_T contains no member of $S[I]$, where the proposition $S[I] \not\subset G_T$ is true if $I=\emptyset$. Using Lemmas 3 and 4, we can show that if G_T is a series or parallel connection, then the solution to G_T can be efficiently obtained from the solutions to component graphs.

LEMMA 5. Let $G_s=H*K$ (of type I), $G_p=H//K$ and $I \subseteq \{1,2,\ldots,\ell\}$. Then we have:

(i) $S[I] \not\subset G_s$ iff $\bigvee_{J \subset I_s} [(S[J] \not\subset H) \wedge (S[\sigma_I(I_s-J)] \not\subset K)]$;

and

(ii) $S[I] \not\subset G_p$ iff $\bigvee_{J \subset I_p} [(S[J] \not\subset H) \wedge (S[\mu_I(I_p-J)] \not\subset K)]$,

where $I_s=\{i$: there exists $S_j \in \mathbf{S}$ s.t. $S_i*S_j \in S[I]\}$ and $I_p=\{i$: there exists $S_j \in \mathbf{S}$ s.t. $S_i//S_j \in S[I]\}$.

We now have the following theorem.

THEOREM 1(2). Let $\mathbf{Q}$ be a property on graphs defined by a finite number of forbidden (induced) subgraphs. Then the decision problem with respect to $\mathbf{Q}$ is linear time computable for every series-parallel graph.

Proof. Let G_T be a terminal-attached graph obtained from a series-parallel graph G by designating two ends of any edge of G as the terminal vertices, so that G_T is TTSP. According to Lemma 2, the problem with respect to $\mathbf{Q}$ on a series-parallel graph G can be reduced to the problem with respect to the property $\mathbf{Q}_T$ on the TTSP graph G_T. Therefore it suffices to show that there exists a set of properties associated with $\mathbf{Q}_T$ that satisfies the requirements (i), (ii) and (iii) of Lemma 1. Consider the following set $\mathbf{P}$ of properties on 2-terminal graphs:

$\mathbf{P}=\{\text{"}S[I]\text{"} : I \subseteq \{1,2,\ldots,\ell\}\}$,

where "S[I]" denotes the property defined by the set S[I] of forbidden 2-terminal subgraphs: a 2-terminal graph satisfies property "S[I]" if it contains no member of S[I] as a 2-terminal subgraph. We write $\mathbf{P}=\{\mathbf{Q}_1,\mathbf{Q}_2,\ldots,\mathbf{Q}_k\}$ where $k=2^{\ell}$. Note that set $\mathbf{P}$ is finite since ℓ is a constant. Then:

(i) The definition of $\mathbf{S}$ implies $\mathbf{B}_T \subset \mathbf{S}$. Thus property $\mathbf{Q}_T$ is identical with the property "S[I]" with $S[I]=\mathbf{B}_T$, and hence $\mathbf{Q}_T \in \mathbf{P}$.

(ii) Since $\mathfrak{l}$ is finite, one can determine in a constant time whether $S[I]\not\subseteq G_{min}$ for every $S[I]$;

(iii) It follows from Lemma 5 that for each $\mathbb{Q}_r\in\mathbb{R}$ there exist sets of properties $\{\mathbb{Q}_{h1},\mathbb{Q}_{h2},\ldots,\mathbb{Q}_{ht}\}\subset\mathbb{R}$ and $\{\mathbb{Q}_{k1},\mathbb{Q}_{k2},\ldots,\mathbb{Q}_{kt}\}\subset\mathbb{R}$ such that

$$G_T\in\mathbb{Q}_r \quad \text{iff} \quad \bigvee_{i=1}^{t}((H\in\mathbb{Q}_{hi})\wedge(K\in\mathbb{Q}_{ki})),$$

for any $G_T=H*K$ (or $H//K$). □

4. Edge deletion problems

In this section we consider the minimum edge deletion problems with respect to a property $\mathbb{Q}$ for series-parallel graphs, in which one would like to determine the minimum number of edges of a given series-parallel graph whose deletion results in a graph satisfying $\mathbb{Q}$. We will show that the problem is also linear time computable if $\mathbb{Q}$ can be defined by a finite number of forbidden (induced) subgraphs.

For a graph $G=(V,E)$ (or 2-terminal graph $G=(V,E,x,y)$) and property $\mathbb{Q}$ on (2-terminal) graphs, define $L(G,\mathbb{Q})$ as follows: if there exists a subset E_s of E such that $G-E_s\in\mathbb{Q}$, then $L(G,\mathbb{Q})$ is the minimum cardinality of such a set E_s; otherwise $L(G,\mathbb{Q})$ is undefined (or ∞). The edge deletion problem asks $L(G,\mathbb{Q})$ for a given G and a fixed $\mathbb{Q}$. Let $\mathbb{Q}$, $\mathbb{Q}_T$ and $\mathbb{R}$ be defined as in the preceding section. Then:

<u>LEMMA 6.</u> Let $G=(V,E)$ be a graph, and let $G_T=(V',E',x,y)$ be any terminal-attached graph of G. Then $L(G,\mathbb{Q})=L(G_T,\mathbb{Q}_T)$.

Lemma 6 implies that the minimum edge deletion problem on a graph can be reduced to the same problem on a 2-terminal graph. The succeeding lemma follows from Lemmas 1 and 3.

<u>LEMMA 7.</u> If G_T is a 2-terminal graph such that $G_T=H*K$ (of type I) (or $G_T=H//K$) for some 2-terminal graphs H and K, then for each $\mathbb{Q}_r\in\mathbb{R}$

$$L(G_T,\mathbb{Q}_r) = \min_{1\leq i\leq t}\{L(H,\mathbb{Q}_{hi})+L(K,\mathbb{Q}_{ki})\}.$$

We now have the following theorem.

THEOREM 3. Let $\mathbb{Q}$ be a property on graphs defined by a finite number of forbidden (induced) subgraphs. Then the minimum edge deletion problem with respect to $\mathbb{Q}$ is linear time computable for every series-parallel graph.

5. Vertex deletion problems

In this section we consider the vertex deletion problems with respect to a property $\mathbb{Q}$ for series-parallel graphs, in which one would like to determine the minimum number of vertices of a given series-parallel graph whose deletion results in a graph satisfying $\mathbb{Q}$. We will show that the vertex deletion problem is also linear time computable if $\mathbb{Q}$ can be defined by a finite number of forbidden (induced) subgraphs.

For a graph $G=(V,E)$ and property $\mathbb{Q}$ on graphs, define $N(G,\mathbb{Q})$ as follows: if there exists $V_S \subseteq V$ such that $G-V_S \in \mathbb{Q}$, then $N(G,\mathbb{Q})$ is the minimum cardinality of such a set V_S; otherwise $N(G,\mathbb{Q})$ is undefined (or ∞). The vertex deletion problem asks $N(G,\mathbb{Q})$ for a given G and a fixed $\mathbb{Q}$.

For a 2-terminal graph $G=(V,E,x,y)$ we consider a vertex deletion problem with an additional constraint that one or both terminals should be deleted. For a property $\mathbb{Q}$ and $m,n=1$ or 0, define $N(G,\mathbb{Q},m,n)$ as follows: if there exist $V_S \subseteq V$ such that (i) $G-V_S \in \mathbb{Q}$, (ii) $x \in V_S$ iff $m=1$, and (iii) $y \in V_S$ iff $n=1$, then $N(G,\mathbb{Q},m,n)$ is the minimum cardinality of such a set V_S; otherwise $N(G,\mathbb{Q},m,n)$ is undefined (or ∞).

Let $\mathbb{Q}$, $\mathbb{Q}_T$ and $\mathbb{R}$ be defined as in Section 3. Then we can reduce a problem on a graph to one on a 2-terminal graph as follows.

LEMMA 8. Let $G=(V,E)$ be a graph, and let $G_T=(V',E',x,y)$ be any terminal-attached graph of G. Then

$$N(G,\mathbb{Q}) = \min_{m,n \in \{0,1\}} N(G_T,\mathbb{Q}_T,m,n).$$

LEMMA 9.

(i) If G_T is a 2-terminal graph such that $G_T=H*K$ (of type I) for 2-terminal graphs H and K, then for $\mathbb{Q}_r \in \mathbb{R}$

$$N(G_T,\mathbb{Q}_r,m,n) = \min\{ \min_{1 \le i \le t} \{N(H,\mathbb{Q}_{hi},m,0)+N(K,\mathbb{Q}_{ki},0,n)\},$$
$$\min_{1 \le i \le t} \{N(H,\mathbb{Q}_{hi},m,1)+N(K,\mathbb{Q}_{ki},1,n)\}-1 \}.$$

(ii) If G_T is a 2-terminal graph such that $G_T=H//K$ for 2-terminal graphs H and K, then

$$N(G_T,Q_r,m,n) = \min_{1\leq i\leq t} \{N(H,Q_{hi},m,n)+N(K,Q_{ki},m,n)\} - (m+n).$$

We now have the following theorem.

THEOREM 4. Let Q be a property on graphs defined by a finite number of forbidden (induced) subgraphs. Then the minimum vertex deletion problem with respect to Q is linear time computable for every series-parallel graph.

6. Properties characterized by homeomorphic subgraphs

In the preceding sections we showed that whenever property Q is defined by a finite number of forbidden (induced) subgraphs, the decision and minimum edge (vertex) deletion problems with respect to Q are all linear time computable. Although there exist graph properties whose characterizations require an infinite number of forbidden subgraphs, some of them can be characterized by a finite number of forbidden "homeomorphic subgraphs". For example, "planarity" is characterized by two forbidden homeomorphic subgraphs K_5 and $K_{3,3}$, while it requires an infinite number of forbidden subgraphs, i.e., all the graphs that are homeomorphic to K_5 or $K_{3,3}$, if one characterizes it by forbidden "subgraphs" instead of "homeomorphic subgraphs".

In this section we will show that if property Q is defined by a finite number of homeomorphic subgraphs, the decision and minimum edge (vertex) deletion problems are also linear time computable.

We now present some more terminology. Let $G_1=(V_1,E_1)$ and $G_2=(V_2,E_2)$ be any two graphs. G_2 is homeomorphic to G_1 if there exist mappings ψ and θ, ψ from E_1 into a set of paths of G_2 and θ from V_1 into V_2, such that, for each edge $(v,w)\in E_1$, path $\psi((v,w))$ has ends $\theta(v)$ and $\theta(w)$, and no two paths $\psi((v_1,w_1))$ and $\psi((v_2,w_2))$ share a vertex except possibly an end of both paths. Next let $G_1=(V_1,E_1,x_1,y_1)$ and $G_2=(V_2,E_2,x_2,y_2)$ be any two 2-terminal graphs. G_2 is 2-terminal homeomorphic to G_1 if (i) the underlying graph of G_2 is homeomorphic to the underlying graph of G_1, (ii) x_2 (or y_2) is virtual if and only if x_1 (or y_1) is virtual, and (iii) the associated mapping θ

satisfies $\theta(x_1)=x_2$ and $\theta(y_1)=y_2$. For a 2-terminal graph G we denote by Hom(G) the set of all the 2-terminal graphs that are 2-terminal homeomorphic to G.

Suppose that property $\mathbb{Q}$ is defined by a finite set of forbidden homeomorphic subgraphs, say $\mathbb{B}=\{B_1,B_2,\ldots,B_q\}$: set $\mathbb{Q}$ consists of all the graphs that contain no subgraph homeomorphic to any B_i, $i=1,2,\ldots,q$. As in the Section 5, let $\mathbb{B}_T$ be the set of all the terminal-attached graphs of $B_1,B_2,\ldots,B_q$. Define the set $\mathbb{B}_h$ of 2-terminal graphs as follows:

$\mathbb{B}_h=\mathbb{B}_T\cup\mathbb{B}_I\cup\mathbb{B}_{II}\cup\mathbb{B}_{III}$;

$\mathbb{B}_I$: the set of all 2-terminal graphs obtained from some $B_i\in\mathbb{B}$ by two operations: replace any edge (u,v) of B_i by a new real terminal z together with two edges (u,z) and (z,v); and designate either an arbitrary vertex of B_i different from z or a newly added isolated virtual vertex as the other terminal;

$\mathbb{B}_{II}$: the set of all the 2-terminal graphs obtained from some $B_i\in\mathbb{B}$ by replacing any two edges (u,v) and (u',v') of B_i by new real terminals x and y together with edges (u,x), (x,v), (u',y) and (y,v'); and

$\mathbb{B}_{III}$: the set of all the 2-terminal graphs obtained from some $B_i\in\mathbb{B}$ by replacing any edge (u,v) of B_i by new real terminals x and y together with edges (u,x), (x,y), and (y,v).

We now define property $\mathbb{Q}_h$ on 2-terminal graphs by the set $\mathbb{B}_h$ of forbidden 2-terminal homeomorphic subgraphs : set $\mathbb{Q}_h$ consists of all the 2-terminal graphs containing no 2-terminal subgraphs that are 2-terminal homeomorphic to any member of $\mathbb{B}_h$. Then we have the following lemma.

<u>LEMMA. 10.</u> Let $G_T=(V',E',x,y)$ be a terminal-attached graph of a graph $G=(V,E)$. Then $G\in\mathbb{Q}$ if and only if $G_T\in\mathbb{Q}_h$.

The following result concerning $\mathbb{Q}_h$ corresponds to Lemmas 6 and 8.

<u>LEMMA 11.</u> If G_T is a terminal-attached graph of a graph $G=(V,E)$, then

(i) $L(G,\mathbb{Q})=L(G_T,\mathbb{Q}_h)$; and

(ii) $N(G,\mathbb{Q})=\min_{m,n\in\{0,1\}} N(G_T,\mathbb{Q}_h,m,n)$.

The preceding Lemmas 10 and 11 imply that the decision problem and the minimum edge (vertex) deletion problem both with respect to property $\mathbb{Q}$ on a graph can be reduced to the same problems with respect to property $\mathbb{Q}_h$ on a 2-terminal graph. In what follows we verify that $\mathbb{Q}_h$ satisfies the requirement of Lemma 1.

We now define a new series separation in terms of its associated connection.

<u>Definition 7.</u> Let $H=(V_H,E_H,x,z_2)$ and $K=(V_K,E_K,z_1,y)$ be 2-terminal graphs. If both z_1 and z_2 are real vertices and the sum of degrees of z_1 in K and z_2 in H is two, then a <u>series connection of type III</u> of H and K is a 2-terminal graph G_s obtained from the union of H and K by identifying z_1 and z_2 and replacing the two series edges incident to the identified vertex by a single edge. Then H and K are called <u>series separations of type III</u> of G_s.

From now on we write $G=H*_hK$ if H and K are series separations of type I, II or III of G.

We can now define the set $\mathbb{S}$ of forbidden 2-terminal homeomorphic subgraphs as the set of all the 2-terminal graphs that are members of $\mathbb{B}_h$ or can be obtained from a member of $\mathbb{B}_h$ by a sequence of series and parallel separations of all the types. We write $\mathbb{S}=\{S_1,S_2,\ldots,S_\ell\}$. It should be noted that $\mathbb{B}_h$, and hence $\mathbb{S}$, are finite sets. For $i=1,2,\ldots,\ell$ and a subset I of $\{1,2,\ldots,\ell\}$, define S[I] and $\mu_I(i)$ as in Section 3, while define $\sigma_I(i)$ as follows :

$$\sigma_I(i)=\{\ j\ :S_j\in\mathbb{S}\text{ and }S_i*_hS_j\in S[I]\}$$

We write $\mathrm{Hom}(S_r)\subset G_T$ if G_T contains at least one member of the set $\mathrm{Hom}(S_r)$ as a 2-terminal subgraph. The following lemma corresponds to Lemma 4 of Section 3.

<u>LEMMA 12.</u> Let G_T be a 2-terminal graph such that $G_T=H*K$ (or $H//K$) where $H=(V_H,E_H,a,b)$ and $K=(V_K,E_K,c,d)$, and let $S_r\in\mathbb{S}$. Then $\mathrm{Hom}(S_r)\subset G_T$ if and only if there exist $S_f,S_g\in\mathbb{S}$ such that $S_r=S_f*_hS_g$ $(S_f//S_g)$, $\mathrm{Hom}(S_f)\subset H$, and $\mathrm{Hom}(S_g)\subset K$.

Using the preceding lemma, we obtain the following result, where we write $\mathrm{Hom}(S[I])\not\subset G_s$ if G_s contains no member of the set $\mathrm{Hom}(S[I])$ as a 2-terminal subgraph.

<u>LEMMA 13.</u> Let G_s and G_p be 2-terminal graphs such that

G_s=H*K (of type I) and G_p=H//K, and let $I \subset \{1,2,\ldots,\ell\}$. Then;

(i) $Hom(S[I]) \not\subset G_s$ iff

$$\bigvee_{J \subset I_s} [(Hom(S[J]) \not\subset H) \wedge (Hom(S[\sigma_I(I_s-J)]) \not\subset K)];$$

and

(ii) $Hom(S[I]) \not\subset G_p$ iff

$$\bigvee_{J \subset I_p} [(Hom(S[J]) \not\subset H) \wedge (Hom(S[\mu_I(I_p-J)]) \not\subset K)],$$

where

$I_s=\{i$: there exists $S_j \in \mathbf{S}$ such that $S_i *_h S_j \in S[I]\}$;

and

$I_p=\{i$: there exists $S_j \in \mathbf{S}$ such that $S_i // S_j \in S[I]\}$.

We now have the following theorem by Lemmas 1 and 10-13.

THEOREM 5. Let $\mathbb{Q}$ be a property on graphs defined by a finite number of forbidden homeomorphic subgraphs. Then the decision problem and the minimum edge (vertex) deletion problem, both with respect to $\mathbb{Q}$, are linear time computable for every series-parallel graph.

Acknowledgement. This work was partly supported by the Grant in Aid for Scientific Research of the Ministry of Education, Science and Culture of Japan under Grant: Cooperative Research (A) 435013 (1980).

REFERENCES

[1] A. V. Aho, J. E. Hopcroft and J. D. Ullman, The Design and Analysis of Computer Algorithms, Addison-Wesley, Reading, Mass. 1974.

[2] M. Boulala and J. Uhry, Polytope des independants d'un graphe series-parallel, Discrete Math., 27, pp. 225-243 (1979).

[3] G. Chartrand, D. Geller and S. Hedetniemi, Graphs with forbidden subgraphs, J. of Combinatorial Theory, 10, pp. 12-41 (1971).

[4] R. J. Duffin, Topology of series parallel networks, J. Math. and Appli. 10, pp. 303-318 (1965).

[5] J. Edmonds, Paths, trees, and flowers, Canad. Math. 17, pp. 449-467 (1965).

[6] S. Even and O. Kariv, An $O(n^{2.5})$ algorithm for maximum matching in general graphs, Proc. IEEE 16th Symp. on FOCS, pp. 100-112 (1975).

[7] M. R. Garey, D. S. Johnson and L. Stockmeyer, Some simplified NP-complete graph problems, Theoretical Computer Science, 1, pp. 237-267 (1976).

[8] J. E. Hopcroft and R. E. Tarjan, Dividing a graph into triconnected components, SIAM J. Comput., 2, 3, pp. 135-158 (1973).

[9] F. O. Hadlock, Finding a maximum cut of a planar graph in polynomial time, SIAM J. Comput., 4, pp. 221-225 (1975).
[10] F. Harary, Graph Theory, Addison-Wesley, Reading, Mass. 1969.
[11] S. T. Hedetniemi, Hereditary properties of graphs, J. Combinatorial Theory (B), 14, pp. 94-99 (1973).
[12] M. S. Krishnamoorthy and N. Deo, Node-deletion NP-complete problems, SIAM J. Comput., 8, 4, pp. 619-625 (1979).
[13] D. G. Kirkpatrick and P. Hell, On the completeness of a generalized matching problem, Proc. 10th ACM Symp. on Theory of Computing (1978).
[14] T. Kikuno, N. Yoshida and Y. Kakuda, Dominating set in planar graphs, Tech. Report AL79-9, Inst. Elect. Commun. Eng. Japan, pp. 21-30 (1979).
[15] J. M. Lewis, On the complexity of the maximum subgraph problem, Proc. of the 10th ACM Symp. on Theory of Computing, pp. 265-274 (1978).
[16] C. L. Monma and J. B. Sidney, Sequencing with series-parallel procedure constraints, TR 347, Sch. of OR/IE, Cornell University (1979).
[17] E. F. Moore and C. E. Shannon, Reliable circuits using reliable relays I-II, J. Franklin Inst., 262, 3, p. 191, and 4, p. 281 (1956).
[18] T. Nishizeki and N. Saito, Necessary and sufficient condition for a graph to be three-terminal series- parallel-cascade, J. of Combinatorial Theory B, 24, 3, pp. 344-361 (1978).
[19] T. Nishizeki, K. Takamizawa and N. Saito, Algorithms for detecting series-parallel graphs and D-charts, Trans. of Inst. Elect. Commun. Eng. Japan, 59, 3, pp. 259-260 (1976).
[20] N. Tomizawa, On a specialization sequence from general matroids to ladder graphs with special emphasis on the characterization of ladder matroids, RAAG Research Notes, Third Series, No. 191 (1973).
[21] J. Valdes, R. E. Tarjan and E. L. Lawler, The recognition of series-parallel digraph, Proc. of 11th Ann. ACM Symp. on Theory of Computing, 1979.
[22] T. Watanabe, T. Ae and A. Nakamura, On the node cover problem of planar graphs, Proc. of 1979 ISCAS, pp. 78-81 (1979).
[23] M. Yannakakis, Node- and edge-deletion NP-complete problems, Proc of the 10th ACM Symp. on Theory of Computing, pp. 253-264 (1978).

A GRAPH-PLANARIZATION ALGORITHM AND ITS APPLICATION TO RANDOM GRAPHS

T. Ozawa and H. Takahashi
Department of Electrical Engineering
Faculty of Engineering, Kyoto University
Kyoto, Japan 606

Abstract. In this paper presented are a graph-planarization algorithm and the results obtained by the application of the algorithm to random graphs. The algorithm tests the subgraph of the given graph G for planarity and if the subgraph fails the test, it deletes a minimum number of edges necessary for planarization. The subgraph has one vertex at the beginning, and the number of its vertices is increased one by one until all the vertices of G are included in it. The result from the application of the algorithm to random graphs indicates that the time complexity of the algorithm is $O(n^p)$ with $p=1.4\sim1.5$ in average, where n is the number of vertices of G.

1. Introduction

Based on the planarity-testing algorithm by Lempel, Even and Cederbaum[1], a graph-planarization algorithm using PQ-trees is presented. The outline of the algorithm is as follows. First, a numbering called an st-numbering is given to the vertices of the given graph. Next, starting from the first vertex and following the st-numbering, the algorithm adds a vertex and its outgoing edges to the subgraph already obtained. Then it tests the planarity of the new subgraph, and if nonplanar, deletes a minimum number of edges necessary to obtain a planar subgraph. Once a new planar subgraph is obtained, the algorithm again adds one more vertex, and so on.

The number of edges deleted by the algorithm depends on the st-numbering and, of course, on the graph. Thus the algorithm is applied to random graphs and some statistical data are obtained. They show very interesting properties of the algorithm and random graphs, which would be useful for designing probabilistic algorithms for graphs. The properties of planarized graph can be predictied with great certainty from the original graph.

2. Definitions

(a) Graph: The graph to be planarized is denoted by G. G has vertex set V and edge set E. The numbers of vertices and edges are denoted by n and e respectively, and the average vertex degree, by $\bar{d}(\bar{d}=2e/n)$.

(b) PQ-tree: The definitions concerning a PQ-tree are due to reference [2]. Let U be a universal set and S, a subset of U. A PQ-tree is a date-structure introduced to obtain, among all the possible sequences of the elements of U, all the sequences in which the elements of S are consecutive. In general, a PQ-tree has a tree-structure from a root to leaves. The leaves correspond to the elements of U. Reading the leaves of the tree from left to right gives an allowable sequence of the elements of U, and is called the frontier of the tree. A branching point in the tree-structure is a P-node or a Q-node, and

(1) the children of a P-node can be permuted arbitrarily, and

(2) the children of a Q-node can be reversed.

When S is given, the PQ-tree is transformed, under the restrictions (1) and (2) above, so that the elements of S are consecutive in the frontier. If the transformation is possible, the PQ-tree is called reducible. Then a new PQ-tree is constructed satisfying the condition that the elements of S be consecutive. The operation to obtain the new tree is called the reduction of the tree.

A PQ-tree is drawn on a plane with the root at the top and the leaves at the bottom. A node and its children in the tree differ in hight by one.

(c) St-numbering: Given a graph G and two vertices s and t in G. A numbering satisfying the following conditions is called an st-numbering for G. Let the number of vertex x be denoted by f(x). Conditions: (i) $f(s)=1$ and $f(t)=n$; (ii) for $x \neq s$ or t, there exist two vertices y and z such that $f(y)<f(x)<f(z)$ and y and z are adjacent to x. It is always possible to determine an st-numbering for a biconnected graph. If an st-numbering is determined, an edge in G is oriented so that it comes out from a vertex with a smaller number and goes into a vertex with a larger number.

3. Planarization Algorithm

Let G be a biconnected graph.

[Algorithm PLAN]

<u>Step 1.</u> Choose two vertices s and t in G, and determine an st-numbering for G. Construct PQ-tree T_1 consisting of a leaf corresponding to vertex 1 of G. Set $N \leftarrow 1$.

<u>Step 2.</u> For vertex N of G, construct PQ-tree T_{NN} consisting of a P-node and its children. The P-node is the root and its children are all leaves corresponding to the vertices into which the edges from vertex N go. Add T_{NN} to T_N by replacing the leaf in T_N corresponding to vertex N with the root of T_{NN}. Let T_{N+1} be the resultant PQ-tree. Set $N \leftarrow N+1$.

<u>Step 3.</u> Let S be the set of all the leaves in T_N corresponding to vertex N of G. If T_N is reducible for S, then go to step 5.

<u>Step 4.</u> Delete a <u>minimum</u> number of leaves in T_N such that T_N becomes reducible.

<u>Step 5.</u> Reduce T_N. If N=n, stop. If N<n, go to step 2.

If PQ-trees are used to implement the planarity-testing algorithm of reference [1], the above algorithm except step 4 will be obtained.

<u>4. Deletion of Leaves</u>

<u>4.1 Step 4 of PLAN</u>

The following definitions are given first.

(a) S-leaves, S-trees, S-root and S-nodes: The leaves of S are called S-leaves. The subtree of T_N which contains all the S-leaves in its frontier, and has the minimum height possible, is called an S-tree. (The S-tree is the pertinent tree of reference [2].) The root of the S-tree is called the S-root, and a node in the S-tree having at least one S-leaf as its descendant, is called an S-node.

(b) The following four types of nodes are defined for the nodes in the S-tree.

Type B node: A node whose descendant leaves are all S-leaves.

Type W node: A node none of whose descendant leaves are S-leaves.

Type H node: A node such that the frontier of its descendant leaves has consecutive S-leaves either on the left or on the right end of the frontier. Non-S-leaves are also consecutive in the frontier.

Type A node: A node such that the frontier of its descendant leaves has consecutive S-leaves on the middle and consecutive non-S-leaves on the ends of the frontier (on both sides of the consecutive S-leaves).

A leaf is either type B or type W. The minimum number of leaves which need be deleted to make an S-node into type B, W, H and A are denoted by b, w, h and a respectively. A type B or type W node is regarded, if necessary, as a special case of a type H or type A node, when h or a is computed. The total number of descendant leaves of a node is denoted by l. We have the following proposition.

[Proposition]

A necessary and sufficient condition for a PQ-tree with given S to be reducible is that the S-root is of one of the types B, H and A.

Based on the above proposition, the step 4 of PLAN is performed in the following four substeps.

[Step 4 of PLAN]

Step 4.1 Search T_N for the S-tree starting from S-leaves and going up from children to parents. At the same time count, for each S-node, the number of S-nodes contained in its children. Let tne number be denoted by n_s.

Step 4.2 Compute b, w, h and a for each S-node by algorithm SCAN given below.

Step 4.3 When b, h and a for the S-root are obtained, the minimum of them determines the type of the S-root which makes T_N reducible with minimum deletion of edges. Once the type of the S-root is determined, the types of its descendant are sequentially determined, first its children and then its grandchildren, and so on. The nodes in T_N are first labeled B, W, H or A according to the types thus determined, and then processed as described in section 4.3.

When a new PQ-tree T_{N+1} is constructed at step 2 of PLAN, the new P-node is given a number which is larger than the number of its parent. The root of T_1 is given number 1. These numbers are utilized to obtain the S-tree efficiently.

4.2 Computation of the Minimum Number of Leaves to Be Deleted

(a) Computation of l: When T_{NN} is constructed at step 2 of PLAN, the number of leaves which the P-node has is equal to the number of edges coming out of vertex N in G. Let this number be d_N. When T_{NN} is added to T_N, the number l for the P-node is set to d_N, and the number l for each of its ancestor nodes is changed as $l \leftarrow l + d_N$.

(b) Computation of b, w, h and a: The S-tree is scanned sequentially from the S-leaves to their parents and then to their ancestors. A queue of nodes is prepared for this scanning. A stack is also prepared for the determination of the types of nodes which takes place in the reverse order of the scanning.

[Algorithm SCAN]

1° Put S-leaves into the queue and the stack. For each S-leaf set $w=1$.

2° Let X be the first node of the queue. For X set $b=l-w$. Compute h and a for X by the method given below.

3° If X is the S-root, stop.

4° Add w for X to w for the parent of X.

5° Set $n_s \leftarrow n_s - 1$ for the parent of X. If new $n_s \geq 1$, go to 2°. If $n_s=0$, put the parent of X at the end of the queue and the stack. Go to 2°.

For a leaf $h=0$ and $a=0$. Consider a node X which is not of the desired type. Its children are numbered from 1 to m. The numbers b, w, h and a for child i(i=1,2,..,m) of X are denoted by b_i, w_i, h_i and a_i respectively.

[Theorem 1] If X is a P-node,

$$h=\sum_{i=1}^{m} min\{w_i,b_i\}-\max_{1\leq i\leq m}(min\{w_i,b_i\}-h_i), \tag{1}$$

$$a=min\{a_I,a_{II}\} \tag{2}$$

where

$$a_I=\sum_{i=1}^{m} min\{w_i,b_i\}-\max_{1\leq i\neq j\leq m}(min\{w_i,b_i\}-h_i+min\{w_j,b_j\}-h_j), \tag{3}$$

$$a_{II}=\sum_{i=1}^{m} w_i-\max_{1\leq i\leq m}(w_i-a_i). \tag{4}$$

(Proof) In order to change X to type H with a minimum number of deleted edges it is necessary and sufficient to assign type H to one of its children which gives $\max_i(min\{w_i,b_i\}-h_i)$, and to each of the other children, type B if $b_i \leq w_i$, or type W if $b_i > w_i$. Thus eq.(1) follows. In order to change X to type A two ways are possible. The first one is to assign type H to two of its children and to each of the other children, either type B or type W. The second one is to assign type A to one of children and type W to all the other children. The minimum number of edges to be deleted in the first can be computed similarly to h, and is given by eq.(3). To obtain a minimum number of edges deleted in the second, the child with $\max_i(w_i-a_i)$ is assigned type A, and eq.(4) follows.

Obviously the smaller of the two gives a.

[Theorem 2] If X is a Q-node,

$$h=\min_{1\leq k\leq m}\left(\min\left\{\sum_{i=1}^{k-1}(w_i-b_i)-b_k+\sum_{i=1}^{m}b_i,\ \sum_{i=1}^{k-1}(b_i-w_i)-w_k+\sum_{i=1}^{m}w_i\right\}+h_k\right) \tag{5}$$

$$a=\min\{a_I,a_{II}\} \tag{6}$$

where

$$a_I=\sum_{i=1}^{m}b_i-\max_{1\leq j<k\leq m}(y_j+z_k) \tag{7}$$

$$y_j=\sum_{i=1}^{j-1}(b_i-w_i)+b_j-h_j \tag{8}$$

$$z_k=\sum_{i=k+1}^{m}(b_i-w_i)+b_k-h_k\ , \tag{9}$$

$$a_{II}=\sum_{i=1}^{m}w_i-\max_{1\leq i\leq m}(w_i-a_i). \tag{10}$$

(Proof) In order to change node X to type H, it is necessary and sufficient to assign type H to one of its children, type B(or W) to the left siblings of the child and type W(or B) to the right siblings. The number of deleted leaves is, then

$$\sum_{i=1}^{k-1}w_i+h_k+\sum_{i=k+1}^{m}b_i \quad\text{or}\quad \sum_{i=1}^{k-1}b_i+h_k+\sum_{i=k+1}^{m}w_i\ ,$$

and eq.(5) follows. Next, there are two possible ways to change X to type A. The first one is to assign type H to two of its children, type B to all the children inside of the two and type W to all the children outside of the two. Let j and k be the two children assigned type H, then the number of leaves deleted is

$$\sum_{i=1}^{j-1}w_i+h_j+\sum_{i=j+1}^{k-1}b_i+h_k+\sum_{i=k+1}^{m}w_i,$$

and eq.(7) follows. The second way is to assign type A to one of the children of X and type W to all the other. The minimum number of leaves to be deleted can be derived similarly to the case where X is a P-node.

To compute eqs.(1)(3)(4)(5) and (10) it is sufficient to scan the children of X once from child 1 to child m. To compute eq.(7) the children of X are scanned once from child 1 to child m and once from child m to child 1. An algorithm for computing a_I is shown below. The maximum of y_i for $1 \leq i \leq j$ which is obtained by scanning from child 1 to child j, is denoted by L_j. The number of the child which gives the maximum is recorded at C_j. $L_{k-1}+z_k$ obtained by scanning from child m to child k is denoted by R_k and $max\ R_i (m \leq i \leq k)$ is denoted by M. The number of the child which gives this maximum is recorded at c.

[Algorithm QA1]

1° $L_1 \leftarrow b_1 - h_1$, $C_1 \leftarrow 1$ and $j \leftarrow 1$.

2° $j \leftarrow j+1$. If $j=m$, go to 4°.

3° $L_j \leftarrow L_{j-1}+h_{j-1}-w_{j-1}+b_j-h_j$. If $L_j > L_{j-1}$, then $C_j \leftarrow j$ and go to 2°. If $L_j \leq L_{j-1}$, then $L_j \leftarrow L_{j-1}$, $C_j \leftarrow C_{j-1}$ and go to 2°.

4° $z_m \leftarrow b_m - h_m$, $R_m \leftarrow L_{m-1}+z_m$, $M \leftarrow R_m$, $c \leftarrow m$ and $k \leftarrow m$.

5° $k \leftarrow k-1$. If $k=1$, let $a_I = (b$ of node X$)-M$, and stop. The number of the children of type H giving a_I are c and C_c.

6° $z_k \leftarrow z_{k+1}+h_{k+1}-w_{k+1}+b_k-h_k$ and $R_k \leftarrow L_{k-1}+z_k$. If $R_k > M$, then $M \leftarrow R_k$, $c \leftarrow k$ and go to 5°. If $R_k \leq M$, go to 5°.

In some case the minimum deletion of edges can be obtained by deleting an S-leaf or a non-S-leaf. In such a case the non-S-leaf is deleted, since it can be expected that the number of deleted edges will be less when algorithm PLAN proceeds to a vertex with a larger number. In our computer program the above algorithm QA1 is modified to include this operation.

4.3 Deletion Procedure

In step 4.3 of PLAN the nodes which have been put in the stack by SCAN are retrieved one by one and labeled. From the label of a node the children to be deleted can be determined. If the children deleted are leaves, they are recorded in a list, and if not, they are labeled D. If a node labeled D is not an S-node, it is put in a queue. A node with label D is taken out later from the stack or the queue, and is processed in the same way as above.

5. Reduction

The label of a node X in the S-tree and the structure of the subtree which has X as the root, can be classified into several patterns, and thus the reduction procedure for each of the patterns can be formulated.

It is only necessary to find a pattern for X and then apply the formula for the pattern to modify the S-tree. This operation corresponds to the templete matching of reference [2], but since the final step in this reduction is to replace the consecutive S-leaves with one leaf, the reduction formulae can be simpler than those in reference [2]. For the simplified formulae see reference [3].

6. Computational Complexity

The most time-consuming procedures in the steps obtaining the S-tree for a vertex in G and reducing it, are that to determine the types of S-nodes by computing the numbers b, w, h and a, and that to apply the reduction formulae. These procedures are repeated for S-nodes. The number of S-nodes varies depending on G, but its upper bound can be given as follows. The PQ-tree T_N represents a subgraph with vertices 1, 2,.., and N of G. The leaves and Q-nodes of T_N correspond to a part of edges and biconnected components of the subgraph respectively. Each of these components contains at least one edge which does not correspond to a leaf. Thus the sum of the numbers of leaves and Q-nodes in T_N is no more than the number of edges in the subgraph. The number of P-nodes in T_N is no more than the number of vertices in the subgraph. Thus the total number of nodes including leaves in T_N is no more than the sum of the numbers of edges and vertices of the subgraph. This sum is no more than e+n.

The steps for the S-tree are repeated at most n times. Thus the time complexity of PLAN is no more than $O(n(e+n))$.

7. Application of PLAN to Random Graphs

Algorithm PLAN was computer programmed and applied to random graphs. The number n of vertices of generated graphs ranges from 30 to 150, and the average vertex degree $\bar{d}$=6, 8, 10 or 12. Note $\bar{d} \ll n$.

7.1 General Description

PQ-tree T_N for large N usually contains one large Q-node, which represents a large biconnected component(a component with many edges and vertices). The reason for getting such a large biconnected component is conjectured as follows. Even if there exist more than one large biconnected components they will be connected together after a small increase of N, because the probability for existence of edges between the vertices in these components and vertex N, is large. S-leaves are, in general, scattered around under the Q-node, and thus most of them are deleted leaving only one, two or three of them. (Note that the average indegree of a planar graph is less than or equal to three.) A non-S-leaves is rarely deleted.

7.2 Dependence of Deleted Edges on St-numberings

The number of deleted edges, denoted by e_d, for planarization depends on st-numberings. An example of the frequency distribution of e_d obtained from 200 st-numberings is shown in Fig. 1. This example and other 15 examples for n=50, 80, 100 and 120 indicate that e_d is rather constant for various st-numberings, that is, the standard deviation of e_d is far smaller than the average of e_d. It is also found that the standard deviation and the average are approximately the same for a small number and large number of trial st-numberings. Fig. 2 shows an example. This means they can be predicted with rather small number of trial st-numberings, and then the lower limit of e_d which can be obtained by PLAN, is

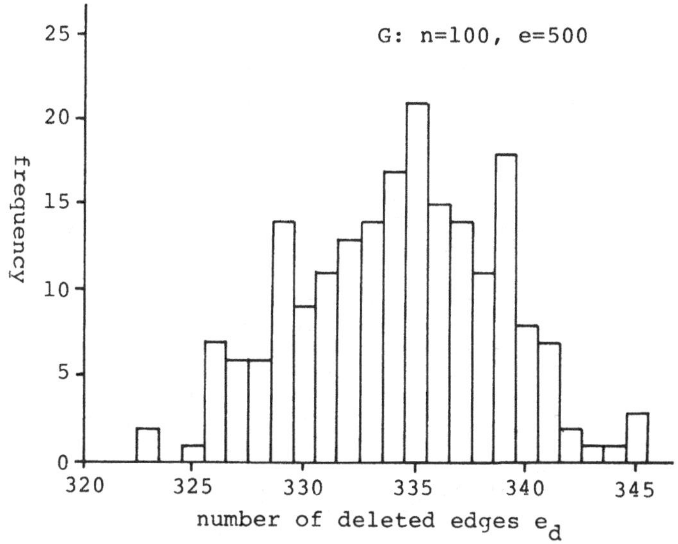

Fig. 1 Frequency distribution of the number of deleted edges e_d for various st-numberings. The average is 332.5, and the standard deviation is 4.3.

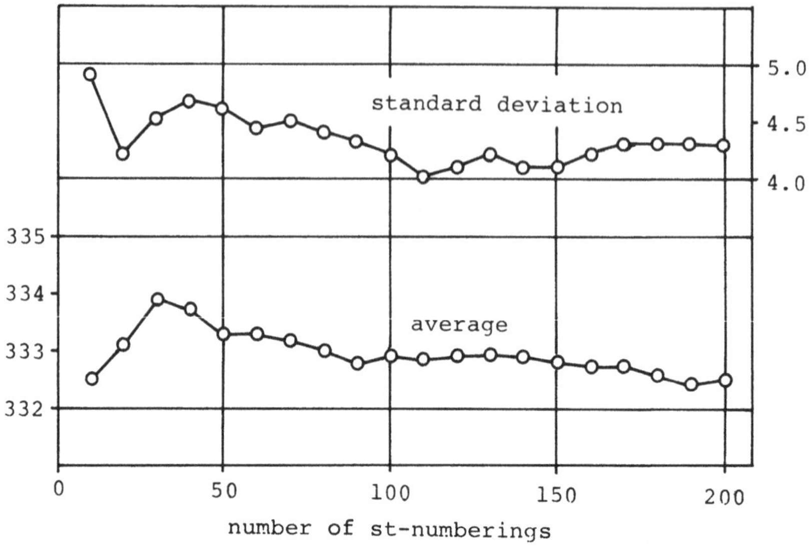

Fig. 2 Variation of the average and the standard deviation of e_d for the number of st-numberings.

estimated from them.

Table 1 shows the ranges(in upper cases) and the averages(in lower cases) of e_d taken over 10 different st-numberings for a graph with specified n and $\bar{d}$.

Table 1 The ranges of the averages of e_d.

$\bar{d}$ \ n	30	50	70	100	120	150
6	32 ∿ 43	71 ∿ 79	102∿115	158∿162	207∿210	
	38	76	109	160	209	
8	54 ∿ 62	106∿116	156∿166	241∿251	289∿305	383∿394
	59	113	162	245	298	388
10	77 ∿ 87	151∿160	217∿228	325∿338	402∿413	514∿531
	83	155	223	334	410	524
12	106∿112	191∿203	278∿290	419∿433	511∿523	658∿668
	109	196	286	425	517	663

7.3 Dependence of e_d on graphs

The average of e_d for 10 st-numberings is obtained for each graph with specified n and $\bar{d}$, and then the range and the average of the averages for 10 different graphs with the same n and $\bar{d}$ are obtained. The results for various n and $\bar{d}$ are shown in Table 2.

Table 2 Variation of e_d for 10 graphs.

$\bar{d}$ \ n	30	50	70	100	120	150
8	57∿60	106∿113	162∿166	241∿249	296∿305	383∿391
	58	111	164	245	300	387
10	82∿84	149∿155	222∿227	330∿337	405∿412	518∿527
	83	151	224	333	408	523
12	108∿110	193∿197	283∿287	420∿428	512∿519	655∿664
	109	195	286	424	517	660

This table indicates that e_d is rather constant for various graphs, if n and $\bar{d}$ are the same.

The average of the average vertex degrees, denoted by $\bar{d}_p$, of 10 planarized graphs is plotted in Fig. 3 for various n. The parameters in the figure are the average vertex degree $\bar{d}$ of the original graphs and the ratio $\beta=\bar{d}/(n-1)$, which is the ratio of the number of edges of G to that of the complete graph with the same number of vertices. (It is expected that a maximal planar graph is obtained from a complete graph.) From this figure the number of edges of a planarized graph can be predicted with great certainty from the original graph.

7.4 Computation Time

The average computation time required for planarization vs the number of vertices of the graphs is shown in Fig. 4. Ten different graphs with specified n and $\bar{d}$, and ten different st-numberings for each of the graphs were tried. (Thus the average is taken over 100 applications of the algorithm for each pair of n and $\bar{d}$.) From this figure it is seen that the computation time is of $O(n^p)$ with $p=1.41\sim1.44$. The computer used is FACOM M200 of the Data Processing Center at Kyoto University, Kyoto, Japan.

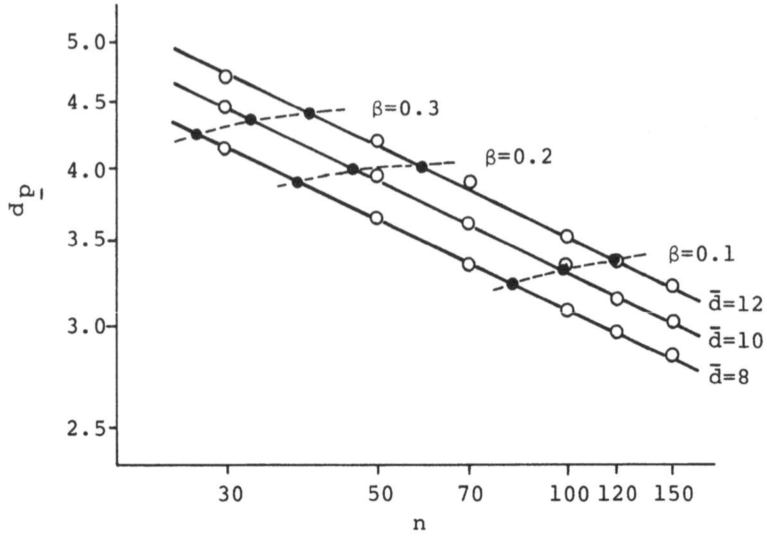

Fig. 3 Average vertex-degree of planarized graphs vs number of vertices of the original graphs.

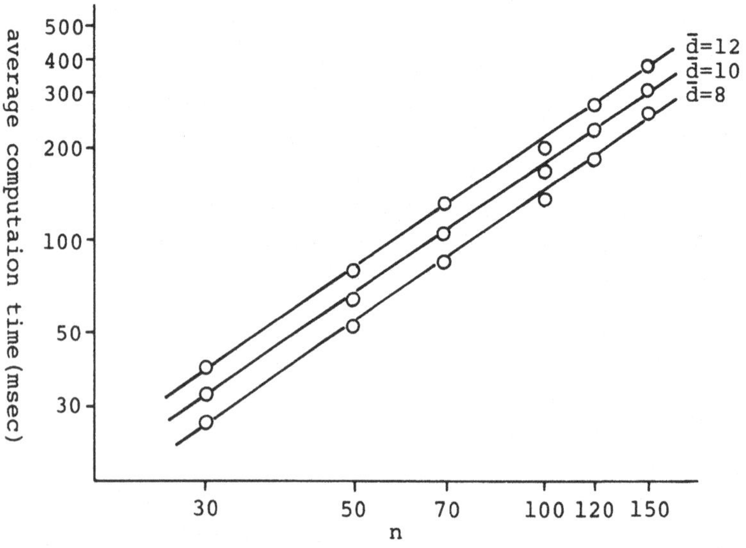

Fig. 4 Average computation time for planarization vs number of vertices of the original graphs.

. Concluding Remarks

The planarization algorithm using PQ-trees has an advantage, over that sing path embedding[4], that the mapping of planarized graphs can be asily obtained from the PQ-trees. From the results as shown in Fig. 1, t is expected that the algorithm gives e_d which is very close to the inimum required for planarization. If so, PLAN is an efficient approx-mation algorithm for the maximum planarization problem which has been roved to be NP-complete[5]. The computational results obtained here ould be useful for studying the properties of random graphs[6].

cknowledgements This work was supported in part by the Grant in Aid or Scientific Research of the Ministry of Education, Science and Cul-ure of Japan under Grant: Cooperative Reseach (A) 435013(1979).

efernces

1] Lempel, A., Even, S. and Cederbaum, I. "An algorithm for planarity testing of graphs," Theory of Graphs, International Symposium, Rome, July 1966, Rosenstiel, P. edit., pp.215-232, Gordon & Breach, N. Y., 1967.

2] Booth, K. S., and Lueker, G. S. "Testing for the consecutive ones property, interval graphs and graph planarity using PQ-trees," J. Computer and Syst. Scie., vol.13, pp.335-379, 1976.

3] Ozawa, T and Takahashi, H. "An algorithm for planarization of graphs using PQ-trees," Trans. Information Processing Society of Japan, vol.22, pp.9-15, 1981; and also Tech. Report, Inst. Electronics and Communication Engineers of Japan, Circuits and Systems, CAS79-150, Jan. 1980.

4] Chiba, T., Nishioka, I. and Shirakawa, I. "An algorithm of maximal planarization of graphs," 1979 International Symposium on Circuits and Systems Proc. pp.649-653, 1979.

5] Garey, M. and Johnson, D.:"Computers and Intractability," W. H. Freeman and Co., Reading, England, 1979.

6] Ozawa, T. and Nishizeki, T. "Properties of certain types of random graphs," 1979 International Symposium on Circuits and Systems Proc., pp.88-91, 1979.

SOME COMMON PROPERTIES FOR REGULARIZABLE GRAPHS, EDGE-CRITICAL GRAPHS AND B-GRAPHS

Claude Berge
Universite de Paris 6
Paris, France

1. Introduction

The purpose of this paper is to display some relations between different classes of graphs, in particular:

- the edge-critical graphs,
- the well-covered graphs ("every maximal stable set is maximum"),
- the B-graphs ("each vertex is contained in some maximum stable set"),
- the regularizable graphs,
- the quasi-regularizable graphs.

Though some of the proofs have already appeared somewhere else, we shall give them in full for the basic lemmas. No use of the Farkas lemma will be made (as for similar researches about hypergraphs) and this paper is self contained.

2. Edge-critical Graphs

Let G be a simple graph with vertex-set X. For $x \in X$, let Γx denote the set of all neighbours of x; if $A \subseteq X$. put $\Gamma A = \cup \Gamma x$ if $A \neq \emptyset$, and $\Gamma A = \emptyset$ if $A = \emptyset$. Let $\alpha(G)$ denote the stability number, i.e. the largest number of independent vertices in G. An edge e of G is <u>α-critical</u> if

$$\alpha(G-e) > \alpha(G).$$

G is <u>α-edge-critical</u> or <u>edge-critical</u> if every edge is α-critical. This concept, introduced by Zykov [24], has been studied by many authors (see Plummer [15], Erdös-Gallai [8], Hajnal [11], Berge [3], George [10], Andrasfai [1], Suranyi [22], etc...)

In this paper we shall write $G \in \mathcal{G}_1$ if G is edge-critical and has no connected component isomorphic to K_1 (isolated vertex) or K_2

(isolated edge). We shall also consider some more general classes of graphs. We write $G \in \mathcal{G}_2$ if each vertex is of degree ≥ 2 and incident to at least one critical edge. An obvious result is:

Proposition 1. Every graph in $\mathcal{G}_1$ is also in $\mathcal{G}_2$.
Proof. It suffices to show that an edge-critical connected graph different from K_1 or K_2 has no vertex of degree 1. Let a be a vertex with $d_G(a)=1$. Since G is connected and has at least three vertices, there exists a vertex x with $[a,x] \in G$. Since $G \neq K_2$, and $d_G(a)=1$, there exists a vertex $b \neq a$ adjacent to x. Since $[b,x]$ is a critical edge, there exists a set S of cardinality $\alpha(G)+1$ which contains only one edge, namely the edge $[b,x]$. Hence $a \notin S$, and $(S-\{x\}) \cup \{a\}$ is a stable set of cardinality $\alpha(G)+1$, a contradiction.

Q.E.D.

Definition. We shall write $G \in \mathcal{G}_3$ if for each vertex x of G there exists a maximum stable set T_x such that $x \notin T_x$, $x \not\subset T_x$.

Proposition 2. Every graph in $\mathcal{G}_2$ is also in $\mathcal{G}_3$.
Proof. Let x be a vertex of a graph G in $\mathcal{G}_2$. Thus, x is incident to a critical edge $[x,b]$, and there exists at least one edge $[x,a] \neq [x,b]$. Also, there exists a set S_{bx} of cardinality $\alpha(G)+1$ which contains only one edge, namely $[b,x]$. So $x \in S_{bx}$, $a \notin S_{bx}$. Hence, $T=S_{bx}-\{x\}$ is a maximum stable set and $x \notin T$; since $a \notin T$, we have also $T \not\supset \Gamma x$. Q.E.D.

THEOREM 1. In a graph $G \in \mathcal{G}_3$, every stable set S satisfies $|\Gamma S| > |S|$.
Proof. We shall assume that G is connected without loss of generality.

We shall show, by induction on $|S|$, that $|\Gamma S| > |S|$ for every stable set S.

First, let $S=\{x\}$ be a singleton. Then x is not an isolated vertex (because $T_x \cup \{x\}$ would be a stable set larger than T_x). Also, x is not incident to only one edge, say $[x,y]$, because $x \notin T_x$, hence $y \in T_x$, hence $\Gamma x \subset T_x$, a contradiction. Thus $|\Gamma S| > |S|$.

Assume that every stable set S with cardinality $\leq$ p-1 satisfies $|\Gamma S| > |S|$, and consider a stable set S with cardinality $p > 1$. Let $a \in S$; we have

$$|\Gamma S \cap T_a| \geq |S-T_a|$$

Otherwise, $|\Gamma S \cap T_a| < |S-T_a|$, and $T_a-(\Gamma S \cap T_a) \cup (S-T_a)$ would be a stable set larger than T_a, a contradiction.

Case 1: $S\cap T_a=\emptyset$. Since $\Gamma a-T_a\neq\emptyset$,

$$|\Gamma S| \geq |\Gamma S\cap T_a| + |\Gamma a-T_a| > |\Gamma S\cap T_a| \geq |S-T_a|=|S|.$$

Case 2: $S\cap T_a\neq\emptyset$. Then $S\cap T_a$ is a stable set with cardinality $\leq p-1$, and by the induction hypothesis, $|\Gamma(S\cap T_a)| > |S\cap T_a|$. Hence

$$|\Gamma S| \geq |\Gamma(S\cap T_a)|+|\Gamma S\cap T_a| > |S\cap T_a|+|S-T_a| = |S|.$$

In both cases we have $|\Gamma S| > |S|$, which completes the proof.

Q.E.D.

Note that THEOREM 1 generalizes a result of Hajnal [11] who has shown that in an edge-critical graph, every stable set S satisfies $|\Gamma S| \geq |S|$.

3. Regularizable graphs and quasi-regularizable graphs

Let G be a multigraph with no loops. We denote by m(G) the number of edges in G, by $\Delta(G)$ the maximum degree of its vertices, by $\nu(G)$ the matching number, i.e. the maximum size of a matching ("set of independent edges"), and by $\tau(G)$ the transversal number $= n-\alpha(G)$. For an integer k and an edge e of G, we say that we multiply e by k if we replace e by k parallel edges; if k=0, multiplying e by k means removing e. The graph kG is the graph obtained from G by multiplying each edge by k. We say that a graph G is regularizable if by multiplying each edge by an integer ≥ 1, we get a regular multigraph (of degree $\neq 0$). We say that G is quasi-regularizable if by multiplying each edge by an integer ≥ 0, we get a regular multigraph (of degree $\neq 0$),

In this section, we shall denote:

$\mathcal{G}_4$ = class of all regularizable graphs which have no bipartite connected components;

$\mathcal{G}_5$ = class of all regularizable graphs;

$\mathcal{G}_6$ = class of all quasi-regularizable graphs.

Proposition 3. Every graph in $\mathcal{G}_4$ is also in $\mathcal{G}_5$, and every graph in $\mathcal{G}_5$ is also in $\mathcal{G}_6$. The converses are not true (for example, the graph P_4 is quasi-regularizable but not regularizable.)

A fractional transversal of G is a non-negative function t(x), defined for $x\in X$, such that for each edge [x,y]

$$t(x)+t(y) \geq 1.$$

$\tau^*(G)$ denotes the minimum of $\Sigma_{x\in X}t(x)$ for all fractional transversals t.

A <u>k-transversal</u> of G is a function t(x) on X such that:

(i) $t(x) \in \{0,1,2,\ldots,k\}$,

(ii) $t(x)+t(y) \geq k$ for every edge [x,y] of G.

$\tau_k(G)$ denotes the minimum of $\Sigma_{x \in X} t(x)$ when t ranges over all the k-transversals of G. Thus $\tau_1(G)$ is the usual transversal number $\tau(G)$, i.e. the minimum cardinality of a set $T \subset X$ which meets all the edges. A partial graph H of kG is called a <u>k-matching</u> if $\Delta(H) \leq k$. So a 1-matching is an ordinary matching.

Denote by $\nu_k(G)$ the maximum number of edges in a k-matching. Thus $\nu_1(G)=\nu(G)$ is the usual matching number.

<u>Lemma 1</u>. For every graph G,

$\nu_k(G)/k \leq \tau^*(G) \leq \tau_k(G)/k$.

Checking these inequalities is easy.

<u>Lemma 2.</u> Let G be a simple graph. Then there exists an optimal 2-matching H of G such that each connected component of H is either a single vertex or a pair of parallel edges ("double edge") or an odd cycle. For every 2-matching of that kind there exists an optimal 2-transversal with values: 0 for a singleton of H, (0,2) or (1,1) for the two vertices belonging to a double edge of H, 1 for a vertex belonging to an odd cycle of H.

<u>Proof</u>. We may assume that G is connected. Let H be a maximum 2-matching. Every connected component of H which is a path or a cycle of even length can be replaced by a set of pairwise disjoint double-edges without changing m(H). No component of H is an odd path (i.e. a path of odd length) since m(H) is maximum. Thus a connected component of H is either a simple vertex or a double edge or an odd cycle. Now we shall label each vertex with 0,1 or 2, by an iterative procedure described by the following rules:

(1) label with 0 each vertex which is a singleton of H;

(2) label with 2 each vertex which is adjacent in G to a vertex previously labelled with 0;

(3) label with 0 every vertex which is adjacent in H to a vertex previously labelled with 2;

(4) every vertex which cannot be labelled by the iterative procedure described by rules (1),(2), and (3) will be labelled 1.

No odd chain, starting from a singleton of H and consisting alternately of edges of G-H and of double-edges of H, ends with a singleton because such a chain would constitute a connected component of a 2-matching H' with $m(H') > m(H)$. Similarly no odd chain of that kind can end in an odd cycle of H. No odd chain of that kind can cross itself at a vertex labelled with 0 (because there would be a better 2-matching having as connected components an odd cycle and a set of double edges).

Thus a unique label $t(x)$ is given to each vertex x by the above rules; furthermore,

$t(x)=0$ if x is a singleton of H,

$t(x)=2$ and $t(y)=0$ (or vice versa) if $[x,y]$ is a double-edge connectable to a singleton (otherwise $t(x)=t(y)=1$), $t(x)=1$ if x belongs to an odd cycle of H.

The rule (2) shows that $t(x)$ is a 2-transversal of G. Furthermore, by lemma 1,

$$m(H)/2 \leq \nu_2(G)/2 \leq \tau^*(G) \leq \tau_2(G)/2 \leq \Sigma_{x\in X} t(x) = m(H)/2.$$

Therefore, these inequalities hold as equalities; and $t(x)$ is an optimal 2-transversal and H is an optimal 2-matching. Q.E.D.

Lemma 3. For every graph G,

$$\nu(G) = \min_k \nu_k(G)/k \leq \max_k \nu_k(G)/k = \nu_2(G)/2 = \tau^*(G)$$
$$= \tau_2(G)/2 = \min_k \tau_k(G)/k \leq \max_k \tau_k(G)/k = \tau(G).$$

Proof. - We have $\nu(G) \geq \inf \nu_k(G)/k$ because $\nu(G)=\nu_1(G)$.

- We have $\nu(G) \leq \inf \nu_k(G)/k$: let H be a maximum matching; so kH is a k-matching, and

$$\nu(G) = m(H) = m(kH)/k \leq \nu_k(G)/k.$$

Hence $\nu(G) = \min \nu_k(G)/k$.

- We have $\tau(G) \geq \sup_k \tau_k(G)/k$.

Let T be a minimal transversal set , with characteristic function $t(x)$. Then $kt(x)$ is a k-transversal; hence:

$$\tau(G)=|T|=\Sigma kt(x)/p \geq \tau_k(G)/k$$

- We have $\tau(G) \leq \sup \tau_k(G)/k$, because $\tau(G)=\tau_1(G)$. Hence, $\tau(G) = \max \tau_k(G)/k$.

- The other equalities follow from lemma 1 and lemma 2.

Q.E.D.

THEOREM 2. For a graph G, the following conditions are equivalent:

(1) G is quasi-regularizable;

(2) $t(x)\equiv 1$ is an optimal 2-transversal;

(3) G has a partial graph whose connected components are either a K_2 or an odd cycle;

(4) $|\Gamma S| \geq |S|$ for every stable set S.

Proof. (1) implies (2). If G is quasi-regularizable and has n vertices, there exists a k-regular graph $H \subseteq kG$, and by counting in two different ways the edges of the incident graph of H, we get $kn=2m(H)$. Hence:

$$n/2 = m(H)/k \leq \nu_k(G)/k \leq \tau^*(G) = \tau_2(G)/2 \leq n/2$$

(since $t(x) \equiv 1$ is a 2-transversal of G). Thus, the quasi-regularizablity implies $\tau_2(G) = n$. So the 2-transversal $t(x) \equiv 1$ is an optimal one.

(2) implies (1). By lemma 3 we see that $\tau^*(G) = n/2$ implies $\nu_2(G) = n$; so by lemma 2 we can cover the vertex-set of G with isolated double-edges and odd cycles; consequently G is quasi-regularizable.

(2) implies (3) (as above).

(3) implies (2) (obvious).

(2) implies (4).

Let S be a stable set. Put :

$t(x)=0$ if $x \in S$,

$t(x)=2$ if $x \in \Gamma S$,

$t(x)=1$ otherwise.

Clearly, $t(x)$ is a 2-transversal, and by (2), $\Sigma t(x) \geq n$. Hence

$|\Gamma S|-|S| = \Sigma_x (t(x)-1) \geq n-n = 0.$

(4) implies (2). Let $t(x)$ be a 2-transversal; clearly, $S=\{x|t(x)=0\}$ is a stable set and $\Gamma S \subseteq \{x|t(x)=2\}$. Hence

$$\Sigma_x t(x) = n + \Sigma_x (t(x)-1) \geq n+|\Gamma S|-|S| \geq n.$$

Hence the 2-transversal identical to 1 is an optimal one. Q.E.D.

COROLLARY. Let G be a connected graph of even order such that every pair of vertex-disjoint odd cycles is linked by an edge. A necessary and sufficient condition that G possess a perfect matching is that $|\Gamma S| \geq |S|$ for every stable set S.

Proof. By Theorem 2, $|\Gamma S| \geq |S|$ for every stable set S if and only if G can be covered with a set of K_2's and of odd cycles (vertex-disjoint). The number of odd cycles is even, and each pair of odd cycles, which is linked by an edge, can be covered by a set of K_2's. Thus G can be covered with disjoint K_2's, i.e. a perfect matching. Q.E.D

REMARK. This corollary has been proved by different methods by Fulkerson, McAndrew, Hoffman [9]. Theorem 2 was partly found by Tutte([23]) who proved in 1952 the following result: G has a perfect 2-matching iff for every $A \subseteq X$ the number of connected components of

G_{X-A} which are isolated vertices is $\leq |A|$.

A similar condition for the existence of a perfect 2-matching without K_3 was found by CORNUEJOLS and PULLEYBLANK ([7]). In [17], PULLEYBLANK shows also that G has a perfect 2-matching iff for every $A \subseteq X$,

$$|\{x \mid x \in X-A,\ \Gamma x \subseteq A\}| \leq |A|.$$

Note that in Theorem 2, (2) can be replaced by:

(2') For every $A \subseteq X$, $|\Gamma A| \geq |A|$.

<u>THEOREM 3</u>. For a simple graph G, the following conditions are equivalent:

(1) G is regularizable and has no bipartite connected component;

(2) the optimal 2-transversal is unique and is defined by $t(x) \equiv 1$;

(3) $|\Gamma S| > |S|$ for every stable set S.

<u>Proof</u>. (1) <u>implies</u> (2). Let G be a graph and let H be a regular multigraph obtained from G by edge-multiplication. Then

$$\tau_2(G) = 2\tau^*(G) = 2\tau^*(H) = 2m(H)/\Delta(H) = 2n(H)/2 = n.$$

Thus, $t(x) \equiv 1$ is an optimal 2-transversal for G.

Now, assume that there exists another optimal 2-transversal $t'(x)$, and for s=0,1,2, put

$$A_s = \{x \mid x \in X,\ t'(x) = s\}.$$

Then $|A_0| = |A_2| \neq 0$. The set A_0 is stable (otherwise $t'(x)$ would not be 2-transversal), and $\Gamma A_0 \subseteq A_2$. We have $\Gamma A_0 = A_2$ (otherwise, $t'(x)$ would not be optimal; a better 2-transversal can be obtained from $t'(x)$ by replacing a 2 by a 1. Since H is regular,

$$\Delta(H)|A_0| = m_H(A_0, A_2)$$
$$\leq \Sigma_{x \in A_2} m_H(x, A_0) \leq |A_2| (H) = \Delta(H)|A_0|.$$

Hence $m_H(x, A_0) = \Delta(H)$ for all $x \in A_2$, and no edge goes out of $A_0 \cup A_2$. Since G is connected, its vertex set is $A_0 \cup A_2$ and G is a bipartite graph having two vertex classes with the same cardinality. This contradicts the hypothesis.

(2) <u>implies</u> (3). Let S be a stable set, and let $H \subseteq 2G$ be an optimal 2-matching as described in Lemma 2.

Since $t(x) \equiv 1$ is an optimal 2-transversal, we have $\tau_2(G) = n$, so the connected components of H are either double edges or odd cycles. Hence

$$|\Gamma_G S| \geq |\Gamma_H S| \geq |S|.$$

If $|\Gamma_G S| = |S|$, it would follow that all the components of H meeting S are double edges. We can then define a 2-transversal $t'(x)$ by putting

$t'(x)=0$ if $x\in S$,

2 if $x\in \Gamma S$,

1 if $x\in X-(S\cup\Gamma S)$.

Since $t'(x)$ would also be an optimal 2-transversal of G, this contradicts the uniqueness of the optimal 2-transversal. Thus $|\Gamma S| > |S|$.

(3) implies (1). Now assume that $|\Gamma S| > |S|$ for every stable set S. Let H be a bipartite graph whose vertex-classes are two copies X and $\bar{X}$ of the vertex set of G, the vertices $x\in X$ and $\bar{y}\in\bar{X}$ being joined by an edge in H if and only if x and y are adjacent in G.

Let $B\subseteq X$, $B\neq\emptyset$, $B\neq X$, be a set such that the subgraph G_B has no isolated vertex. Then $\Gamma_H(B)\supseteq\bar{B}$. Now let $S\subseteq X$ be a set such that G_S has only isolated vertices. Then S is a stable set of G, and by (3),

$|\Gamma_H S|=|\Gamma_G S| > |S|$.

So, for every set $A=B\cup S$, $A\neq\emptyset$, $A\neq X$, we have

$|\Gamma_H A| > |A|$,

noting that $\Gamma_H S\cap\bar{B}=\emptyset$ if there are no edges between B and S.

First, we shall show that each edge $[a,\bar{b}]$ of H belongs to at least one perfect matching, that is , the subgraph H' of H induced by $(X\cup\bar{X})-\{a,\bar{b}\}$ has a perfect matching. For every $A\subset X-\{a\}$,

$|\Gamma_{H'}A|=|\Gamma_H A-\{b\}| \geq |\Gamma_H A|-1 \geq |A|$.

Thus, by König's theorem, H has such a matching.

Consequently, for each edge $[a,b]$ of G, there exists a 2-matching which saturates all the vertices and which uses the edge $[a,b]$. The union of all these possible 2-matchings defines a regular multigraph which is from G by edge-multiplications. Thus G is regularizable.

Q.E.D.

REMARK. It is easy to see that in Theorem 3, (3) can be replaced by

(3') For every non-empty set A, $|\Gamma A| > |A|$.

Theorem 3 was stated as above in [3],[4], but equivalent results were found independently by PULLEYBLANK [17], NEMHAUSER and TROTTER [14], BRUALDI [6]. In fact, those graphs are also called "2-bicritical" by PULLEYBLANK, with the following definition:

(4) For every x, $G_{X-\{x\}}$ is quasi-regularizable.

Clearly (3) implies (4) because every stable S' of $G'=G_{X-\{x\}}$ satisfies $|\Gamma_{G'}S'| \geq |\Gamma_G S'|-1 \geq |S'|$, and (4) follows from Theorem 2. Conversely, if (3) is false, there exists in G a stable S with $|\Gamma_G S| \leq |S|$. So for $x\in\Gamma_G S$, $G'=G_{X-\{x\}}$ satisfies $|\Gamma_{G'}S| < |S|$, and (4) is false.

Proposition 4. Every graph in $\mathcal{G}_3$ is also in $\mathcal{G}_4$.

This follows from Theorem 1 and Theorem 3.

Lemma Let G=(X,Y;E) be a bipartite connected graph. Then G is regularizable if and only if

$|\Gamma S| > |S| \quad (S \subseteq X,\ S \neq X)$,

$|\Gamma T| > |T| \quad (T \subseteq Y,\ T \neq Y)$,

$|X| = |Y| \neq \emptyset$.

Proof. This follows immediately from the theorem of Konig, which gives a necessary and sufficient condition that for each edge [x,y], the subgraph induced by $(X-\{x\}) \cup (Y-\{y\})$ has a perfect matching, that is G has a perfect matching containig [x,y]. (The union of all these perfect matchings gives a regular multigraph, which shows that G is regularizable). Q.E.D.

THEOREM 4. A graph G is regularizable iff $|\Gamma S| \geq |S|$ for every stable set S, and $|\Gamma S| = |S| \Longrightarrow \Gamma(\Gamma S) = S$.

This follows immediately from this lemma and Theorem 3.

In [5], we have also shown that the line-graph of an r-uniform hypergraph with no vertex of degree 1 and no edge meeting less than r other edges is regularizable. An impotant class to be considered is the claw-free graphs, i.e. the graphs which have no induced subgraphs isomorphic to $K_{1,3}$ (for instance, the line-graphs). M. Las Vergnas [13] and D. Sumner [21] have shown independently that a connected claw-free graph with an even number of vertices has a perfect matching (and therefore is quasi-regularizable). A claw-free graph is not always regularizable, as we can see with the following graph: take an even cycle, whose vertices are colored alternately with red and blue, and add a few (at least one) triangular chords connecting two blue vertices at distance 2. Such a graph is called a C-graph; Jaeger and Payan have shown:

THEOREM 5([12]). A connected claw-free graph G is regularizable if and only if G has no pendant vertices and is not a C-graph.

Proof. It suffices to show that a connected claw-free graph G with no pendant vertices and which is not regularizable is a C-graph.

Thus, G is not bipartite (otherwise, a vertex in one vertex-class is adjacent to exactly two vertices in the other class, so G is an even cycle, so G is regularizable, a contradiction).

So, by Theorem 4, there exists a stable set S with $|\Gamma S| \leq |S|$. Each vertex in S has at least 2 neighbours in S (otherwise there is a pendant vertex), and each vertex in ΓS has less than 3 neighbours in S (otherwise there is an induced $K_{1,3}$). So the number of edges $m(S,\Gamma S)$ between S and ΓS satisfies:

$$2|S| \leq \Sigma_{x\in S}\, d(x) = m(S,\Gamma S) \leq 2|\Gamma S| \leq 2|S|.$$

Hence $|S|=|\Gamma S|$ and every vertex in S has exactly two neighbours in ΓS, and every vertex in ΓS has exactly two neighbours in ΓS. Furthermore, a vertex in ΓS has no neighbour in $X-(S\cup\Gamma S)$, and since G is connected, $X=S\cup\Gamma S$.

Since G is not bipartite, $G_{\Gamma S}$ has at least one edge $e=[x,y]$; the vertices x and y have a common neighbour z in S (since G is claw-free). So G is a C-graph. Q.E.D.

The same proof shows that a claw-free graph with no pendant vertex is quasi-regularizable. So, a claw-free graph with no pendant vertex is quasi-regularizable.

4. Well-covered graph

A graph G is <u>well-covered</u>, or $G\in\mathcal{G}_7$, if G has no isolated vertices and if every maximal stable set is also a maximum stable set. This class is independant of $\mathcal{G}_1$. For instance, the graph P_4 (elementary chain with four vertices) is well-covered but is not in $\mathcal{G}_1$; the graph C_9 is in $\mathcal{G}_1$ but is not well-covered. Nevertheless, we shall see that the two classes have similar properties.

A graph G is a <u>B-graph</u>, or $G\in\mathcal{G}_8$, if G has no isolated vertices and if each vertex belongs to some maximum stable set.

<u>Proposition 5</u>. Every well-covered graph is a B-graph.

(Trivial).

<u>Proposition 6</u>. Every graph in $\mathcal{G}_2$ is a B-graph.

(Trivial).

The converse is not true: the graph C_6 is a B-graph, but is not in $\mathcal{G}_2$. The characterizations of well-covered graphs and of B-graph are difficult problems as quoted by Plummer [16]; Ravindra [19] has shown that a 2-connected graph G with no odd cycles of length ≥ 5 is a B-graph if and only if G is isomorphic to K_3, or to K_4, or is a bipartite graph with a perfect matching.

For a graph G with n vertices, a transversal set is the complement of a stable set, and therefore, the cardinality of a minimum transversal set is $\tau(G) = n - \alpha(G)$. A vertex x is <u>τ-critical</u> if $\tau(G-x) \leq \tau(G)$, that is if there exists a maximum stable set S_X which does not contain x. A graph G whose vertices are all τ-critical is said to be <u>τ-vertex-critical</u>, or to be in class $\mathcal{G}_9$.

<u>Proposition 7</u>. Every B-graph is τ-vertex-critical.

(Trivial).

<u>Proposition 8</u>. Every graph in $\mathcal{G}_3$ is τ-vertex-critical.

(Trivial).

The converse is not true. The graph in FIGURE 1 is in $\mathcal{G}_9$ but not in $\mathcal{G}_8$ or in $\mathcal{G}_3$.

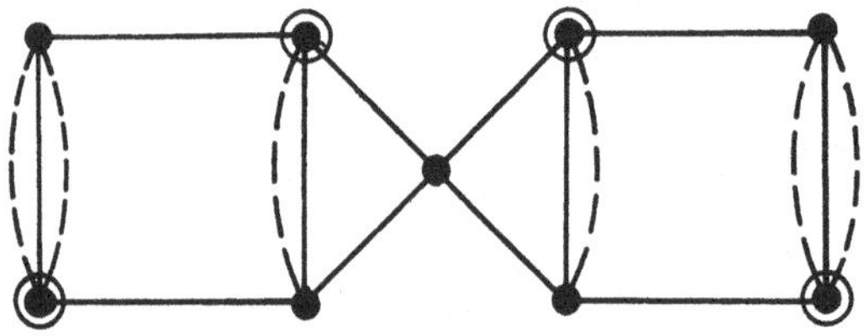

FIGURE 1. $\alpha = 4$

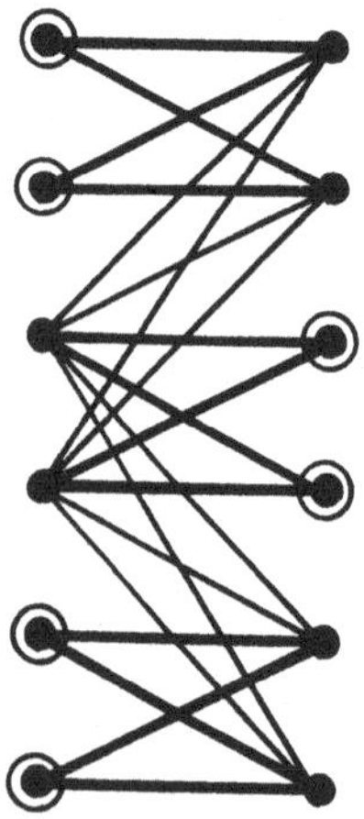

FIGURE 2. $\alpha = 6$

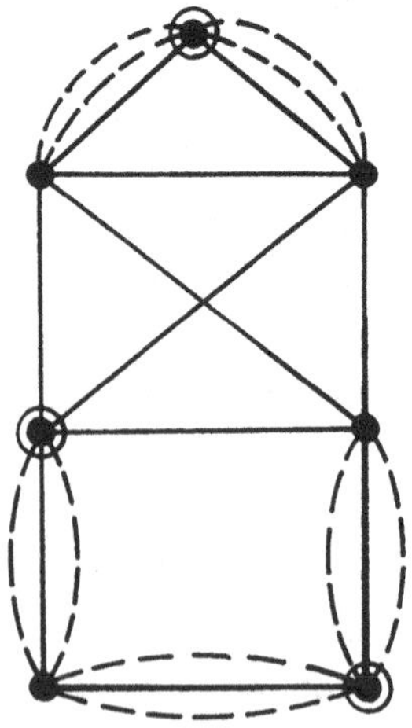

FIGURE 3. $\alpha = 3$

A τ-vertex-critical graph is not necessarily regularizable, as we can see with the graph in FIGURE 2; a graph regularizable is not necessarily τ-vertex-critical, as we can see with the graph represented in FIGURE 3.

However, we shall show that every τ-vertex-critical graph is quasi-regularizable. We first need a lemma.

Lemma. In a graph G, a stable set S is maximum if and only if every stable set T disjoint from S can be matched into S.

Proof. 1. Let S be a maximum stable set, and let T be a disjoint stable set.

Let $H=(T,S;E)$ be the bipartite graph defined by the edges having one end point in T and the other in S.

For $B \subseteq T$, we have $|B| \leq |\Gamma_H B|$ (otherwise, $|B| > |\Gamma_H B|$, and $B \cup (S-\Gamma_H B)$ would be a stable set with cardinality $> |S|$, a contradiction).

Thus, by the theorem of König, there exists a matching between T and S saturating all the vertices in T.

2. Now, assume that every stable set T can be matched into S; let B be a maximum stable set, $B \neq S$; then $T=B-S$ can be matched into S, and therefore into S-B. So, $|B-S| \leq |S-B|$.

Hence $|S| \geq |B|$, and S is a maximum stable set. Q.E.D.

THEOREM 6. Every τ-vertex-critical graph is quasi-regularizable.

Proof. Let G be a τ-vertex-critical graph; so for every vertex a, there exists a maximum stable set T_a with $a \notin T_a$.

Now, we show that $|\Gamma S| \geq |S|$ for every stable set S by induction on $|S|$.

- if $|S|=1$, this is trivial.
- if $|S| = p > 1$, consider a vertex $a \in S$, and a maximum stable set T_a which does not contain a. By the lemma, $S-T_a$ can be matched into T_a, and therefore into T_a-S; also, $S \cap T_a$ can be matched into $X-(S \cap T_a)$, by the induction hypothesis (because $|S-T_a| < |S|= p$). Thus S can be matched into X-S and $|\Gamma S| \geq |S|$. Q.E.D.

Remark that the converse is not true; the graph in FIGURE 3 is quasi-regularizable but is not τ-vertex-critical (because all the maximum stable sets contain a).

The results of this section can be summarized by the diagram shown in FIGURE 4.

We see that $G \in \mathcal{G}_4 \not\Rightarrow G \in \mathcal{G}_9$, because the graph in FIGURE 3 is regularizable and not τ-vertex-critical (because of the point a). Also, $G \in \mathcal{G}_9 \not\Rightarrow G \in \mathcal{G}_5$, because the graph in FIGURE 2 belongs to $\mathcal{G}_7$, $\mathcal{G}_8$, $\mathcal{G}_9$, but not to $\mathcal{G}_5$.

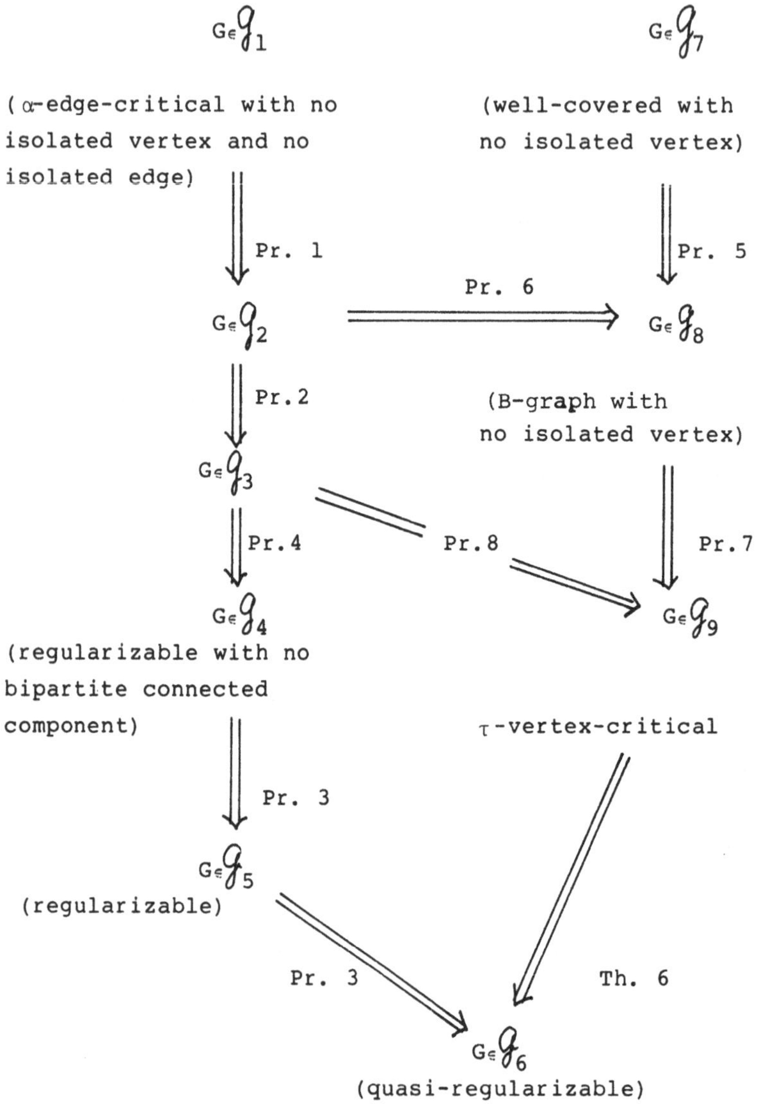

FIGURE 4

5. Case of bipartite graphs

If G is bipartite, we have $G \notin \mathcal{G}_1$, $G \notin \mathcal{G}_2$, $G \notin \mathcal{G}_3$, $G \in \mathcal{G}_4$, and the other properties considered in the preceding sections are easier to characterize.

We have:

<u>Proposition 9</u>. For a bipartite graph $G=(X,Y;E)$, the following properties are equivalent:

- G is quasi-regularizable,
- G has a perfect matching,
- G is a B-graph,
- G is τ-vertex-critical.

<u>Proof</u>. If G is quasi-regularizable, then G has a perfect matching by Theorem 2 (characterization 3).

If G has a perfect matching, then X is a minimum transversal set (by the König theorem), hence X and Y are both maximum stable sets; so G is a B-graph.

If G is a B-graph, then G is τ-vertex-critical, by Proposition 5.

If G is τ-vertex critical, then G is quasi-regularizable, by Theorem 6. Q.E.D.

<u>Proposition 10</u>. (Ravindra [18]). A tree T is well-covered if and only if its pendant edges constitute a perfect matching.

<u>Proof</u>. 1. An edge is <u>pendant</u> if it is incident to a vertex of degree 1. Let G be a graph (not necessarily a tree) whose pendant edges constitute a perfect matching M; then the pendant vertices constitute a stable set of cardinality $n/2$, and $\alpha(G)= n-\tau(G) \leq n-|M|= n/2$. So $\alpha(G)= n/2$. If a stable set S_0 has less than $n/2$ elements, there exists an edge $e\in M$ which does not meet S_0, so S_0 plus the pendant vertex attached to e is also a stable set. This shows that every maximal stable set is also maximum, i.e. $G\in\mathcal{G}_7$.

2. Now, let T be a well-covered tree. So, $T\in\mathcal{G}_8$, and since T is bipartite, T has a perfect matching M (by Proposition 7 and Theorem 6).

Hence, $\alpha(T)= n-\tau(T)= n-|M|= n/2$, and a maximal stable set has exactly one point in each edge of M.

Now, let $e=[a,b]\in M$, and assume that e is not a pendant edge. Then there exists two edges $[b,b']$ and $[a,a']$ with $a'\neq b'$, $[a',b']\notin T$ (since T has no cycle). Therefore, the maximal stable set which contains a' and b' does not meet $\{a,b\}$ and cannot be maximum: a contradiction. Thus, every edge in M is pendant (and every pendant edge is in M, because the matching M is perfect). So T has the required property.

Q.E.D.

Lemma. Let G be a well-covered graph having a perfect matching M such that no alternating chain constitute two disjoint odd cycles linked by an odd chain. Then for each edge $[a,b] \in M$, the set $\{a,b\} \cup \Gamma a \cup \Gamma b$ induces on G a complete-bipartite graph.

Proof. By a theorem of Sterboul [20], if there exists a perfect matching of the described kind, then $\tau(G) = \nu(G)$. Hence $\alpha(G) = n - \tau(G) = n - \nu(G) = n/2$.

So, a maximum stable set has exactly one point in each edge of M.

Let $[a,b] \in M$. If a' is a neighbour of a and b' a neighbour of b, then $a' \neq b'$ (otherwise a maximum stable set containing $\{a'\}$ cannot meet $[a,b]$). Also, $[a',b']$ is an edge of G (otherwise a maximum stable set containing $\{a',b'\}$ does not meet $[a,b]$).

So $\{a,b\} \cup \Gamma a \cup \Gamma b$ induces on G a complete bipartite graph.

Q.E.D.

Proposition 11. Let G be a connected regularizable bipartite graph; then G is well-covered if and only if G is isomorphic to a complete bipartite graph $K_{r,r}$.

Proof. Clearly $K_{r,r}$ is well-covered.

Conversely, Let $G=(X,Y;E)$ be a well-covered bipartite graph. If G is not isomorphic to a complete-bipartite graph $K_{r,s}$, then there exists a $x \in X$ and a $y \in Y$ whose distance $d(x,y)$ is larger than 1, so there exists a set $\{x,b,a,y\}$ which induces a P_4. The edge $[a,b]$ belongs to some perfect matching M (since a regular bipartite multigraph has the edge-coloring-property). Applying the lemma with the edge $[a,b]$, we get a contradiction.

Thus G is isomorphic to $K_{r,s}$, and since G is regularizable, $|\Gamma S| \geq |S|$ for all stable set S, hence r=s. Q.E.D.

REFERENCES

[1] B. Andrásfai, On critical graphs, Théorie des Graphes (Rome I.C.C.), Paris, (1967), 9-19.

[2] C. Berge, Graphes et Hypergraphes (Dunod, Paris, 1970).

[3] C. Berge, Une propriete des graphes k-stables critiques, Combinatorial Structures (Gordon and Breach, New York, 1970) 7-11.

[4] C. Berge, Regularizable Graphs, Proc. I.S.I. Conference on Graph Theory, Calcutta, 1976.

[5] C. Berge, Regularizable Graphs, Annals of Discrete Math. 3 (1978) 11-19.

[6] R. A. Brualdi, Combinatorial Properties of symmetric non-negative matricies, Coll. Th. Combinat. Rome, 2 (1976) 99-120.

[7] G. Cornuejols, W. Pulleyblank, A matching problem with side conditions, Discrete Math. 29 (1980) 135-139.

[8] P. Erdős, T. Gallai, On the minimal number of vertices representing the edges of a graph, Publ. Math. Inst. Hung. Acad. Sci. 6 (1961) 181-203.
[9] D. R. Fulkerson, A. J. Hoffman, M. H. McAndrew, Some properties of graphs with multiple edges, Can. J. Math. (1965) 166-177.
[10] A. George, On line-critical graphs, Thesis, Vanderbilt Univ., Nashville, TN (1971).
[11] A. Hajnal, A theorem on k-saturated graphs, Can. J. Math. 17 (1965) 720-772.
[12] F. Jaeger, C. Payan, A class of regularizable graphs, Annals of Discrete Math. 3 (1978) 125-127.
[13] M. Las Vergnas, A note on matchings, Acts Coll. Brussells, CER, 17, 1975, 255-260.
[14] G. L. Nemhauser, L. E. Trotter, Vertex packings: structural properties and algorithms, Math. Programming 8 (1975) 232-248.
[15] M. D. Plummer, On a family of line critical graphs, Monatsh. Math. 71 (1967) 40-48.
[16] M. D. Plummer, Some covering concepts in Graphs, J. Comb. Theory B (1970) 46-48.
[17] W. R. Pulleyblank, Minimum node covers and 2-bicritical graphs, Math. Programming 17 (1979) 91-103.
[18] G. Ravindra, Well coverd Graphs, I.I.T. Madras (1976).
[19] G. Ravindra, B-Graphs, Symposium on Graph Theory, I.S.I. (1976).
[20] F. Sterboul, A characterization of the graphs in which the transversal number equals the matching number, J. Comb. Theory B 27 (1979) 228-229.
[21] D. P. Sumner, Graphs with 1-factors, Proc. Am. Math. Soc. 42, 1974, 8-12.
[22] L. Suranyi, On line-critical graphs, Infinite and finite sets, (North Holland, Amsterdam, 1975) 1411-1444.
[23] W. Tutte, The factors of graphs, Canad. J. Math. 4 (1952) 314-328.
[24] A. A. Zykov, On some properties of linear complexes, Math. USSR Sb. 24 (1949) 163-188.

"DUALITIES" IN GRAPH THEORY AND IN THE RELATED FIELDS VIEWED FROM THE METATHEORETICAL STANDPOINT

M. Iri

Department of Mathematical Engineering and Instrumentation Physics
Faculty of Engineering, University of Tokyo
Hongo, Bunkyo-ku, Tokyo, Japan 113

Abstract. The importance is emphasized of distinguishing clearly among different kinds of concepts usually referred to as "duality". Those different kinds of dualities concentrate in the "dual graph", wherefrom confusion is sometimes given rise to. The importance is illustrated by "new" theorems and concepts which are derived by understanding correctly the difference of the concepts.

1. Introduction

The concept of duality, or of being dual, is familiar in graph theory, network theory, mathematical programming, etc. It is as old as projective geometry. It is so familiar and appears so simple that most textbooks and papers deal with it in a very informal manner. However, actually, there are basically two different kinds of concepts usually called "duality", of which one is the duality *in* a theory and the other is the duality *of* a theory. Although the two kinds of concepts are closely related to each other, the confusion between them sometimes leads to meaningless arguments.

In other words, there are many types of "duality theorems" in the theory of graphs, the theory of mathematical programming, etc., which are *proved within* the theory, whereas, sometimes, the theory, either in part or as a whole, has a symmetric structure to be called "duality". The former is a *theoretical* concept (i.e., a concept *in the theory*), whereas the latter is a *metatheoretical* concept (i.e., a concept outside of the theory, or *in the metatheory*). The duality theorems in mathematical programming, the Alexander-type duality theorems in algebraic topology, Pontrjagin's duality theorem for topological groups are of the former kind; the widest known duality in projective geometry (or, in general, that in lattice theory) is of the latter kind.

Thus, from the metatheoretical standpoint, it is also interesting to investigate whether a duality theorem in a theory with a duality structure (such as graph theory) is self-dual or not, because one is apt to regard a duality theorem as a self-dual theorem on no sound basis.

In the following, the concepts of duality and duality theorems connected with graphs are re-viewed from the metatheoretical standpoint. Specifically, it is remarked that the nonexistence of a dual graph does not contradict the duality of graph theory but reinforces it, that there are $4 = 2 \times 2$ kinds of triangular inequalities for distances and capacities on networks, and that the concept of reciprocity in linear systems theory such as electric network theory may be related to the coexistence of the metatheoretical duality and the theoretical.

All the technical materials on which the arguments in the present paper are based, are found in references [1], [2], [3] and [4]. For the first-order and higher-order predicate calculi, any introductory books and papers (e.g. [5], [6], [7]) on mathematical logic may be referred to.

2. Duality of a Theory and Duality Theorems in a Theory

Let us define that a "theory" T is a collection S of "sentences" written in the language of the first-order or the higher-order predicate calculus. Some of those sentences are axioms, and others are theorems. Usually —— especially, for an application-oriented theory —— a certain universe is fixed together with an interpretation, i.e., all the sentences of the theory are true on that universe under that interpretation.

In the following, however, we shall not describe a sentence of a theory in the form of a closed well-formed formula of the predicate calculus, but, more informally, in the ordinary plain language —— the same language in which the text of this paper is written ——, for we hope it will be far more legible and there is no fear of confusion or misunderstanding.

We assume that there is a subset D (possibly empty) of predicates as well as an involutive bijection

$$\psi : D \to D , \qquad \psi \circ \psi = \mathrm{id}_D . \tag{1}$$

It should be noted that most of mathematical expressions in the present paper, such as those in (1), are "metatheoretical", i.e., outside of the theory in question. The ψ induces a mapping of S to $\psi(S)$ in a natural way, where the image $\psi(s)$ of a sentence s in S is defined to be a sentence obtained from s by replacing each occurrence in s of every predicate p in D by $\psi(p)$ (in particular, if no predicate in D occurs in s, we put $\psi(s) = s$).

$\psi(S)$ does not in general coincide with S, but, if it does, i.e., if

$$\psi(S) = S \ , \tag{2}$$

then the theory T is said to have the dual structure with respect to (ψ, D), or the duality (ψ, D) holds in T. (Any theory has the trivial dual structure with respect to $(\psi, \emptyset)$.) Even if the entire theory has not a dual structure, it may happen that part of it, i.e., not S but a subset S' of S, has one. In such a case we say that that part of the theory has the dual structure.

For any theory and any (ψ, D), we may find the (maximal) part $\hat{S}$ having the dual structure with respect to (ψ, D) by means of the equation

$$\hat{S} = S \cap \psi(S) \ . \tag{3}$$

Since those predicates which do not occur in $\hat{S}$ are inessential, only the subset $\hat{D}$ obtained from D by removing them, as well as the restriction $\hat{\psi}$ of ψ to $\hat{D}$, is of significance. Thus, that part of the theory which consists of sentences of $\hat{S}$ has the dual structure with respect to $(\hat{\psi}, \hat{D})$. It is usual that we are interested mainly in those sentences of $\hat{S}$ in which at least one predicate from $\hat{D}$ occurs.

Two sentences s_1 and s_2 of $\hat{S}$ are said to be *the dual* of each other if $s_1 = \psi(s_2)$ (equivalently, $s_2 = \psi(s_1)$), or, more generally, if s_1 and $\psi(s_2)$ is logically equivalent: $s_1 \equiv \psi(s_2)$. In particular, a sentence s such that $s \equiv \psi(s)$ is said to be *self-dual*.

In the case of graph theory, we usually put

$$D = \{\text{arc, cycle, cocycle, circuit, cocircuit, tree, cotree, } \cdots\} \tag{4}$$ *[1]

and

$$\psi(\text{arc}) = \text{arc}, \qquad \psi(\text{cycle}) = \text{cocycle}, \qquad \text{etc.} \tag{5}$$

Thus, the sentences*[2]

[A ring sum of elementary cycles is the union of elementary cycles.]

and

[A ring sum of elementary cocycles is the union of elementary cocycles.]

are the dual of each other, and the sentences

[A tree is a maximal cycle-free subset of arcs.]

and

[A cotree is a maximal cocycle-free subset of arcs.]

are also the dual of each other. The sentence

[A circuit and a cocircuit are orthogonal to each other under a suitably defined product operation.]

is self-dual, and so is the sentence

[The complement of a tree is a cotree, and vice versa.]

It should be remarked that no predicate related to vertices belongs to D, nor does the most important predicate of *being a graph*.

Matroid theory may be regarded as a theory which is developed with those sentences in graph theory as axioms which belong to the part of graph theory having the dual structure.

---

*1: This is an informal description. To be more formal, we should describe, e.g., "the predicate of *being an arc*", "the predicate of *being a cycle*", etc.
Among a number of different terminologies and notations in the existing literature on graph theory, we shall follow those in [8] as far as possible.

*2: Here, as well as in the following, the informal description of a sentence of a theory is written in the brackets.

In contrast with the duality *of* a theory, the conventional characterization of duality theorems *in* a theory is somewhat vague, although the mathematical contents of the theorems themselves are clear and rigorous. However, it may be said that, in most cases, a bilinear form which can be regarded as the inner product of two vectors from dual vector spaces or modules plays a fundamental role in the theorem. Thus, Pontrjagin's duality theorem in topological group theory [9] states the relation between the topological structures of two topological groups G_1 and G_2 which determine each other by means of a bilinear map $\omega : G_1 \times G_2 \to C$ to the unit circle C. The Alexander-type duality theorems in algebraic topology [10] are based on the inner product between the family of chain groups and that of cochain groups of a complex. Likewise, the duality theorem in linear programming can be regarded as a theorem stating the relation between a subspace of a vector space and a subspace of the dual space, the two subspaces being defined by mutually contragredient constraint matrices [11].

Since duality theorems are objects *in* a theory, there is little to discuss about them from the metatheoretical viewpoint.

3. Problems related to the Concept of Dual Graphs

The concept of dual graphs is in an interesting situation from our standpoint. Among possible different definitions of dual graphs, we shall adopt here the following.

> [Two graphs G_1 and G_2 are said to be dual to each other, or G_i is *a* dual of G_j $(i \neq j)$, if they have the same set of arcs (or, more exactly, their arc sets are in one-to-one correspondence with each other), and if every cycle in one of them corresponds to a cocycle in the other, and vice versa.] (6)

This sentence (definition) is obviously self-dual. It will probably because the definition of dual graphs is self-dual that the concept of dual graphs itself is apt to be regarded as a core concept connected with the duality of graph theory. However, it should be emphasized by all means that the concept of dual graphs is primarily *within* the theory of graphs, and is not directly connected with the duality of the theory.

Sometimes, it is said that *the duality of graph theory is restricted because not every graph has its dual*, but that the theory of matroids has the complete duality because every matroid has its dual. However, the existence of a dual is evidently not connected with the duality of a theory. Contrarily, and even paradoxically, the assertion of the nonexistence of dual graph is an evidence which supports the duality of graph theory. In fact, the sentence in graph theory

[There is a graph having no dual.]

is itself self-dual, so that it is within that part of graph theory which has the dual structure.

As has been shown, the concept of dual graphs is in a crucial position between theory and metatheory. There is another path connecting the level of metatheory and that of theory with respect to graphs. It is the so-called orthogonality of the cycle space and the cocycle space of a graph [1]. The former space is a subspace of the vector space V of the 1-dimensional chain group of the graph as a 1-dimensional topological complex, and the latter is a subspace of the vector space V^*, dual to V, of the cochain group. Thus, the sentence

[The cycle space and the cocycle space of a graph are orghogonal, or complementary, to each other in the mutually dual vector spaces defined with the arc set as the basis vectors.]

is a self-dual theorem of graph theory. Therefore, it is possible to define the concept of dual graphs in another way, i.e. by saying that

[Two graphs G_1 and G_2 on the same arc set are dual if and only if their cycle spaces are the orthogonal complement of each other.] (7)

So long as graphs are concerned, there is no connotative difference between the two definitions of dual graphs, i.e., one (6) based on the correspondence of the concepts of cycles and cocycles in the duality of the theory, and the other (7) based on the orthogonality of the related vector spaces.

Curiously enough, these two definitions, when extended to network theory, lead us to different definitions of dual networks. To be specific, let us consider linear electric networks. In electric network theory, the duality (ψ, D) of graph theory, exemplified in (4) and (5), is extended into $(\tilde{\psi}, \tilde{D})$:

$$\tilde{D} = D \cup \{\text{current, voltage, impedance, admittance, } \cdots\} \qquad (8)$$

and

$$\tilde{\psi}|_D = \psi, \qquad \tilde{\psi}\ (\text{current}) = \text{voltage}, \quad \tilde{\psi}\ (\text{impedance}) = \text{admittance}, \quad \ldots\ldots\ . \qquad (9)$$

The most fundamental laws in electric network theory, i.e., Kirchhoff's current and voltage laws, may be stated as

[The vector whose components are currents in arcs should belong to the cycle space of the graph.]

and

[The vector whose components are voltages across arcs should belong to the cocycle space of the graph.]

The two laws are obviously the dual of each other with respect to the duality $(\tilde{\psi}, \tilde{D})$. Thus, the duality of graph theory is naturally extended to electric network theory through the extension (8), (9) of ψ and D.

The concept of dual graphs is extended to that of dual electric networks accordingly; i.e.,

[Two electric networks N_1 and N_2 are said to be dual to each other, or N_i is *a* dual of N_j $(i \neq j)$, if their graphs are dual to each other, and if the physical characteristics of arcs in one of them correspond to those in the other under the correspondence $(\tilde{\psi}, \tilde{D})$.] (10)

According to this definition, if the current-voltage relation in N_1 is expressed as

$$E_1 = Z_1 I_1 \qquad (11)$$

then that in N_2 is expressed as

$$I_2 = Y_2 E_2 \qquad (12)$$

and

$$Y_2 = Z_1 , \tag{13}$$

where E_i and I_i are, respectively, the voltage vector and the current vector in N_i $(i = 1, 2)$, and Z_1 is the impedance matrix for arcs of N_1 and Y_2 is the admittance matrix for arcs of N_2.

What will happen if the extension is made on the basis of the relation (7). As has already been noted, nothing new will happen as for the underlying graphs. However, the set of linear constraint equations for currents and voltages in N_1 and that for currents and voltages in N_2 should be related to each other in terms of orthogonality or complementarity in the dual vector spaces. More precisely, the Z_1 in (11) and the Y_2 in (12) should be connected with each other by the equation

$$Z_1^t + Y_2 = 0 \qquad \text{or} \qquad Y_2 = -Z_1^t . \tag{14}$$

In fact, (14) is necessary and sufficient for the orthogonality:

$$E_1^t \cdot E_2 + I_1^t \cdot I_2 = 0 .$$

The distinction between (13) and (14) is clear. This distinction was explicitly pointed out in [3], and further generalized in [4], together with discussions on its network-theoretical implications. Comparing (14) with (13), the minus sign before Z_1^t in (14) is physically not so important, whereas the transposition seems to be essential. Thus, the two definitions of dual networks coincide, up to a minus sign, with each other for "reciprocal networks" and for them only. (The reciprocity may be defined in terms of the symmetry of impedance or admittance matrix.) If they do not coincide with each other, it turns out that the two networks are "adjoint" with each other in electrical terminology.

As has been shown so far, careful consideration on duality will open new vistas to electric network theory.

4. Triangular Inequalities in Network Flow Theory [2]

Triangular inequalities in network flow theory afford another example which shows the importance of precise understanding of duality concept.

As a natural extension of the duality in graph theory, network flow theory has the dual structure with respect to $(\bar{\psi}, \bar{D})$, where

$$\bar{D} = D \cup \{\text{flow, tension, capacity, distance}, \cdots\} \tag{15}$$

and

$$\bar{\psi}|_D = \psi\,, \qquad \begin{array}{l} \bar{\psi}(\text{flow}) = \text{tension}\,, \\ \bar{\psi}(\text{capacity}) = \text{distance}\,, \\ \cdots\cdots\cdots \end{array} \tag{16}$$

with ψ in (5) and D in (4) (cf. [2], [12], etc.). Thus, the maximum-flow problem on a capacitated network is the dual of the shortest-path problem on a network with distances defined on arcs. (It will be worth noting that, in order to provide network flow theory with as much dual structure as possible, the concept of vertices should be expelled from the theory wherever possible; e.g., by replacing the entrance-exit pair (source-sink pair) in a two-terminal problem by a fictitious "reference arc" connecting the pair of vertices.)

The best known triangular inequality is the one for distances, which is ordinarily described as

"For any three vertices v_1, v_2, v_3 on a network N with distances defined on arcs, the distance d_{ij} along the shortest path in N from v_i to v_j $(i \neq j)$ satisfies the inequality: $d_{13} \leqq d_{12} + d_{23}$." (17)

Since the maximum-flow problem was formulated, another triangular inequality has been noticed [13], which is ordinarily described as

"For any three vertices v_1, v_2, v_3 on a capacitated network N, the terminal-pair capacity c_{ij}, i.e., the value of the maximum flow through N, from v_i to v_j $(i \neq j)$ satisfies the inequality: $c_{13} \leqq \min(c_{12}, c_{23})$." (18)

We are tempted to regard these two theorems (17) and (18) as the "dual" theorems because they are basic triangular inequalities in the dual problems. However, a little careful contemplation will make us aware that it is impossible to extend the ordinary duality of graph theory to that of network theory so as to make (17) and (18) the dual of each other.

In order to look for the dual of (17) (and that of (18)), if there is any, we have first to rewrite the statement of the triangular inequality into a dualizable form. It is in fact possible. (17) can be rewritten as

[On a network N with distances defined on arcs, we choose three arcs a_1, a_2, a_3 such that $\{-a_1, a_2, a_3\}$ is a circuit. Let d_i denote the value of the solution of the shortest-path problem with a_i as the reference arc on the network which is obtained from N by deleting (opening) the other two arcs a_j, a_k $(j, k \neq i)$. Then, we have $d_1 \leqq d_2 + d_3$.] (19)

Once (17) is rewritten in this form, it is straightforward to describe the dual "theorem" for a capacitated network as follows (see Figs. 1 and 2):

[On a capacitated network N, we choose three arcs a_1, a_2, a_3 such that $\{-a_1, a_2, a_3\}$ is a cocircuit. Let c_i denote the value of the solution of the maximum-flow problem with a_i as the reference arc on the network which is obtained from N by contracting (shortening) the other two arcs a_j, a_k $(j, k \neq i)$. Then we have $c_1 \leqq c_2 + c_3$.] (20)

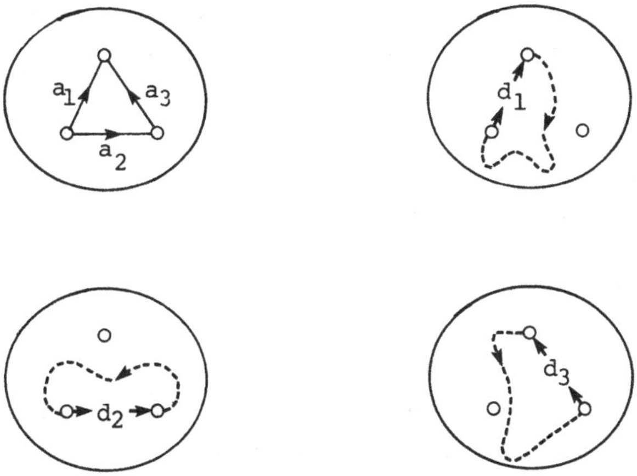

$d_1 \leqq d_2 + d_3$

Fig. 1. Triangular inequality for the shortest-path problem.

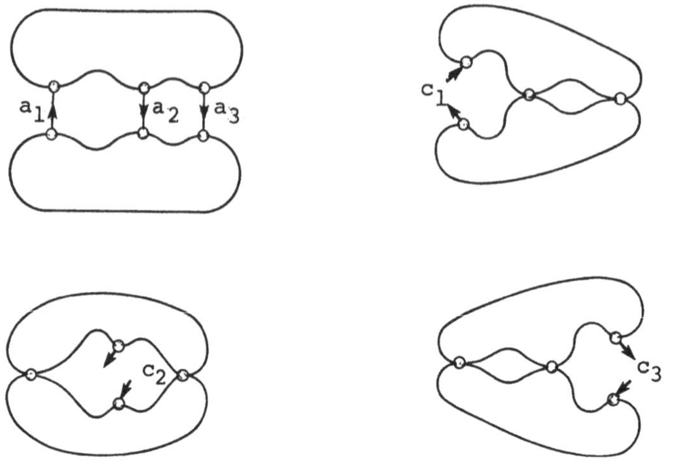

$c_1 \leqq c_2 + c_3$

Fig. 2. Another triangular inequality for the maximum-flow problem.

Similarly, we have the dualizable form of (18):

[On a capacitated network N, we choose three arcs a_1, a_2, a_3 such that $\{-a_1, a_2, a_3\}$ is a circuit. Let c_i denote the value of the solution of the maximum-flow problem with a_i as the reference arc on the network obtained from N by deleting (opening) the other two arcs a_j, a_k $(j, k \neq i)$. Then we have $c_1 \geqq \min(c_2, c_3)$.], (21)

and its dual (see Figs. 3 and 4):

[On a network N with distances defined on arcs, we choose three arcs a_1, a_2, a_3 such that $\{-a_1, a_2, a_3\}$ is a cocircuit. Let d_i denote the value of the solution of the shortest-path problem with a_i as the reference arc on the network obtained from N by contracting (shortening) the other two arcs a_j and a_k $(j, k \neq i)$. Then we have $d_1 \geqq \min(d_2, d_3)$.] (22)

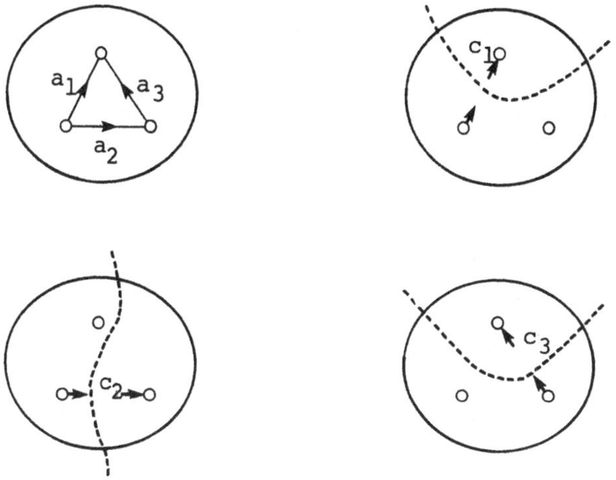

$$c_1 \geqq \min(c_2,\ c_3)$$

Fig. 3. Triangular inequality for the maximum-flow problem.

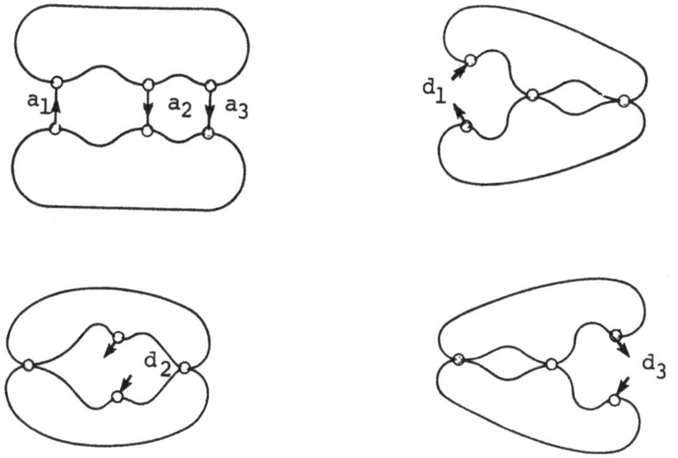

$$d_1 \geqq \min(d_2,\ d_3)$$

Fig. 4. Another triangular inequality for the shortest-path problem.

References

[1] Iri, M.: Metatheoretical considerations on duality. *RAAG Research Notes*, Third Series, No. 124, February 1968.

[2] Iri, M.: *Network Flow, Transportation and Scheduling — Theory and Algorithms*. Academic Press, New York, 1969.

[3] Iri, M.; Recski, A.: Reflection on the concepts of dual, inverse and adjoint networks (in Japanese). *Papers of the Technical Group on Circuits and Systems*, Institute of Electronics and Communication Engineers of Japan, CAS 79-78 (September 1979). (English translation available)

[4] Iri, M.; Recski, A.: Reflection on the concepts of dual, inverse and adjoint networks, II — Towards a qualitative theory (in Japanese). *Papers of the Technical Group on Circuits and Systems*, Institute of Electronics and Communication Engineers of Japan, CAS 79-133 (January 1980). (English translation available)

[5] Kemeny, J. G.: A new approach to semantics — Part I; Part II. *Journal of Symbolic Logic*, Vol. 21, No. 1 (March 1956), pp. 1-27; No. 2 (June 1956), pp. 149-161.

[6] Robinson, A.: *On the Metamathematics of Algebra*. North-Holland Publishing Co., Amsterdam, 1951.

[7] Smullyan, R. M.: *First-Order Logic*. Springer-Verlag, Berlin, 1968.

[8] Berge, C.: *Graphes et Hypergraphes*. Dunod, Paris, 1970.

[9] Pontrjagin, L.: *Topological Groups*. Princeton University Press, Princeton, 1946.

[10] Lefschetz, S.: *Algebraic Topology*. American Mathematical Society Colloquium Publications, Vol. 27, New York, 1942.

[11] Iri, M.: *Linear Programming* (in Japanese). Hakujitsu-sha, Tokyo, 1973.

[12] Berge, C.; Ghouila-Houri, A.: *Programmes, Jeux et Réseaux de Transport*. Dunod, Paris, 1962.

[13] Ford, L. R., Jr.; Fulkerson, D. R.: *Flows in Networks*, Princeton University Press, Princeton, 1962.

ON CENTRAL TREES OF A GRAPH *

S. Shinoda
Department of Electrical Engineering
Faculty of Science and Engineering
Chuo University
1-13-27, Kasuga, Bunkyo-ku, Tokyo, Japan
phone (03) 813-4171 Ext.511

T. Kawamoto
Department of Electrical and Electronic Engineering
Faculty of Engineering
Tokyo Institute of Technology
2-12-1, O-okayama, Meguro-ku, Tokyo, Japan
phone (03) 726-1111 Ext.2565

Abstract. The concept of central trees of a graph has attracted our attention in relation to electrical network theory. Until now, however, only a few properties of central trees have been clarified. In this paper, in connection with the critical sets of the edge set of a graph, some new theorems on central trees of the graph are presented. Also, a few examples are included to illustrate the applications of these theorems.

1. Introduction

The concept of central trees of a graph was originally introduced in 1966 by Deo [1] in relation to the reduction of the amount of labor involved in Mayeda and Seshu's method of generating all trees of a graph and subsequently considered in 1968 by Malik [2] and in 1971 by Amoia and Cottafava [3]. Also, its close relation to the formulation of a new network equation called "the 2-nd hybrid equation" (which will

* The main part of this paper was presented at the 14-th Asilomar conference on Circuits, Systems and Computers held on November 17-19,1980 at Pacific Grove, California, U.S.A.

be shown in the appendix) was pointed out in 1971 by Kishi and Kajitani [4] and subsequently considered in 1979 by Kajitani [5] in a new context. Until now, however, only a few properties of central trees have been clarified [3,6,7,8].

In this paper, in connection with the critical sets of the edge set of a graph, some new theorems on central trees of the graph are given as a few extensions of the results obtained already in [6,7].

Throughout this paper, we adopt the usual set-theoretic conventions: set union, set intersection, set inclusion, proper inclusion and set difference are denoted by the familiar symbols $\cup$, $\cap$, $\subseteq$, $\subset$ and -, respectively. The empty set is denoted by $\emptyset$ and the cardinality of a set A is denoted by $|A|$.

2. Critical Sets

Throughout this paper, G is used to denote a nonseparable graph of rank r[G] and nullity n[G], and E is used to denote the edge set of G.

For any subset S of E, a graph obtained from G by deleting all edges in $E - S$ is denoted by $G \cdot S$, and a graph obtained from G by contracting all edges in $E - S$ is denoted by $G \times S$. $G \cdot S$ and $G \times S$ are called a subgraph and a contraction of G, respectively. For $R \subseteq S \subseteq E$, a graph obtained from G by deleting all edges in $E - S$ and then contracting all edges in $S - R$ is denoted by $(G \cdot S) \times R$, which is called a minor of G. Then, for $R \subseteq S \subseteq E$, we have the relations:

$$
\begin{aligned}
(G \cdot S) \cdot R &= G \cdot R, \\
(G \times S) \times R &= G \times R, \\
(G \cdot S) \times R &= (G \times (\overline{S} \cup R)) \cdot R, \\
(G \times S) \cdot R &= (G \cdot (\overline{S} \cup R)) \times R
\end{aligned}
\tag{1}
$$

where $\overline{S} = E - S$. The ranks of $G \cdot S$, $G \times S$ and $(G \cdot S) \times R$ are denoted by $r[G \cdot S]$, $r[G \times S]$ and $r[(G \cdot S) \times R]$, respectively, and the nullities of $G \cdot S$, $G \times S$ and $(G \cdot S) \times R$ are denoted by $n[G \cdot S]$, $n[G \times S]$ and $n[(G \cdot S) \times R]$, respectively. Then,

(i) for $R \subseteq S \subseteq E$,

$$r[G \cdot S] = r[G \cdot R] + r[(G \cdot S) \times (S - R)], \tag{2}$$

(ii) for $R \subseteq S \subseteq E$,

$$r[(G \cdot S) \times R] + n[(G \cdot S) \times R] = |R|, \tag{3}$$

(iii) $$r[G \cdot \emptyset] = 0, \tag{4}$$

(iv) for $e \in E$,

$$r[G \cdot \{e\}] = 1, \tag{5}$$

(v) for $R \subseteq S \subseteq E$,

$$r[G \cdot R] \leq r[G \cdot S], \tag{6}$$

(vi) for $R, S \subseteq E$,

$$r[G \cdot R] + r[G \cdot S] \geq r[G \cdot (R \cup S)] + r[G \cdot (R \cap S)]. \tag{7}$$

For any α such that $0 \leq \alpha < \infty$, and for any subset S of E,

$$f_\alpha(S) = \alpha|S| - r[G \cdot S] \tag{8}$$

is called the deficiency of S with respect to α. A subset S_α of E is called a <u>critical set</u> of E with respect to α if

$$f_\alpha(S_\alpha) = \max_{S \subseteq E} f_\alpha(S). \tag{9}$$

Then, we can easily prove from (7) that if S_α^1 and S_α^2 are two critical sets of E with respect to α, then $S_\alpha^1 \cup S_\alpha^2$ and $S_\alpha^1 \cap S_\alpha^2$ are also critical sets of E with respect to α. Now, let F_α be the family of all the critical sets of E with respect to α, then we see that F_α has a unique minimal member $S_\alpha^{(0)}$ and a unique maximal member $S_\alpha^{(\infty)}$, and also we see that for any critical set S of F_α

$$S_\alpha^{(0)} \subseteq S \subseteq S_\alpha^{(\infty)} \tag{10}$$

is satisfied. Let $E_\alpha^+ = S_\alpha^{(0)}$, $E_\alpha^o = S_\alpha^{(\infty)} - S_\alpha^{(0)}$ and $E_\alpha^- = E - S_\alpha^{(\infty)}$. Here, such a unique tripartition $(E_\alpha^+, E_\alpha^o, E_\alpha^-)$ of E is called the principal partition of E with respect to α. In particular, in case of $\alpha = 1/2$, $(E_\alpha^+, E_\alpha^o, E_\alpha^-)$ is nothing but the principal partition of E defined in 1967 by Kishi and Kajitani [9,10,11]. Next, let us denote all the maximal critical sets of E with respect to all α satisfying $0 \leq \alpha < \infty$ by $S_{\alpha_0}^{(\infty)}$ ($= \emptyset$), $S_{\alpha_1}^{(\infty)}$, $S_{\alpha_2}^{(\infty)}$, ..., $S_{\alpha_k}^{(\infty)}$, $S_{\alpha_{k+1}}^{(\infty)}$ ($= E$) such that

$$\emptyset = S_{\alpha_0}^{(\infty)} \subset S_{\alpha_1}^{(\infty)} \subset S_{\alpha_2}^{(\infty)} \subset \cdots \subset S_{\alpha_k}^{(\infty)} \subset S_{\alpha_{k+1}}^{(\infty)} = E \tag{11}$$

where $0 \leq \alpha_0 < c_1$, $c_1 \leq \alpha_1 < c_2$, $c_2 \leq \alpha_2 < c_3$, ..., $c_k \leq \alpha_k < c_{k+1}$, $c_{k+1} \leq \alpha_{k+1} < \infty$ and

$$c_i = \min_{S_{\alpha_{i-1}}^{(\infty)} \subset S \subseteq E} \frac{r[G \cdot S] - r[G \cdot S_{\alpha_{i-1}}^{(\infty)}]}{|S - S_{\alpha_{i-1}}^{(\infty)}|} \tag{12}$$

$$= \min_{S_{\alpha_{i-1}}^{(\infty)} \subset S \subsetneq E} \frac{r[(G \times \overline{S_{\alpha_{i-1}}^{(\infty)}}) \cdot (\overline{S_{\alpha_{i-1}}^{(\infty)}} - \overline{S})]}{|\overline{S_{\alpha_{i-1}}^{(\infty)}} - \overline{S}|} \tag{13}$$

Here such numbers c_i are called the critical numbers of E, and a partition $(X_0, X_1, X_2, \ldots, X_k)$ of E such that

$$X_i = S_{\alpha_i}^{(\infty)} - S_{\alpha_{i-1}}^{(\infty)} \quad (i = 0, 1, 2, \ldots, k) \tag{14}$$

is called the principal partition of E with respect to all α such that $0 \leqq \alpha < \infty$, which was given in 1976 by Tomizawa [12].

Here, it should be noted that all the critical sets of E with respect to all α such that $0 \leqq \alpha < \infty$ can be obtained by Tomizawa's algorithm[12].

3. Central Trees and Their Properties in Connection with Critical Sets

A tree T_s of G is called a central tree of G if

$$r[G \cdot \overline{T_s}] \leqq r[G \cdot \overline{T}] \tag{15}$$

for every tree T of G where $\overline{T_s} = E - T_s$ and $\overline{T} = E - T$ [1].

[Theorem 1]

If, for a critical set S_{α_i} of E with respect to α_i such that $c_i \leqq \alpha_i < c_{i+1}$, there exists a tree T_s of G such that

$$\text{(1-1)} \quad S_{\alpha_i} \supseteq \overline{T_s} = E - T_s, \tag{16}$$

$$\text{(1-2)} \quad 1 > c_i|S_{\alpha_i} - \overline{T_s}| - r[(G \cdot S_{\alpha_i}) \times (S_{\alpha_i} - \overline{T_s})] \tag{17}$$

are satisfied, then T_s is a central tree of G.

[Proof]

Since, for a critical set S_{α_i} of E $(c_i \leqq \alpha_i < c_{i+1})$ and for any subset S of E,

$$\alpha_i|S_{\alpha_i}| - r[G \cdot S_{\alpha_i}] \geqq \alpha_i|S| - r[G \cdot S] \tag{18}$$

is always satisfied, we have

$$\alpha_i|S_{\alpha_i}| - r[G \cdot S_{\alpha_i}] \geqq \alpha_i|\overline{T}| - r[G \cdot \overline{T}] \tag{19}$$

for every tree T of G.

Now, suppose that there exists a tree T_s of G such that the condition (1-1) is satisfied, then we have the relations:

$$|S_{\alpha_i}| = |\overline{T}_s| + |S_{\alpha_i} - \overline{T}_s| , \qquad (20)$$

$$r[G \cdot S_{\alpha_i}] = r[G \cdot \overline{T}_s] + r[(G \cdot S_{\alpha_i}) \times (S_{\alpha_i} - \overline{T}_s)] \qquad (21)$$

from which it follows that for every tree T of G we have

$$\alpha_i |S_{\alpha_i} - \overline{T}_s| - r[(G \cdot S_{\alpha_i}) \times (S_{\alpha_i} - \overline{T}_s)]$$
$$\geqq r[G \cdot \overline{T}_s] - r[G \cdot \overline{T}] \qquad (22)$$

because $|\overline{T}_s| = |\overline{T}|$. Here, considering $c_i \leqq \alpha_i < c_{i+1}$, we have

$$c_i |S_{\alpha_i} - \overline{T}_s| - r[(G \cdot S_{\alpha_i}) \times (S_{\alpha_i} - \overline{T}_s)]$$
$$\geqq r[G \cdot \overline{T}_s] - r[G \cdot \overline{T}] \qquad (23)$$

for every tree of G. Furthermore, suppose that the condition (1-2) is satisfied, then for every tree T of G we have

$$1 > r[G \cdot \overline{T}_s] - r[G \cdot \overline{T}] \qquad (24)$$

from which it follows that for every tree T of G

$$r[G \cdot \overline{T}_s] \geqq r[G \cdot \overline{T}] \qquad (25)$$

because both $r[G \cdot \overline{T}_s]$ and $r[G \cdot \overline{T}]$ are non-negarive integers. Hence we see that the theorem is true. (END)

[Corollary 1-1]

If, for a critical sets S_{α_i} of E with respect to α_i such that $c_i \leqq \alpha_i < c_{i+1}$, there exists a tree T_s of G such that

$$(1\text{-}1) \quad S_{\alpha_i} \supseteq \overline{T}_s , \qquad (16)$$

$$(1\text{-}3) \quad 1 > c_i |S_{\alpha_i} - \overline{T}_s| \qquad (26)$$

are satisfied, then T_s is a central tree of G.

[Proof]

This is obvious from the theorem 1 and the non-negative integrality of $r[(G \cdot S_{\alpha_i}) \times (S_{\alpha_i} - \overline{T}_s)]$. (END)

[Example 1]

Let G be a graph shown in Fig. 1(a). Then E = { 1, 2, 3, 4, 5, 6, 7, 8, 9, 10, 11, 12, 13, 14, 15 } and all the critical sets of E with respect to all α such that $0 \leqq \alpha < \infty$ are

$$S_{\alpha_0} = S_{\alpha_0}^{(\infty)} = \emptyset ,$$

$$S^1_{\alpha_1} \qquad\qquad = \{6,\ 7,\ 8,\ 9,\ 10,\ 11,\ 12,\ 13,\ 14,\ 15\}$$

$$S^2_{\alpha_1} = S^{(\infty)}_{\alpha_1} = \{4,\ 5,\ 6,\ 7,\ 8,\ 9,\ 10,\ 11,\ 12,\ 13,\ 14,\ 15\}$$

$$S_{\alpha_2} = S^{(\infty)}_{\alpha_2} = \{1,\ 2,\ 3\} \cup S^{(\infty)}_{\alpha_1} = E$$

where $0 \leq \alpha_0 < c_1$, $c_1 \leq \alpha_1 < c_2$, $c_2 \leq \alpha_2 < \infty$, $c_1 = 1/2$ and $c_2 = 2/3$.

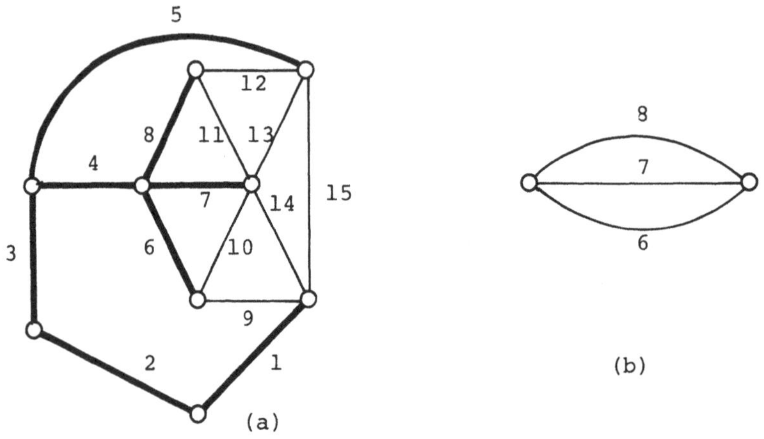

Fig. 1 Graphs for Example 1.

Now, if we choose $T_s = \{1,\ 2,\ 3,\ 4,\ 5,\ 6,\ 7,\ 8\}$ as a tree of G, then for the critical set $S^1_{\alpha_1}$ we have the relations:

$$S^1_{\alpha_1} \supseteq \overline{T}_s = \{9,\ 10,\ 11,\ 12,\ 13,\ 14,\ 15\}\ ,$$

$$|S^1_{\alpha_1} - \overline{T}_s| = |\{6,\ 7,\ 8\}| = 3,$$

$$r[(G \cdot S^1_{\alpha_1}) \times (S^1_{\alpha_1} - \overline{T}_s)] = 1$$

where $(G \cdot S^1_{\alpha_1}) \times (S^1_{\alpha_1} - \overline{T}_s)$ is shown in Fig. 1(b), and consequently we have

$$1 > c_1|S^1_{\alpha_1} - \overline{T}_s| - r[(G \cdot S^1_{\alpha_1}) \times (S^1_{\alpha_1} - \overline{T}_s)] = (1/2) \times 3 - 1 = 1/2.$$

Hence we see from the theorem 1 that T_s is a central tree of G.

(END)

[Example 2]

Let G be a graph shown in Fig. 2. Then $E = \{1,\ 2,\ 3,\ 4,\ 5,\ 6,\ 7,\ 8,\ 9,\ 10,\ 11,\ 12,\ 13,\ 14\}$ and all the critical sets of E with respect to all α such that $0 \leq \alpha < \infty$ are

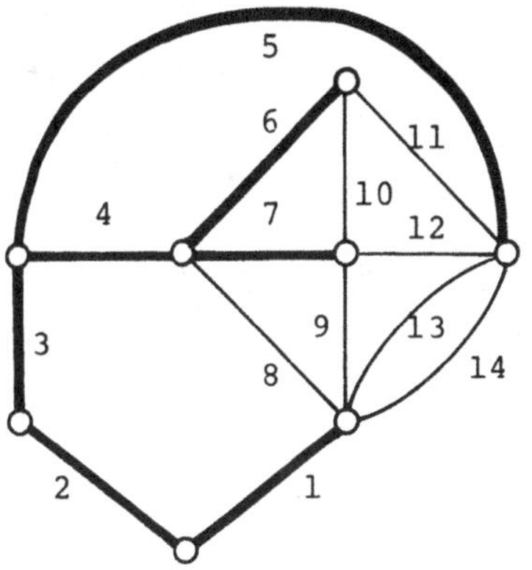

Fig. 2 A Graph for Example 2

$S_{\alpha_0} = S_{\alpha_0}^{(\infty)} = \emptyset$,

$S_{\alpha_1} = S_{\alpha_1}^{(\infty)} = \{6, 7, 8, 9, 10, 11, 12, 13, 14\}$,

$S_{\alpha_2} = S_{\alpha_2}^{(\infty)} = \{4, 5\} \cup S_{\alpha_1}^{(\infty)}$,

$S_{\alpha_3} = S_{\alpha_3}^{(\infty)} = \{1, 2, 3\} \cup S_{\alpha_2}^{(\infty)} = E$

where $0 \leqq \alpha_0 < c_1$, $c_1 \leqq \alpha_1 < c_2$, $c_2 \leqq \alpha_2 < c_3$, $c_3 \leqq \alpha_3 < \infty$, $c_1 = 4/9$, $c_2 = 1/2$ and $c_3 = 2/3$. Now, if we choose $T_s = \{1, 2, 3, 4, 5, 6, 7\}$ as a tree of G, then for the critical sets S_{α_1} we have the relations:

$S_{\alpha_1} \supseteq \overline{T_s} = \{8, 9, 10, 11, 12, 13, 14\}$,

$|S_{\alpha_1} - \overline{T_s}| = |\{6, 7\}| = 2$,

from which it follows that

$1 > c_1 |S_{\alpha_1} - \overline{T_s}| = (4/9) \times 2 = 8/9$.

Hence we see from the corollary 1-2 that T_s is a central tree of G.

(END)

[Theorem 2]

If, for a critical set S_{α_i} of E with respect to α_i such that $c_i \leqq \alpha_i < c_{i+1}$, there exists a tree T_s of G such that

(2-1) $S_{\alpha_i} \subseteq \overline{T_s} = E - T_s$, (27)

(2-2) $1 > (1 - \alpha_i) \, |\overline{T_s} - S_{\alpha_i}| - n[(G \cdot \overline{T_s}) \times (\overline{T_s} - S_{\alpha_i})]$ (28)

are satisfied, then T_s is a central tree of G.

[Proof]

As in the proof of the theorem 1, for a critical set S_{α_i} of E and for every tree T of G, there holds

$$\alpha_i |S_{\alpha_i}| - r[G \cdot S_{\alpha_i}] \geqq \alpha_i |\overline{T}| - r[G \cdot \overline{T}]. \quad (19)$$

Now, suppose that there exists a tree T_s of G such that the condition (2-1) is satisfied, then we have the relations:

$$|\overline{T}_s| = |S_{\alpha_i}| + |\overline{T}_s - S_{\alpha_i}| , \quad (29)$$

$$r[G \cdot \overline{T}_s] = r[G \cdot S_{\alpha_i}] + r[(G \cdot \overline{T}_s) \times (\overline{T}_s - S_{\alpha_i})]$$

from which it follows that for every tree T of G we have

$$- \alpha_i |\overline{T}_s - S_{\alpha_i}| + r[(G \cdot \overline{T}_s) \times (\overline{T}_s - S_{\alpha_i})]$$

$$\geqq r[G \cdot \overline{T}_s] - r[G \cdot \overline{T}] \quad (30)$$

because $|\overline{T}_s| = |\overline{T}|$. Since

$$|\overline{T}_s - S_{\alpha_i}| = r[(G \cdot \overline{T}_s) \times (\overline{T}_s - S_{\alpha_i})] + n[(G \cdot \overline{T}_s) \times (\overline{T}_s - S_{\alpha_i})] \quad (31)$$

is satisfied, we have

$$(1 - \alpha_i) |\overline{T}_s - S_{\alpha_i}| - n[(G \cdot \overline{T}_s) \times (\overline{T}_s - S_{\alpha_i})]$$

$$\geqq r[(G \cdot \overline{T}_s] - r[G \cdot \overline{T}] \quad (32)$$

for every tree T of G. Furthermore, suppose that the condition (2-2) is satisfied, then for every tree T of G we have

$$1 > r[G \cdot \overline{T}_s] - r[G \cdot \overline{T}] \quad (33)$$

from which it follows that for every tree T of G

$$r[G \cdot \overline{T}_s] \leqq r[G \cdot \overline{T}] \quad (34)$$

because both $r[G \cdot \overline{T}_s]$ and $r[G \cdot \overline{T}]$ are non-negative integers. Hence we see that the theorem is true. (END)

[Corollary 2-1]

If, for a critical set S_{α_i} of E with respect to α_i such that $c_i \leqq \alpha_i < c_{i+1}$, there exists a tree T_s of G such that

$$\text{(2-1)} \quad S_{\alpha_i} \subseteq \overline{T}_s , \quad (27)$$

$$\text{(2-2)} \quad 1 > (1 - \alpha_i) |\overline{T}_s - S_{\alpha_i}| \quad (35)$$

are satisfied, then T_s is a central tree of G.

[Proof] This is obvious from the theorem 2. (END)

[Example 3]

Let G be a graph shown in Fig. 3. Then E = {1, 2, 3, 4, 5, 6, 7, 8, 9, 10, 11, 12, 13, 14, 15, 16} and all the critical sets of E with respect to all α such that $0 \leqq \alpha < \infty$ are

$$S_{\alpha_0} = S_{\alpha_0}^{(\infty)} = \emptyset ,$$

$$S_{\alpha_1} = S_{\alpha_1}^{(\infty)} = \{14, 15, 16\} ,$$

$$S_{\alpha_2}^{1} = \{12, 13\} \cup S_{\alpha_1}^{(\infty)} ,$$

$$S_{\alpha_2}^{2} = \{10, 11, 12, 13\} \cup S_{\alpha_1}^{(\infty)} ,$$

$$S_{\alpha_2}^{3} = \{8, 9, 12, 13\} \cup S_{\alpha_1}^{(\infty)} ,$$

$$S_{\alpha_2}^{4} = S_{\alpha_2}^{(\infty)} = \{8, 9, 10, 11, 12, 13\} \cup S_{\alpha_1}^{(\infty)} ,$$

$$S_{\alpha_3} = S_{\alpha_3}^{(\infty)} = \{1, 2, 3, 4, 5, 6, 7\} \cup S_{\alpha_2}^{(\infty)} = E$$

where $0 \leqq \alpha_0 < c_1$, $c_1 \leqq \alpha_1 < c_2$, $c_2 \leqq \alpha_2 < c_3$, $c_3 \leqq \alpha_3 < \infty$, $c_1 = 1/3$, $c_2 = 1/2$ and $c_3 = 4/7$.

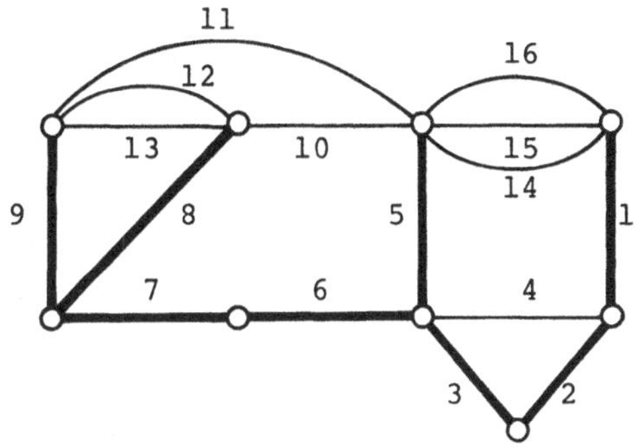

Fig. 3 A Graph for Example 3.

Now, if we choose $T_s^{(1)} = \{1, 2, 3, 5, 6, 7, 8, 9\}$ as a tree of G, then for the critical set $S_{\alpha_2}^{2}$ we have the relations

$$S_{\alpha_2}^{2} \subsetneqq \overline{T_s^{(1)}} = \{4, 10, 11, 12, 13, 14, 15, 16\} ,$$

$$|\overline{T_s^{(1)}} - S_{\alpha_2}^{2}| = |\{4\}| = 1$$

from which it follows that

$$1 > (1 - \alpha_2)|\overline{T_s^{(1)}} - S_{\alpha_2}^2| = (1 - \alpha_2) \times 1 = 1 - \alpha_2$$

Thus, $\alpha_2 > 0$. Here, since there exists α_2 such that $\alpha_2 > 0$ and $c_2 = 1/2 \leqq \alpha_2 < c_3 = 4/7$, we see from the corollary 2-1 that $T_s^{(1)}$ is a central tree of G.

On the other hand, if we choose $T_s^{(2)} = \{1, 2, 4, 5, 6, 7, 10, 11\}$ as a tree of G, then for the critical set $S_{\alpha_2}^3$ we have the relations:

$$S_{\alpha_2}^3 \subseteq \overline{T_s^{(2)}} = \{3, 8, 9, 12, 13, 14, 15, 16\},$$

$$|\overline{T_s^{(2)}} - S_{\alpha_2}^3| = |\{3\}| = 1$$

from which it follows that

$$1 > (1 - \alpha_2)|\overline{T_s^{(2)}} - S_{\alpha_2}^3| = 1 - \alpha_2 .$$

Accordingly, we get $\alpha_2 > 0$. Since there exists α_2 such that $\alpha_2 > 0$ and $c_2 = 1/2 \leqq \alpha_2 < c_3 = 4/7$, we also see from the corollary 2-1 that $T_s^{(2)}$ is a central tree of G.

(END)

Now, considering that the condition (2-1) is equivalent to

$$(2'\text{-}1) \quad T_s \subseteq \overline{S_{\alpha_i}} = E - S_{\alpha_i} \qquad (36)$$

we have the relations

$$\overline{T_s} - S_{\alpha_i} = \overline{S_{\alpha_i}} - T_s , \qquad (37)$$

$$(G \cdot \overline{T_s}) \times (\overline{T_s} - S_{\alpha_i}) = (G \times \overline{S_{\alpha_i}}) \cdot (\overline{S_{\alpha_i}} - T_s) \qquad (38)$$

from which it follows that the theorem 2 and its corollary 2-1 can be rewritten as follows:

[Theorem 2']

If, for a critical set S_{α_i} of E with respect to α_i such that $c_i \leqq \alpha_i < c_{i+1}$, there exists a tree T_s of G such that

$$(2'\text{-}1) \quad T_s \subseteq \overline{S_{\alpha_i}} , \qquad (36)$$

$$(2'\text{-}2) \quad 1 > (1 - \alpha_i)|\overline{S_{\alpha_i}} - T_s| - n[(G \times \overline{S_{\alpha_i}}) \cdot (\overline{S_{\alpha_i}} - T_s)] \qquad (39)$$

are satisfied, then T_s is a central tree of G. (END)

[Corollary 2'-1]

If, for a critical set S_{α_i} of E with respect to α_i such that $c_i \leqq \alpha_i < c_{i+1}$, there exists a tree T_s of G such that

Acknowledgement

The authors would like to express their thanks to Prof. Y.Kajitani of Tokyo Institute of Technology, Tokyo, and Prof. C.Ishida of Niigata University, Niigata, for their comments.

References

[1] N. Deo: A central tree, IEEE Trans. Circuit Theory; Vol. CT-13, pp.439-440, 1960.

[2] N. R. Malik: On Deo's central tree concept; IEEE Trans. Circuit Theory, Vol. CT-15, pp.283-284, 1968.

[3] V. Amoia and G. Cottafava: Invariance properties of central trees; IEEE Trans. Circuit Theory, Vol. CT-18, pp,465-467, 1971.

[4] G. Kishi and Y. Kajitani: Generalized topological degree of freedom in analysis of LCR networks; Papers of the Technical Group on Circuit and System Theory of Inst. Elec. Comm. Eng. Japan, No.CT 71-19, pp.1-13, July 1971.

[5] Y. Kajitani: The semibasis in network analysis and graph theoretical degree of freedom; IEEE Trans. Circuits and Systems, Vol.CAS-26, pp.846-854, 1979.

[6] T. Kawamoto, Y. Kajitani and S. Shinoda: New theorems on central trees described in connection with the principal partition of a graph, Papers of the Thchnical Group on Circuit and System Theory of Inst. Elec. Comm. Eng. Japan, No.CST77-109, pp. 63-69, Dec. 1977.

[7] S. Shinoda, M. Kitano and C. Ishida: Two theorems in connection with partitions of graphs; Papers of the Technical Group on Circuits and Systems of Inst. Elec. Comm. Eng. Japan, No.CAS79-146, pp.1-6, Jan. 1980.

[8] S. Shinoda and K. Saishu: Conditions for an incidence set to be a central tree, ibid., No.CAS80-6, pp. 41-46, Apr. 1980.

[9] G. Kishi and Y. Kajitani: On maximally distinct trees, Proceedings of the Fifth Annual Allerton Conference on Circuit and System Theory, University of Illinois, pp.635-643, Oct. 1967.

[11] S. Shinoda: Principal partitions of graphs with applications to graph and network problems, Proc. of Inst. Elec. Comm. Eng. Japan, Vol.62, pp.763-772, 1979.

(2'-1) $T_s \subseteq \overline{S}_{\alpha_i}$, (36)

(2'-3) $1 > (1 - \alpha_i)|\overline{S}_{\alpha_i} - T_s|$ (40)

are satisfied, then T_s is a central tree of G. (END)

Also, as a special case of the theorem 1 and 2, the following known theorem and corollary can be derived:

[Theorem 3]

If, for a critical set S_{α_i} of E with respect to α_i such that $c_i \leqq \alpha_i < c_{i+1}$, there exists a tree T_s of G such that

(3-1) $T_s = \overline{S}_{\alpha_i}$ (41)

is satisfied, then T_s is a central tree of G. (END)

[Corollary 3-1]

If there exists a tree T_s of G such that for a critical set $S_{1/2}$ of E with respect to 1/2 there holds

(3-2) $T_s = \overline{S}_{1/2}$, (42)

then T_s is a central tree of G. (END)

This corollary was given and proved in 1977 by Kawamoto, Kajitani and Shinoda [6]. In 1980, as an extension of the corollary, the theorem 3 was proved in an elegant way by Shinoda, Kitano and Ishida [7]. Indeed it was the proof technique of the theorem 3 shown in [7] that suggested the present investigation.

4. Conclusions

In this paper, in connection with the critical sets of the edge set of a nonseparable graph, some new theorems on central trees of the graph have been given as a few extensions of the results obtained already in [6, 7].

Since all the critical sets of the edge set of a nonseparable graph can be easily obtained by Tomizawa's algorithm [12], the theorems and their corollaries presented in this paper may be very useful.

[12] N. Tomizawa: Strongly irreducible matroids and principal partitions of a matroid into strongly irreducible minors, Trans. Inst. Elec. comm. Eng. Japan, Vol. J59-A, pp.83-91, 1976.

Appendix The 2-nd hybrid equation and a central tree

Let N(G) be an electrical network whose underlying graph is G and whose edge-immittance matrix is a non-singular diagonal matrix. Each edge κ in N(G) is represented by either (a) or (b) of Fig. A where

- s : complex variable in the Laplace transformation;
- $v_\kappa(s)$: voltage of edge κ ;
- $i_\kappa(s)$: current of edge κ ;
- $e_\kappa(s)$: voltage of voltage source in edge κ ;
- $j_\kappa(s)$: current of current source in edge κ ;
- $z_\kappa(s)$: edge-impedance of edge κ ; and
- $y_\kappa(s)$: edge-admittance of edge κ .

Among $v_\kappa(s)$, $e_\kappa(s)$, $i_\kappa(s)$, $j_\kappa(s)$, $z_\kappa(s)$ and $y_\kappa(s)$ there holds either

$$v_\kappa(s) = z_\kappa(s) \cdot (i_\kappa(s) + j_\kappa(s)) - e_\kappa(s) \qquad \text{(A-1)}$$

or

$$i_\kappa(s) = y_\kappa(s) \cdot (v_\kappa(s) + e_\kappa(s)) - j_\kappa(s). \qquad \text{(A-2)}$$

Here, (A-1) or (A-2) are called the <u>v-i relations</u> of edge κ .

For a tree t of G, t* is a tree of G which is at the maximal distance from the tree t. $\bar{t}$ and $\bar{t}^*$ are the cotrees of t and t*, respectively. Since each edge in $\bar{t} \cap \bar{t}^*$, together with some (or all) edges in $\bar{t} \cap t^*$, defines the fundamental tieset with respect to t*, it follows from Kirchhoff's voltage law that the voltages of the edges in $\bar{t} \cap \bar{t}^*$ can be uniquely expressed as the linear combinations of the voltages of the edges in $\bar{t} \cap t^*$.

Now, applying the v-i relations to the edges in $\bar{t}$, we see that the currents of the edges in $\bar{t}$ can be uniquely expressed as the linear combinations of the voltages of the edges in $\bar{t} \cap t^*$. Also, since each edge in t defines the fundamental cutset with respect to t, it follows from Kirchhoff's current law that the currents of the edges in t can be uniquely expressed as the linear combinations of the voltages of the edges in $\bar{t} \cap t^*$.

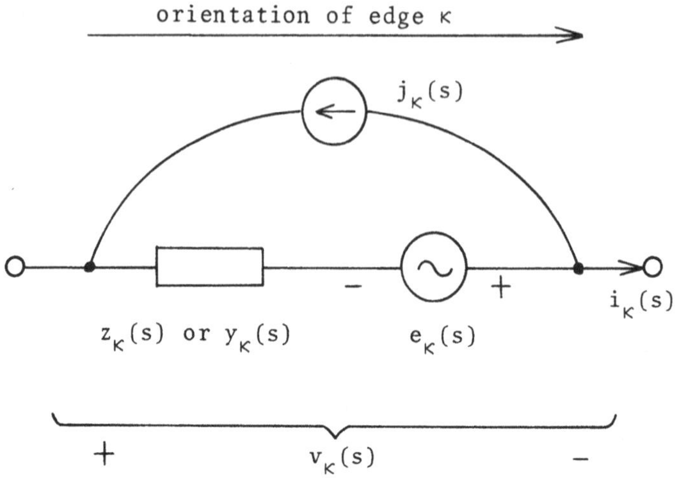

(a)

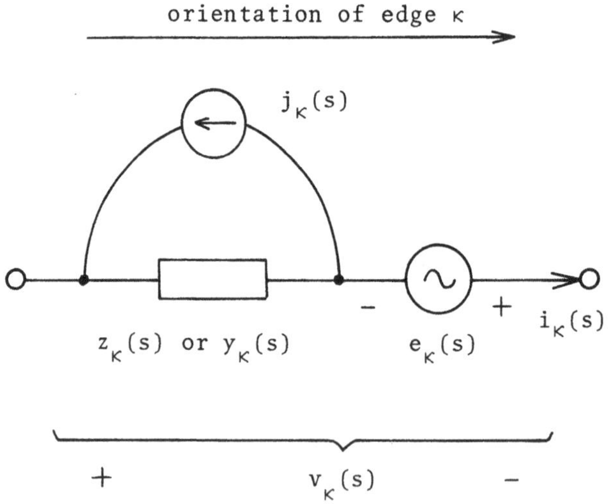

(b)

Fig. A An edge κ in N(G).

Moreover, applying the v-i relations to the edges in t, we see that the voltages of the edges in t can be uniquely expressed as the linear combinations of the voltages of the edges in $\bar{t} \cap t^*$. Namely, we see from the above that the voltages and the currents of all edges of N(G) can be uniquely expressed as the linear combinations of the voltages of the edges in $\bar{t} \cap t^*$.

Here, substituting the voltages of all edges of N(G) expressed as the linear combinations of the voltages of the edges in $\bar{t} \cap t^*$ into a system of Kirchhoff's voltage equations based on the fundamental tie-sets in G which are defined by the edges in $\bar{t} \cap t^*$ with respect to t, we obtain a system of equations whose variables are the voltages of the edges in $\bar{t} \cap t^*$. Such a system of equations is called the 2-nd hybrid equation of N(G), since the elements in the coefficient matrix of the 2-nd hybrid equation are expressed in quadratic polynomials of edge-immittances.

The order of the 2-nd hybrid equations is $d(t) = |\bar{t} \cap t^*|$. d(t) varies under the choice of t. Since d(t) is the distance between t and t*, and since t is called a central tree of G if $d(t) \leqq d(t')$ for every tree t' of G, we see that the 2-nd hybrid equation of minimum order can be obtained by choosing a central tree of G as t.

The above was originally pointed out in 1971 by Kishi and Kijitani [4] and subsequently considered in 1979 by Kajitani in a new context [5].

ON POLYNOMIAL TIME COMPUTABLE PROBLEMS

T. Kasai
Dept. of Computer Science, The University of
Electro-communications, 1-5-1 Chofugaoka,
Chofu-shi, Tokyo, 182, JAPAN

A. Adachi
Dept. of Academic and Scientific Program,
IBM, JAPAN

Abstract. In this paper, we investigate problems which require $O(n^k)$ time, for each interger k, where n is the size of input. Also, we present a number of problems which require exponential time.

1. Introduction

A number of complete problems in various complexity classes are reported. Jones and Laaser [5] showed some familiar problems which are complete in deterministic polynomial time with respect to log space reducibility. A great number of familiar problems have been reported which are complete in NP (nondeterministic polynomial time) [1], [3], [6]. Even and Tarjan [4] considered generalized Hex and showed that the problem to determine who wins the game if each player plays perfectly is complete in polynomial space. Schaefer [9] derived some two-person games from NP complete problems which are complete in polynomial space. However compelling the circumstantial evidence may be, no one has yet been able to prove that NP complete or polynomial space complete problems are actually intractable, and also there are few authors to distinguish the degree of the polynomial when the time complexity of a given algorithm is polynomial. There is general agreement that if problems have no polynomial time algorithm they are intractable. Some problems, however, in the class P are not always tractable. In this point of view, it is significant to find the concrete degree of the polynomial which represent the time complexity of a problem.

In this paper, a technique to obtain a lower bound of the time complexity of problems is introduced. We consider k-pebble games for each integer k, which involves moving pebbles according to certain rules, initially k pebbles are placed on certain places. The goal of the game is to put a pebble on a particular place. We show that the problem to determine whether or not the first player has a forced win in a (2k+1)-pebble game requires $O(n^k)$ time. A rough discussion such as to determine whether or not a given problem belongs to NP is independent of the machine model and the way of defining the size of problems, since any of the commonly used machine models can be simulated by any other with only a polynomial loss in running time and no matter what criteria the size is defined, they differ from each other by polynomial order. However, in precise discussion, for example, in the discussion whether the computation of a problem requires $O(n^k)$ time or $O(n^{k+1})$ time, the complexity heavily depends on machine models and the definition of the size of problems.

From these points, we introduce a somewhat stronger notion of reducibility. Using this reducibility, we show that the game, so called "Cat and 2k+2 Mice problem" requires $O(n^k)$ time. The basic results are also applied to show that certain problems are complete in exponential time. We consider a game, so called "Chinese checkers game," and a game similar to the "Towers of Hanoi." It has been shown that the winning strategy problems of these games are exponential time complete.

2. Preliminaries

In this section, some fundamental notions are introduced for the study of polynomial time computability.

Definition 2.1 A two-person game G is a tripple $G = (X,E,s)$, where:

(1) X is a finite set, an elenent of X is called a position,

(2) E is a subset of $X \times X$, an element of E is called a rule, we sometimes write $x \to y$ for an element (x,y) of E,

(3) s, in X, is called the starting position.

At the beginning of the game, the first player is in position s. If $(x,y) \in E$ for any $x, y \in X$, then a player in his turn may move the position x to the position y. The winner is the player who makes the other player unable to move.

Definition 2.2 A pebble game is a quadruple $G = (X,R,S,t)$, where:

(1) X is a finite set of nodes, the number of node is called the order of G,

(2) $R \subseteq \{(x,y,z) | x,y,z \in X, x \neq y, y \neq z, z \neq x\}$ is called a set of rules.

(3) S is a subset of X; the number of nodes in S is called the rank of G,

(4) t is a node in X, called the terminal node.

A pebble game of rank k is simply called k-pebble game.

A pebble game is played by two plyers, P_1 and P_2, who alternatively move pebbles on the pebble game, with P_1 playing first. At the beginning of the pebble game, pebbles are placed on all nodes of S. If $(x,y,z) \in R$ and pebbles are placed on x,y but not on z, then we can move a pebble from x to z. The winner is the player who puts a pebble on the terminal node or who makes the other player unable to move.

More formally the two-person game represented by a pebble game is stated as follows.

Definition 2.3 A two-person game induced from a pebble game $G = (X,R,S,t)$ is a triple $\overline{G} = (\overline{X},E,S)$, where:

(1) $\overline{X} = \{A | A \subseteq X, \#(A) = \#(S)\}$, $\#(A)$ denotes the number of elements in A,

(2) $E = \{(A,B) | A,B \in \overline{X}, t \notin A, (x,y,z) \in R, x,y \in A, z \notin A, B = (A - \{x\}) \cup \{z\}\}$.

Throughout this paper, by Turing machines, we mean a single tape Turing machine.

Definition 2.4 We denote by N the set of all natural numbers. A problem is a triple (Σ,L,σ), where Σ is an alphabet, L is a subset of Σ^*, and σ is a computable function from Σ^* to N. When Σ and σ are understood, we simply write L instead of (Σ,L,σ). The function σ is called the size function of L, and for each $w \in \Sigma^*$, $\sigma(w)$ is the size of w.

Definition 2.5 Let L Σ^* be an arbitrary problem. Suppose that σ is the size function associated with L. Then L is said to be $T(n)$ time computable with respect to the size iff there exists a Turing machine such that for any input x, the computation terminates within $T(\sigma(x))$ steps. We say that a problem L requires $T(n)$ time iff for any T', if $\inf_n T'(n)/T(n) = 0$ then L can not be solved within $T'(n)$ time. In general, we write $T' \ll T$ if $\inf_n T'(n)/T(n) = 0$ for two functions T and T'.

A Turing machine M is said to be T(n) time bounded with respect to the size σ iff for any input x, the computation terminates within $T(\sigma(x))$ steps. When the size is defined to be the length of inputs, i. e., $\sigma(x) = |x|$, we simply say that M is T(n) time bounded.

Definition 2.6 Let T and Z be functions from N to N, such that for any $m, n \in N$, if $m < n$ then $Z(m) < Z(n)$. Let L_1 and L_2 be problems. Let σ_1 and σ_2 be sizes of L_1 and L_2, respectively. Then L_1 is (T,Z)-reducible iff there exists a function f from Σ_1^* to Σ_2^* which satisfies the following:

(1) For any $x \in \Sigma_1^*$, $x \in L_1$ iff $f(x) \in L_2$,

(2) There exists a Turing machine which computes the function f, and for any x, the computation of f terminates within $T(\sigma_1(x))$ steps,

(3) For any $x \in \Sigma_1^*$, $\sigma_2(f(x)) < z(\sigma_1(x)$.

Lemma 2.1 Let L_1 and L_2 be problems with the size function σ_1 and σ_2, respectively. Suppose that L_1 is (T,Z)-reducible to L_2 and $T << T_1$. If the computation of L_1 requires T_1 time with respect to the size σ_1, then the computation of L_2 requires $T_1 \cdot Z^{-1}$ time with respect to the size σ_2, where $T_1 \cdot Z^{-1}$ stands for the composition of the function T_1 and the inverse function Z^{-1}.

3. Problems which require $O(n^k)$ time.

In this section we consider two problems which require $O(n^k)$ time.

Definition 3.1 For each integer k, k-pebble game problem is the problem when a k-pebble game is played by two persons to determine whether the first player has a wining strategy, that is, a way to win the game. In the k-pebble game problem, the size is defined to be the number of nodes.

Theorem 3.1 The 2k+1-pebble game problem requires $O(n^k)$ time.

The proof is done by showing that any $O(n^k)$ time computable problem is (O(n log n), O(n))-reducible to the 2k+1 pebble game problem. The outline of the proof is as follows: From a given $O(n^k)$ time bounded Turing machine M and an input x of length n, we construct 2k+1 pebble game such that M accepts x if and only if the first player has a forced win in the $2k+1$ pebble game, and furthermore, the construction can be performed under $(O(n \log n), O(n))$-reducibility.

Definition 3.2 A cat and mice game is a 5-tuple $G = (X,E,S,a,t)$ where: X is a finite set of nodes, $E \subseteq X \times X$ is the set of edges, S is a subset of X, and a and t are elements of $X-S$. The size of G is defined to be the number of nodes. If the number of elements of S is k, then G is called a cat and k-mice game. The game is played on the directed graph (X,E). At the beginning of the game, mice occupy all nodes of S, and the cat occupies the node a. The cat and one of the mice alternate moves according to a single edge of the graph with the cat moving first. The cat wins if the cat and one of the mice occupy the same node. The mice wins if one of the mice reaches the goal t before being caught.

Theorem 3.2 The cat and $2k+2$ mice game problem requires $O(n^k)$ time.

The proof is done by showing that the $2k+1$ pebble game problem is $(O(n \log n), O(n))$-reducible to the cat and $2k+2$ mice problem.

4. Problems which requier exponential time.

In this secrion, the basic results are applied to show that certain games are exponential time complete. From Theorems 3.1 and 3.2, it follows the followings.

Theorem 4.1 (i) The two-person pebble game problem requires exponential time. (ii) The cat and mice problem requires exponential time.

Definition 4.1 A Chinese checkers game is $G = (N,E,W,B,t)$, where N is a finite set of nodes, $E \subseteq N^2$ is the set of edges, W and B are subsets of N such that $W \cap B = \emptyset$, and t is an element of N.

A Chinese checkers game G is a game played on the graph (N,E) between two players, White and Black. White moves first. Initially, White stones are placed on each node of W and black stones are placed on each node of B. Suppose that (x,y) and (y,z) are edges of E. If there are a white stone on x, a black stone on y and no stone on z, then White in his turn can move the stone from x to z. Similarly, if a black stone is on x, a white stone is on y and no stone is on z, then Black can move the black stone from x to z. The player wins if after his move he has a stone on his color on the node t or the other player cannot move any stone of his color.

Theorem 4.2 The problem to determine whether there is a winning strategy in a Chinese checkers game require exponential time.

Definition 4.2 Let Z be the set of integers. A peg game is $G = (V,m,n)$, where $m, n \in N$ and V is a finite subset of Z^n such that $(v_1,\cdots,v_n) \in V$ implies $v_1+v_2+\cdots+v_n = 0$.

A peg game can be considered as the game described as follows. There are n pegs fixed upright of a board, and m disks. Each disk has a hole in its center. An element $y = (y_1,\cdots,y_n)$ of N^n represents that y_i disks are threaded on the i-th peg, $i = 1, 2,\cdots, n$. A rule $v = (v_1,\cdots,v_n) \in V$ means that for each i, if $v_i \geqq 0$ then we put v_i disks on the i-th peg, and if $v_i < 0$ we remove $-v_i$ disks from the i-th peg. Initially, all disks are threaded on the first peg. The object of the game is to transfer all disks to the n-th peg. In the two-person game, when two players althernatively move disks by the rules, the player wins if after his move all disks are on the n-th peg.

Theorem 4.3 A two-person peg game problem requires exponential time.

References

[1] A. V. Aho, J. E. Hopcroft and J. D. Ullman. The Design and Analysis of Computer Algorithms, Addison-Wesley, Reading, MA, 1974.

[2] A. K. Chandra and L. J. Stockmeyer, Alternation, Proc. 17th Ann. IEEE Symp. on Foundation of Computer Sciences, 1976, pp.98-108.

[3] S. A. Cook, The complexity of theorem-proving procedures, Proc. 3rd ACM Symp. on Theory of Computing, 1971, pp.151-158.

[4] S. Even and R. R. Tarjan, A combinatorial problem which is complete in polynomial space, J. Assc. Comput. Mach., 23(1976), pp.710-719.

[5] W. D. Jones and W. T. Laaser, Complete problems for deterministic

polynomial time, Theoretical Comput. Sci., 3(1977), pp.105-117.

[6] R. M. Karp, Reducibility among combinatorial problems, Complexity of Computer Computations, R. E. Miller and J. w. Thatcher, eds., Plenum Press, New York, 1972, pp.85-104.

[7] T. Kasai, A. Adachi and S. Iwata, Classes of pebble games and complete problems, SIAM J. Comput. 8(1979) pp.574-586.

[8] T. Kasai and A. Adachi, A characterization of time complexity by simple loop programs, J. Comput. System Sci., 20(1980) pp.1-17.

[9] T. J. Schaefer, Complexity of decision problems based on finite two-person perfect-information games, Proc. 8th Ann. ACM Symp. on Theory of Computing, 1976, pp.41-49.

HOMOMORPHISMS OF GRAPHS AND THEIR GLOBAL MAPS

Masakazu Nasu
Research Institute of Electrical Communication
Tohoku University, Sendai, Japan

1. Introduction

For directed graphs G_1 and G_2, a homomorphism h of G_1 into G_2 is, roughly speaking, a mapping of the set of arcs of G_1 into the set of arcs of G_2 that preserves the adjacency of arcs. It is naturally extended to a mapping h^* of the set of paths in G_1 into the set of paths in G_2, which is called the extension of h. Also, h naturally induces a mapping h_∞ of the set of bisequences over G_1 into the set of bisequences over G_2, which is called the global map of h. In [9], Hedlund describes the properties of endomorphisms of the shift dynamical system. In [10], using results in [9] and graph-theoretical approaches, the author further investigated the properties of global maps of one-dimentional tessellation automata ("global maps of one-dimensional tessellation automata" and "endomorphisms of the shift dynamical system" are names for the same notion in different fields). Many notions and results in [9] and [10] can be naturally generalized to extensions and global maps of homomorphisms between strongly connected graphs so that we have a new area of graph theory [13][14].

In this paper, we survey a part of the results obtained in [13]and [14] which is mainly concerned with uniformly finite-to-one and onto global maps of homomorphisms between strongly connected graphs.

Most of our results except for Theorem 1 can be considered as generalizations of results described somewhere in [9] and [10]. (We do not say why they can be considered so and which result in [9] or [10] each of them corresponds to. These are found in [13] and [14]. See also [15].) As a generalization of the shift dynamical systems, a class of symbolic flows known as irreducible subshifts of finite type has been studied. Global maps of homomorphisms between strongly connected graphs are closely related to homomorphisms of symbolic flows between irreducible subshifts of finite type, and our results can be directly applied to them. These applications are contained in [13] and [14]. Related results on symbolic flows are found in the works of Coven and Paul [3] [4] [5].

2. Basic definitions

A graph (directed graph with labeled points and labeled arcs) G is defined to be a triple $\langle P, A, \zeta \rangle$ where P is a finite set of elements called points, A is a finite set of elements called arcs and ζ is a mapping of A into $P \times P$. If $\zeta(a) = (u, v)$ for $a \in A$ and $u, v \in P$, then u and v are the initial endpoint of a and the terminal endpoint of a, respectively, and are denoted by $i(a)$ and $t(a)$, respectively.

A sequence $x = a_1 \cdots a_p$ $(p \geq 1)$ with $a_i \in A$, $i = 1, \cdots, p$, is a path of length p in G if $t(a_i) = i(a_{i+1})$ for $i = 1, \cdots, p-1$. We call $i(a_1)$ and $t(a_p)$ the initial endpoint of x and the terminal endpoint of x, respectively. Every point u of G is a path of length 0 in G whose initial [terminal] endpoint is u. For any path x in G, we denote by $i(x)$ and $t(x)$ the initial endpoint of x and the terminal endpoint of x, respectively, and if $i(x) = u$ and $t(x) = v$, then we often say that x goes from u to v. The set of all paths in G is denoted by $\Pi(G)$. The set of all paths of length p (≥ 0) in G is denoted by $\Pi^{(p)}(G)$.

Let Z be the set of integers. For a graph $G = \langle P, A, \zeta \rangle$, a mapping $\alpha : Z \to A$ is a bisequence over G if $t(\alpha(i)) = i(\alpha(i+1))$ for all $i \in Z$. Let $\Omega(G)$ denote the set of all bisequences over G. If $\alpha \in \Omega(G)$ and $i \in Z$, then $\alpha(i)$ will often be denoted by α_i.

Let $G_1 = \langle P, A, \zeta_1 \rangle$ and $G_2 = \langle Q, B, \zeta_2 \rangle$ be two graphs. A homomorphism h of G_1 into G_2 is a pair (h, ϕ) of a mapping $h : A \to B$ and a mapping $\phi : P \to Q$ such that for any $a \in A$, if $\zeta_1(a) = (u, v)$ with $u, v \in P$, then

$$\zeta_2(h(a)) = (\phi(u), \phi(v)).$$

If G_1 has no isolated point, that is, for each point u of G_1, there exists at least one arc going from or to u, then the homomorphism $h = (h, \phi)$ of G_1 into G_2 is uniquely determined by h. Therefore, when G_1 has no isolated point, we say that h is a homomorphism of G_1 into G_2 and we denote by ϕ_h the unique mapping ϕ such that (h, ϕ) is a homomorphism of G_1 into G_2. In what follows we assume, without loss of generality, that graphs have no isolated point.

A homomorphism $h : A \to B$ of a graph $G_1 = \langle P, A, \zeta_1 \rangle$ into a graph $G_2 = \langle Q, B, \zeta_2 \rangle$ is naturally extended to a mapping $h^* : \Pi(G_1) \to \Pi(G_2)$. That is, we define $h^* : \Pi(G_1) \to \Pi(G_2)$ as follows : For each $x \in \Pi(G_1)$, if the length of x is 0, i.e., x is a point of G_1, then $h^*(x) = \phi_h(x)$, and if $x = a_1 \cdots a_p$ $(p \geq 1)$ with $a_i \in \mathbf{A}$, $i = 1, \cdots, p$, then $h^*(x) = h(a_1) \cdots h(a_p)$. Mapping h^* is called the extension of h. Another mapping is naturally induced by h. We define $h_\infty : \Omega(G_1) \to \Omega(G_2)$ as follows : For $\alpha \in \Omega(G_1)$, $h_\infty(\alpha) = \beta$ where $\beta_i = h(\alpha_i)$ for all $i \in Z$. We call h_∞ the global map of the homomorphism h.

A graph $G = \langle P, A, \zeta \rangle$ is strongly connected if for any $u, v \in P$, there exists a path going from u to v. (Note that by our assumption, $A \neq \phi$.)

For a positive integer k, a mapping $f : X \to Y$ is k-to-one if $|f^{-1}(y)| = k$ for all $y \in f(X)$. A mapping $f : X \to Y$ is constant-to-one if there exists a positive integer k such that f is k-to-one, uniformly finite-to-one if there exists a positive integer k such that $|f^{-1}(y)| \leq k$ for all $y \in Y$, and finite-to-one if $|f^{-1}(y)| < \infty$ for all $y \in Y$.

3. Uniformly finite-to-one and onto extensions and uniformly finite-to-one and onto global maps

In this section, we state some properties of uniformly finite-to-one and onto extensions and uniformly finite-to-one and onto global maps of homomorphisms of graphs.

For a graph G, let M(G) be the adjacency matrix of G (i.e., if G has n points $u_1, \cdots, u_n$, then M(G) is the square matrix (m_{ij}) of order n such that m_{ij} is the number of arcs going from u_i to u_j.) Since M(G) is a non-negative matrix, by Perron-Frobenius Theorem, M(G) has the non-negative characteristic value that the moduli of all the other characteristic values do not exceed (cf. Gantmacher [7]). We denote by r(G) that "maximal" characteristic value of M(G), which is often called the spectral radius of G.

Theorem 1†. Let h be a homomorphism of a graph G_1 into a graph G_2. If h^* is uniformly finite-to-one and onto, then $r(G_1) = r(G_2)$ and the characteristic polynomial of $M(G_1)$ is divided by the characteristic polynomial of $M(G_2)$.

Let h be a homomorphism of a graph G_1 into a graph G_2. Two paths x and y in G_1 are indistinguishable by h if $i(x) = i(y)$, $t(x) = t(y)$, and $h^*(x) = h^*(y)$.

---

† A stronger result than Theorem 1 is found in [13].

Proposition 1. Let G_1 and G_2 be two strongly connected graphs, and let h be a homomorphism of G_1 into G_2. Then the following statements are equivalent. (1) h^* is uniformly finite-to-one. (2) There exist no two distinct paths in G_1 which are indistinguishable by h. (3) h_∞ is uniformly finite-to-one. (4) h_∞ is finite-to-one.

Proposition 2. Let G_1 and G_2 be two graphs such that for each point u of them, there exist at least one arc going to u and at least one arc going from u. Then for any homomorphism h of G_1 into G_2, h^* is onto if and only if h_∞ is onto.

Theorem 2. Let G_1 and G_2 be two strongly connected graphs with $r(G_1) = r(G_2)$. Then for any homomorphism h of G_1 into G_2, h^* is uniformly finite-to-one if and only if h^* is onto.

Let G_1 and G_2 be two strongly connected graphs and let h be a homomorphism of G_1 into G_2. Then, by the above results, we have many statements which are equivalent to the statement that $r(G_1) = r(G_2)$ and h^* is onto. The following are some of them. (1) $r(G_1) = r(G_2)$ and there exist no two distinct paths in G_1 which are indistinguishable by h. (2) h^* is onto and there exist no two distinct paths in G_1 which are indistinguishable by h. (3) h^* is uniformly finite-to-one and onto. (4) h_∞ is uniformly finite-to-one and onto.

Example 1. Let $G = \langle P, A, \zeta \rangle$ be a graph. For any non-negative integer p, we define a graph $L^{(p)}(G)$ as follows. $L^{(0)}(G) = G$. For $p \geq 1$, $L^{(p)}(G) = \langle \Pi^{(p)}(G), \Pi^{(p+1)}(G), \zeta^{(p)} \rangle$ where $\zeta^{(p)}(a_1 \cdots a_{p+1}) = (a_1 \cdots a_p, a_2 \cdots a_{p+1})$ for $a_1 \cdots a_{p+1} \in \Pi^{(p+1)}(G)$ with $a_i \in A$, $i = 1, \cdots, p+1$. We call $L^{(p)}(G)$ the <u>path graph of length p</u> of G. ($L^{(1)}(G)$ is usually known as the <u>line digraph</u> of G (cf. Harary [8]) or the <u>adjoint</u> of G(cf. Berge [2])). Clearly, if G is strongly connected, then $L^{(p)}(G)$ is strongly connected for all $p \geq 0$. For any positive integers p and q with $p \geq q$, we define a mapping $h_{G,p,q} : \Pi^{(p)}(G) \to A$ as follows. For any $a_1 \cdots a_p \in \Pi^{(p)}(G)$ with $a_i \in A$, $h(a_1 \cdots a_p) = a_q$. Then clearly $h_{G,p,q}$ is a homomorphism of $L^{(p-1)}(G)$ into G. If G is a graph such that for each point u of it, there exist at least one arc going to u and at least one arc going from u, then $(h_{G,p,q})^*$ is uniformly finite-to-one and onto and $(h_{G,p,q})_\infty$ is one-to-one and onto. Hence, by Theorem 1, we know that under the same condition for G, $r(L^{(p)}(G)) = r(G)$ and $\psi_{G'}(X)$ is divided by $\psi_G(X)$, where $G' = L^{(p)}(G)$ and we denote by $\psi_H(X)$ the characteristic polynomial of M(H) for any graph H. In fact, Adler and Marcus [1] pointed out a stronger result : For any graph G (without any restriction imposed on it), $\psi_{G'}(X) = X^{m-n}\psi_G(X)$ where $G' = L^{(p)}(G)$, $m = |\Pi^{(p)}(G)|$, n is the number of points of G, and we assume that $\psi_\phi(X) = 1$ for the graph ϕ with no point.

4. Compatible sets and Complete sets

Let $G_1 = \langle P, A, \zeta_1 \rangle$ and $G_2 = \langle Q, B, \zeta_2 \rangle$ be graphs, and let h be a homomorphism of G_1 into G_2. Let $U \subset P$ and let $y \in \Pi(G_2)$. Define

$$C_h(U, y) = \{t(x) \mid x \in \Pi(G_1),\ i(x) \in U,\ h^*(x) = y\}$$

and

$$\bar{C}_h(y, U) = \{i(x) \mid x \in \Pi(G_1),\ t(x) \in U,\ h^*(x) = y\}.$$

For $u \in P$ and $y \in \Pi(G_2)$, we denote $C_h(\{u\}, y)$ [$\bar{C}_h(y, \{u\})$] by $C_h(u, y)$ [$\bar{C}_h(y, u)$]. A subset U of P is called a compatible set [a backward-compatible (abbreviated b-compatible) set] for h if $U = C_h(u, y)$ [$U = \bar{C}_h(y, u)$] for some $u \in P$ and $y \in \Pi(G_2)$.

A subset U of P is a complete set [a backward-complete (abbreviated b-complete) set] for h, if there exists $v \in Q$ such that $U \subset \phi_h^{-1}(v)$, and $C_h(U, y) \neq \phi$ [$\bar{C}_h(y, U) \neq \phi$] for all $y \in \Pi(G_2)$ with $i(y) = v$ [$t(y) = v$].

Theorem 3. Let $G_1 = \langle P, A, \zeta_1 \rangle$ and $G_2 = \langle Q, B, \zeta_2 \rangle$ be two strongly connected graphs with $r(G_1) = r(G_2)$. Let h be a homomorphism of G_1 into G_2 with h^* onto. Then every maximal compatible [b-compatible] set for h is a minimal complete [b-complete] set for h.

Corollary 1. Let G_1 and G_2 be two strongly connected graphs with $r(G_1) = r(G_2)$, and let h be a homomorphism of G_1 into G_2 with h^* onto. Let U be an arbitrary maximal compatible [b-compatible] set for h. Then for any path y in G_2 with $i(y) \in \phi_h(U)$ [$t(y) \in \phi_h(U)$], $C_h(U, y)$ [$\bar{C}_h(y, U)$] is a maximal compatible [b-compatible] set for h.

Proof. Let y be a path in G_2 with $i(y) \in \phi_h(U)$. From Theorem 3, U is a complete set. Hence $C_h(U, y)$ is a complete set. Since U is a compatible set, $C_h(U, y)$ is a compatible set. Let V be a maximal compatible set such that $V \supset C_h(U, y)$. Then from Theorem 3, V is a minimal complete set. Therefore, since $C_h(U, y)$ is a complete set, we have $V = C_h(U, y)$. Therefore $C_h(U, y)$ is a maximal compatible set.

The proof of the second reading is similar.

5. Induced regular homomorphisms

A homomorphism h of a graph G_1 into a graph G_2 is *regular* [*backward-regular* (abbreviated *b-regular*)] if for each point u of G_1 and for each arc b going from [to] $\phi_h(u)$, there exists exactly one arc a going from [to] u with $h(a) = b$.

By virtue of the Corollary 1 in the preceding section, we can introduce the notion of "induced regular [b-regular] homomorphism" which is associated with every homomorphism h between two strongly connected graphs such that h^* is uniformly finite-to-one and onto.

Throughout this section, we assume that $G_1 = \langle P, A, \zeta_1 \rangle$ and $G_2 = \langle Q, B, \zeta_2 \rangle$ are two strongly connected graphs with $r(G_1) = r(G_2)$ and h is a homomorphism of G_1 into G_2 such that h^* is onto.

Denote by $\mathcal{C}_h$ $[\bar{\mathcal{C}}_h]$ the set of all maximal compatible [b-compatible] sets for h. For any $U \subset P$ and $y \in \Pi(G_2)$, we define

$$B_h(U, y) = \{x \in \Pi(G_1) \mid i(x) \in U,\ h^*(x) = y\}$$

and

$$\bar{B}_h(y, U) = \{x \in \Pi(G_1) \mid t(x) \in U,\ h^*(x) = y\}.$$

We define the *bundle-graph induced by h* as the graph $G_h = \langle \mathcal{C}_h, \mathcal{E}_h, \zeta_h \rangle$ where $\mathcal{E}_h$ is the set of all pairs of the form $(U, B_h(U, b))$ where $U \in \mathcal{C}_h$ and $b \in B$ with $i(b) \in \phi_h(U)$, and $\zeta_h : \mathcal{E}_h \to \mathcal{C}_h \times \mathcal{C}_h$ is defined as follows :

$$\zeta_h((U, B_h(U, b))) = (U, C_h(U, b))$$

for all $U \in \mathcal{C}_h$ and $b \in B$ with $i(b) \in \phi_h(U)$. By Corollary 1, $C_h(U, b) \in \mathcal{C}_h$ for any $U \in \mathcal{C}_h$ and $b \in B$ with $i(b) \in \phi_h(U)$. Hence ζ_h is well-defined. Furthermore, we define a mapping $\tilde{h} : \mathcal{E}_h \to B$ as follows :

$$\tilde{h}((U, B_h(U, b))) = b$$

for all $U \in \mathcal{C}_h$ and $b \in B$ with $i(b) \in \phi_h(U)$.

Similarly, the *backward bundle-graph* (abbreviated *b-bundle-graph*) *induced by h* is defined to be the graph $\bar{G}_h = \langle \bar{\mathcal{C}}_h, \bar{\mathcal{E}}_h, \bar{\zeta}_h \rangle$ where $\bar{\mathcal{E}}_h$ is the set of all pairs of the form $(\bar{B}_h(b, U), U)$ where $U \in \bar{\mathcal{C}}_h$ and $b \in B$ with $t(b) \in \phi_h(U)$ and $\bar{\zeta}_h : \bar{\mathcal{E}}_h \to \bar{\mathcal{C}}_h \times \bar{\mathcal{C}}_h$ is defined as follows.

$$\bar{\zeta}_h((\bar{B}_h(b, U), U)) = (\bar{C}_h(b, U), U)$$

for all $U \in \bar{\mathcal{C}}_h$ and $b \in B$ with $t(b) \in \phi_h(U)$. We define a mapping $\bar{h} : \bar{\mathcal{E}}_h \to$

B as follows :

$$\bar{\bar{h}}((\bar{B}_h(b, U), U)) = b$$

for all $U \in \bar{C}_h$ and $b \in B$ with $t(b) \in \phi_h(U)$.

Theorem 4. G_h [$\bar{G}_h$] is a strongly connected graph, $\tilde{h}$ [$\bar{\bar{h}}$] is a regular [b-regular] homomorphism of G_h [$\bar{G}_h$] into G_2, and hence $r(G_h) = r(\bar{G}_h) = r(G_2)$ ($= r(G_1)$).

We call $\tilde{h}$ [$\bar{\bar{h}}$] the <u>induced regular [b-regular] homomorphism of h.</u>

To each path Z of length p (≥ 0) in G_h [$\bar{G}_h$], the subset of paths $B_h(U, y)$ [$\bar{B}_h(y, U)$] of length p in G_1 where $i(Z) = U$ [$t(Z) = U$] and $y = \tilde{h}(Z)$ [$y = \bar{\bar{h}}(Z)$], corresponds and is called the <u>bundle</u> of Z. Clearly each subset of paths of length p in G_1 of the form $B_h(U, y)$ [$\bar{B}_h(y, U)$] where $U \in C_h$ [$U \in \bar{C}_h$] and $y \in \Pi(G_2)$ with $i(y) \in \phi_h(U)$ [$t(y) \in \phi_h(U)$], is the bundle of some path of length p in G_h [$\bar{G}_h$], and is also called a <u>bundle</u> [<u>backward bundle</u>, abbreviated <u>b-bundle</u>] <u>of length p for h.</u>

6. Mergible homomorphisms

In this section, we introduce the notion of "mergible" for homomorphisms between strongly connected graphs with uniformly finite-to-one and onto extensions, and we give an outline of the proof that for each mergible homomorphism h, h_∞ is constant-to-one.

Let G_1 and G_2 be two strongly connected graphs with $r(G_1) = r(G_2)$, and let h be a homomorphism of G_1 into G_2 with h^* onto. Let p be a non-negative integer. We say that h is <u>p bundle-mergible</u> [p <u>b-bundle mergible</u>] if for each bundle [b-bundle] X of length p for h, all paths in X have the same initial [terminal] endpoint. We say that h is <u>mergible</u> if for some non-negative integers p and q, h is both p bundle-mergible and q b-bundle-mergible. We note that h is 0 bundle-mergible [0 b-bundle-mergible] if and only if h is regular [b-regular].

It is easily verified that for a homomorphism h between two strongly connected graphs G_1 and G_2 with $r(G_1) = r(G_2)$, h^* is onto and h is p bundle-mergible [p b-bundle-mergible] if and only if for any two paths x_1 and x_2 of length $\ell \geq p$ in G_1, if $i(x_1) = i(x_2)$ [$t(x_1) = t(x_2)$] and $h^*(x_1) = h^*(x_2)$, then x_1 and x_2 have the same initial [terminal] subpath of length $\ell - p$. (For paths x and y in a graph G, y is an <u>initial subpath</u> [a <u>terminal subpath</u>] of x if there exists a path w in G such that $x = yw$ [$x = wy$]. Here we assume that $i(x)x = xt(x) = x$ for each path x in a graph G.)

Another restatment of the property of being p bundle-mergible [p b-bundle-mergible] is given as the following proposition.

Proposition 3. Let G_1 and G_2 be two strongly connected graphs with $r(G_1) = r(G_2)$ and let h be a homomorphism of G_1 into G_2 with h^* onto. Let p be a non-negative integer. Then h is p bundle-mergible [p b-bundle-mergible] if and only if for any point u of G_1 and $y \in \Pi^{(p)}(G_2)$ with $i(y) = \phi_h(u)$ $[t(y) = \phi_h(u)]$, $C(u, y)$ $[\bar{C}(y, u)]$ is either empty or a maximal compatible [b-compatible] set.

Now we shall state six lemmas used in the proof of the main theorem of this section.

Lemma 1. Let G_1 and G_2 be two strongly connected graphs with $r(G_1) = r(G_2)$, and let h be a homomorphism of G_1 into G_2 with h^* onto. If h is mergible, then the induced regular homomorphism $\tilde{h}$ of h is mergible.

Lemma 2. Let G_1 and G_2 be two strongly connected graphs with $r(G_1) = r(G_2)$, and let h be a homomorphism of G_1 into G_2 with h^* onto. If h is p bundle-mergible [p b-bundle-mergible] for a non-negative integer p, then there exists a one-to-one and onto mapping $\rho: \Omega(G_h) \to \Omega(G_1)$ $[\rho : \Omega(\bar{G}_h) \to \Omega(G_1)]$ such that $\tilde{h}_\infty = h_\infty\rho$ $[\bar{\tilde{h}}_\infty = h_\infty\rho]$.

Let G_1 and G_2 be two strongly connected graphs and let h be a homomorphism of G_1 into G_2. Let n be a non-negative integer. We define a mapping $h^{(n)} : \Pi^{(n+1)}(G_1) \to \Pi^{(n+1)}(G_2)$ by

$$h^{(n)}(x) = h^*(x) \qquad (x \in \Pi^{(n+1)}(G_1)).$$

It is easily seen that $h^{(n)}$ is a homomoprhism of $L^{(n)}(G_1)$ into $L^{(n)}(G_2)$, $(h^{(n)})^*$ is onto if and only if h^* is onto, and if $r(G_1) = r(G_2)$, then $r(L^{(n)}(G_1)) = r(L^{(n)}(G_2))$. (Cf. Example 1.)

Lemma 3. Let G_1 and G_2 be two strongly connected graphs with $r(G_1) = r(G_2)$, and let h be a homomoprhism of G_1 into G_2 with h^* onto. Let n and p be non-negative integers. If h is p bundle-mergible [p b-bundle-mergible], then $h^{(n)}$ is a p bundle-mergible [p b-bundle-mergible] homomorphism of $L^{(n)}(G_1)$ into $L^{(n)}(G_2)$.

Lemma 4. Let G_1 and G_2 be two strongly connected graphs with $r(G_1) = r(G_2)$, and let h be a homomorphism of G_1 into G_2 with h^* onto. Suppose that h is p bundle-mergible [p b-bundle-mergible] for a non-negative integer p. Then any two distinct maximal compatible [b-compatible] sets for $h^{(p)}$ are disjoint.

A homomorphism h between graphs is <u>biregular</u> if h is both regular and b-regular.

Lemma 5. Let h be a regular homomorphism of G_1 into G_2 where G_1 and G_2 are strongly connected graphs. If every two distinct maximal b-compatible sets for h are disjoint, then $\bar{\bar{h}}$ is biregular.

Lemma 6. Let h be a biregular homomorphism of a graph G_1 with $\Omega(G_1) \neq \phi$ into a strongly connected graph G_2. Let G_1 have p points and G_2 have q points. Then h_∞ is p/q-to-one.

Theorem 5. Let G_1 and G_2 be two strongly connected graphs with $r(G_1) = r(G_2)$, and let h be a homomorphism of G_1 into G_2 with h^* onto. If h is mergible, then h_∞ is constant-to-one.

Proof. Assume that h is mergible.

Let $G_3 = G_h$ and let $h_1 = \tilde{h}$. Then from Theorem 4 and Lemma 1, G_3 is a strongly connected graph with $r(G_3) = r(G_2)$ and h_1 is a regular and mergible homomorphism of G_3 into G_2. From Lemma 2, there exists a one-to-one and onto mapping $\rho : \Omega(G_3) \rightarrow \Omega(G_1)$ such that

$$(h_1)_\infty = h_\infty \rho.$$

Since h_1 is regular and mergible, h_1 is 0 bundle-mergible and there exists $p \geq 0$ such that h_1 is p b-bundle mergible. Let $G_5 = L^{(p)}(G_3)$, let $G_4 = L^{(p)}(G_2)$, and let $h_2 = h_1^{(p)}$. Then, $r(G_5) = r(G_4)$, h_2^* is onto, and from Lemma 3, h_2 is 0 bundle-mergible and p b-bundle-mergible. Moreover, from Lemma 4, any two distinct maximal b-compatible sets for h_2 are disjoint. Let $\rho_1 = (h_{G_3,p+1}, 1)_\infty$ and let $\rho_2 = (h_{G_2,p+1}, 1)_\infty$ (cf. Example 1). Then ρ_1 is a one-to-one mapping of $\Omega(G_5)$ onto $\Omega(G_3)$ and ρ_2 is a one-to-one mapping of $\Omega(G_4)$ onto $\Omega(G_2)$, and we have

$$(h_2)_\infty = \rho_2^{-1}(h_1)_\infty \rho_1$$

Let $G_7 = \bar{G}_{h_2}$ and let $h_3 = \bar{\bar{h}}_2$. Then since h_2 is regular (because h_2 is 0 bundle-mergible) and any two distinct maximal b-compatible sets for h_2 are disjoint, it follows from Lemma 5 that h_3 is biregular. Since

h_2 is p b-bundle-mergible, it follows from Lemma 2 that there exists a one-to-one and onto mapping $\rho' : \Omega(G_7) \to \Omega(G_5)$ such that

$$(h_3)_\infty = (h_2)_\infty \rho'.$$

Since h_3 is biregular, it follows from Lemma 6 that $(h_3)_\infty$ is constant-to-one. Therefore, since ρ, ρ_1, ρ_2, and ρ' are one-to-one and onto mappings, it follows that h_∞ is constant-to-one.

7. Characterizations of constant-to-one and onto global maps of homomorphisms between strongly connected graphs.

Let G be a graph with $\Omega(G) \neq \phi$. Two bisequences $\alpha, \beta \in \Omega(G)$ are point-separated if $\mathrm{i}(\alpha_i) \neq \mathrm{i}(\beta_i)$ for all $i \in Z$.

Let G_1 and G_2 be two strongly connected graphs with $r(G_1) = r(G_2)$, and let h be a homomorphism of G_1 into G_2. It is easy to see that if for each $\beta \in \Omega(G_2)$, any two distinct members of $h_\infty^{-1}(\beta)$ are point-separated, then h^* is onto and h is mergible. Moreover, using topological arguments similar to those in Hedlund [9] or those in Ferguson [6] (see the proof of Lemma 2.3 of [6]), we can prove that if h_∞ is constant-to-one, then for each $\beta \in \Omega(G_2)$, any two distinct members of $h_\infty^{-1}(\beta)$ are point-separated. Therefore, using these and Theorem 5, we have the following result.

Theorem 6. Let G_1 and G_2 be two strongly connected graphs and let h be a homomorphism of G_1 into G_2. Then the following statements are equivalent.

(1) h_∞ is constant-to-one and onto.

(2) $r(G_1) = r(G_2)$ and for each $\beta \in \Omega(G_2)$, any two distinct members of $h_\infty^{-1}(\beta)$ are point-separated.

(3) $r(G_1) = r(G_2)$, h^* is onto, and h is mergible.

By the fact stated after Theorem 2, statement (3) in the above theorem can be restated as follows :

(3') h^* is onto, there exist no two distinct paths in G_1 which are indistinguishable by h, and h is mergible.

It is easy to see that there exists an algorithm to determine, for a homomorphism h between two strongly connected graphs G_1 and G_2, whether (3') holds. This gives an algorithm to determine whether h_∞ is constant-to-one and onto for an arbitrary homomorphism h between strongly connected graphs.

As an application of Theorem 6, we have the following result which can be considered as a generalization of Theorem 2 of [12].

Theorem 7. Let G_1, G_2 and G_3 be strongly connected graphs with $r(G_1) = r(G_2) = r(G_3)$, and let h_1 be a homomorphism of G_1 into G_2 and h_2 be a homomorphism of G_2 into G_3. Then if $(h_1h_2)_\infty$ is constant-to-one, then each of $(h_1)_\infty$ and $(h_2)_\infty$ is constant-to-one.

8. One-to-one and onto global maps of homomorphisms between strongly connected graphs.

Let h be a regular [b-regular] homomorphism of G_1 into G_2 and let p be a non-negative integer. We say that h is p definite if for any x_1, $x_2 \in \Pi^{(p)}(G_1)$, $h^*(x_1)= h^*(x_2)$ implies $t(x_1) = t(x_2)$ $[i(x_1) = i(x_2)]$. We say that h is definite if h is p definite for some non-negative integer p.

A definite regular homomorphism is considered to be a generalization of the state transition diagram of an automaton having a definite table, which was introduced by Perles, Rabin, and Shamir [16]. We remark that properties of definite tables and a practical decision procedure for definiteness of tables presented in [16], are straightforwardly extended to definite regular [b-regular] homomorphisms of graphs. We can characterize homomorphisms between strongly connected graphs with one-to-one and onto global maps in terms of definiteness of their induced regular and b-regular homomorphisms.

Theorem 8. Let G_1 and G_2 be two strongly connected graphs with $r(G_1) = r(G_2)$, and let h be a homomorphism of G_1 into G_2 with h^* onto. Let p be a non-negative integer. Then the induced regular [b-regular] homomorphism $\tilde{h}$ $[\bar{\tilde{h}}]$ of h is p definite if and only if h is p b-bundle-mergible [p bundle-mergible] and $U \cap V \neq \phi$ $(|U \cap V| = 1)$ for any $U \in C_h$ and $V \in \bar{C}_h$ with $\phi_h(U) = \phi_h(V)$.

Theorem 9. Let G_1 and G_2 be two strongly connected graphs with $r(G_1) = r(G_2)$, and let h be a homomorphism of G_1 into G_2 with h^* onto. Then h_∞ is one-to-one if and only if h is mergible and $U \cap V = \phi$ $[|U \cap V| = 1]$ for any $U \in C_h$ and $V \in \bar{C}_h$ with $\phi_h(U) = \phi_h(V)$.

By the above two theorems, we have the following result.

Theorem 10. Let G_1 and G_2 be two strongly connected graphs with

$r(G_1) = r(G_2)$, and let h be a homomorphism with h^* onto. Then h_∞ is one-to-one if and only if both the induced regular homomorphism and induced b-regular homomorphism of h are definite.

References

[1] R.L. Adler and B. Marcus, Topological entropy and equivalence of dynamical systems, Memoirs Amer. Math. Soc. 219 (1979).

[2] C. Berge, Graphs and Hypergraphs (North-Holland, Amsterdam, 1973).

[3] E.M. Coven and M.E. Paul, Endomorphisms of irreducible subshifts of finite type, Math. Systems Theory 8 (1974) 167-175.

[4] E.M. Coven and M.E. Paul, Sofic systems, Israel J. Math. 20 (1975) 165-177.

[5] E.M. Coven and M.E. Paul, Finite procedures for sofic systems, Monatsh. Math. 83 (1977) 265-278.

[6] J.D. Ferguson, Some properties of mappings on sequence spaces, Ph. D. Thesis, Yale University, New Haven, CT (1962).

[7] F.R. Gantmacher, The Theory of Matrices, Vol. II (Chelsea, New York, 1959).

[8] F. Harary, Graph Theory (Addison-Wesley, Reading, Mass., 1969).

[9] G.A. Hedlund, Endomorphisms and automorphisms of the shift dynamical system, Math. Systems Theory 3 (1969) 320-375.

[10] M. Nasu, Local maps inducing surjective global maps of one-dimensional tessellation automata, Math. Systems Theory 11 (1978) 327-351.

[11] M. Nasu, An interconnection of local maps inducing onto global maps, Discrete Applied Math. 2 (1980) 125-150.

[12] M. Nasu, Indecomposable local maps of tessellation automata, Math. Systems Theory 13 (1979) 81-93.

[13] M. Nasu, Uniformly finite-to-one and onto extensions of homomorphisms between strongly connected graphs, submitted.

[14] M. Nasu, Constant-to-one and onto global maps of homomorphisms between strongly connected graphs, in preparation.

[15] M. Nasu, Maps of one-dimensional tessellation automata and homomorphisms of graphs, Proc. of The Fifth IBM Symp. on Mathematical Foundations of Computer Science (1980).

[16] M. Perles, M.O. Rabin, and E. Shamir, The theory of definite automata, IEEE Trans. Electr. Comp. EC-12 (1963) 233-243.

ALGORITHMS FOR SOME INTERSECTION GRAPHS

T. Kashiwabara
Dept. of Information and Computer Sciences
Faculty of Engineering Science, Osaka University
Toyonaka, Japan 560

Abstract. Several intersection graphs such as curves-in-the-plane graphs, circular-arc graphs, chordal graphs and interval graphs are reviewed, especially on their recognition algorithms. In this connection graph realization problem is mentioned.

1. Introduction

This report summarizes some already known results on certain intersection graphs. A finite undirected graph $G=(V,E)$ is an intersection graph on intersection model $M=(S,\mathcal{S})$ when there is a 1-1 correspondence f between V and $\mathcal{S}$ such that $(u,v)\in E$ iff $f(u)\cap f(v)\neq\phi$, where $\mathcal{S}$ is a collection of subsets of S. Trivially, any graph is an intersection graph on some appropriate model M [1]. In practical applications, graphs having simple intersection models such as chordal graphs and interval graphs etc. are of interest [2][3].

In the following, several intersection graphs having particular models are considered. They are curves-in-the-plane, chordal, path, interval, circular-arc and circle graphs. Relations between them are mentioned and recognition algorithms and computational complexity of several problems on them are sketched. Connection between path graphs and the graph realization problem is also mentioned.

2. Curves-in-the-plane graphs and circle graphs

Without loss of generality, the set S in intersection model $M=(S,\mathcal{S})$ can be taken to be a plane: Any graph is an intersection graph on the plane. Therefore it is necessary to restrict the family of subsets to have an appropriate property for the purpose of defining a proper subclass of graphs. When every $S'\in\mathcal{S}$ is a connected piece in the plane, the corresponding intersection graphs seem to be a proper subclass of all graphs. In [4], the class of intersection graphs of curves in the plane is introduced.

Definition. Let V be a set of (non self-intersecting) curves in the plane. The corresponding curves-in-the-plane graph has V as the vertex set and two vertices are connected by an edge iff two corresponding curves intersect in the plane. Similarly straight-lines-in-the-plane graph is defined as an intersection graph of straight line segments in the plane.

The following facts are reported.

Theorem 1 General graphs $\supsetneq$ curves-in-the-plane graphs $\supsetneq$ straight-lines-in-the-plane graphs [4].

Fig.1 shows an example which is not a curves-in-the-plane graph, as underlying K_5 is not planar.

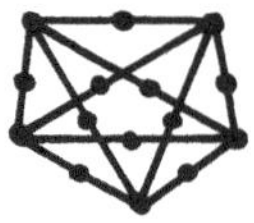

Fig.1

Fig.2

Theorem 2 Every planar graph is a curves-in-the-plane graph [4]. (see Fig. 2)

Theorem 3 The problem of finding the chromatic number for straight-lines-in-the-plane graph is NP-complete [4].

The class of circle graphs is a restricted class of straight-lines-in-the-plane graphs.

Definition A circle graph is an intersection graph of straight line segments in the circle such that two endpoints of each line segment are on the circle.

Fig.3

Complexity of coloring a circle graph is reported.

Theorem 4 Determining the chromatic number of circle graphs is NP-complete [6].

No recognition algorithms for curves-in-the-plane graphs, straight-lines-in-the-plane graphs and circle graphs have been given so far.

3. Circular-arc graphs

Definition A graph is a circular-arc graph iff it is the intersection graph of arcs on a circle.

Fig.4

The class of circular-arc graphs is a proper superset of interval graphs. Though there exists a polynomial time algorithm for determining the chromatic number of interval graphs, the same problem for circular-arc graphs seems intractable. There is reported the following.

Theorem 5 Determining the chromatic number for circular-arc graphs is NP-complete [6].

Unlike chordal graphs, the number of dominant cliques of a circular-arc graph or a circle graph (which is a curves-in-the-plane graph) can grow exponentially. Fig.5 shows an example of such a graph [7][8]. It is a complete n-partite graph of 2n vertices which has 2^n dominant cliques.

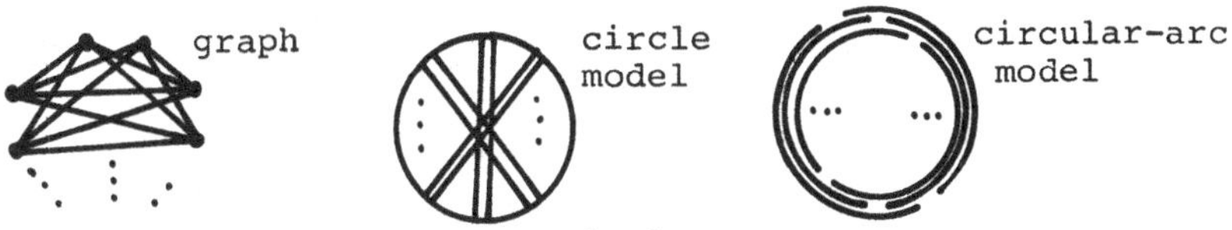

Fig.5

Because of the above fact, efficient recognition algorithms for circle or circular-arc graphs, if exist, cannot use the set of all dominant cliques. This is essentially different from the recognition algorithm for interval graphs which makes use of dominant cliques effectively. An efficient recognition algorithm for circular-arc graphs which searches for an appropriate order of vertices is presented in [8].

4. Subtree graphs (chordal graphs)

In sections 4-6, intersection model on a tree is treated, i.e., the case where the set S in model M is a tree. Also for this case, an arbitrary undirected graph can be an intersection graph if disconnected pieces for $S' \in \mathcal{S}$ are allowed. Restricting the sets in $\mathcal{S}$ to be connected leads to the following definition.

Definition A graph is a subtree graph iff it is the intersection graph of subtrees in a tree. (a tree or a subtree is thought to be connected.)

Related to the Gaussian elimination pivot ordering of symmetric matrices, chordal graphs are known.

Fig.6

<u>Definition</u> A graph is a chordal graph iff every cycle with more than 3 edges has a chord.

In [9], it is proved that the above two classes of graphs coincide with each other.

<u>Theorem 6</u> A graph is a subtree graph iff it is a chordal graph [9].

Any subtree graph has a, so called, rooted tree model as follows.

<u>Definition</u> A model $M=(S,\mathcal{S})$ for a subtree graph is a rooted tree model if

i) the underlying tree S has a root on the left and stretches to the right, i.e., any branch point of the tree S has only one edge incident from the left

ii) the function $x(v)$ is one to one where $x(v)$ is defined as follows. Let $l(v)$ be the point on the tree S which is the leftmost point of the subtree corresponding to vertex v. ($l(v)$ is well defined because of the property of tree S). $x(v)$ is defined as the x-coordinate of $l(v)$.

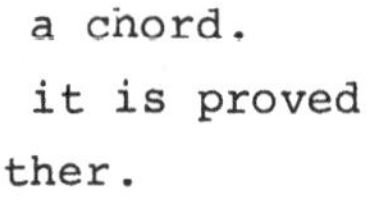

Fig.7

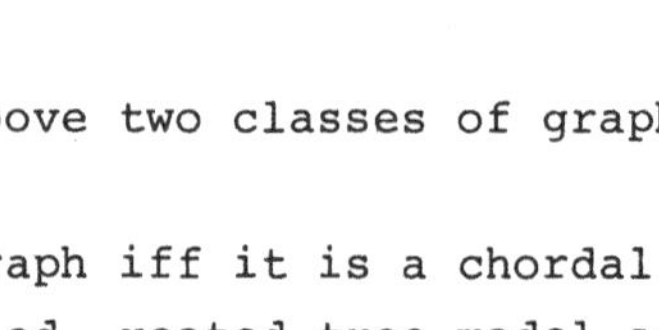

Fig.8

Rooted tree models are not restrictive.

<u>Lemma</u> Let G be any subtree graph and v_1 be any vertex of G. G has a rooted tree model for which $x(v_1)$ is the smallest value among $\{x(v)\}_{v\in V}$.

There is a recognition algorithm for chordal graphs which is based on LBFS [10]. It can be interpreted on the above mentioned intersection models as follows. First, a chordal order can be defined on a rooted tree model.

<u>Definition</u> $v_n, v_{n-1}, \ldots, v_1$ is a chordal order if, for any i $(1\leq i\leq n)$, v_i is a simplicial vertex for the section graph $G(\{v_{i-1},\ldots,v_1\})$, that is, any distinct vertices u,v in $\{w\in V \; ; \; w\in Adj(v_i)\cap\{v_{i-1},\ldots,v_1\}\}$ are connected by an edge.

<u>Theorem 7</u> $v_n, v_{n-1},\ldots,v_1$ is a chordal order of vertices iff $x(v_n)>$

$x(v_{n-1})>\ldots>x(v_1)$ for some rooted tree model.
This is because subtrees corresponding to u and v must pass the point $l(v_i)$ in the corresponding rooted tree model. (see Fig.9)

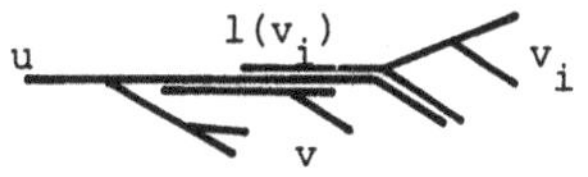

Fig.9

A recognition algorithm for subtree graphs can be divised which tries to construct rooted tree models from the left to the right, in particular, left to right order of l(v) points. Any vertex, say v_1, can be put at the leftmost position on the tree S. The detail of the form of the subtree v_1 and tree S is not determined at this stage. Only the point $l(v_1)$ is fixed. Consider three vertices u,v,w such that u,v, $w \in Adj(v_1)$, $(u,v) \notin E$, $(u,w) \in E$ and $(u,w) \in E$.

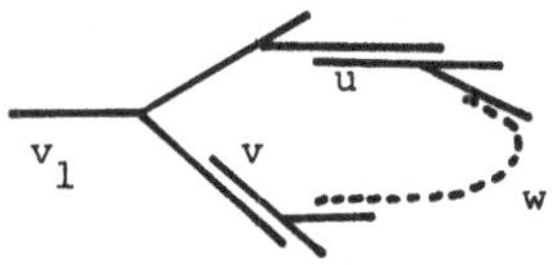

Fig.10

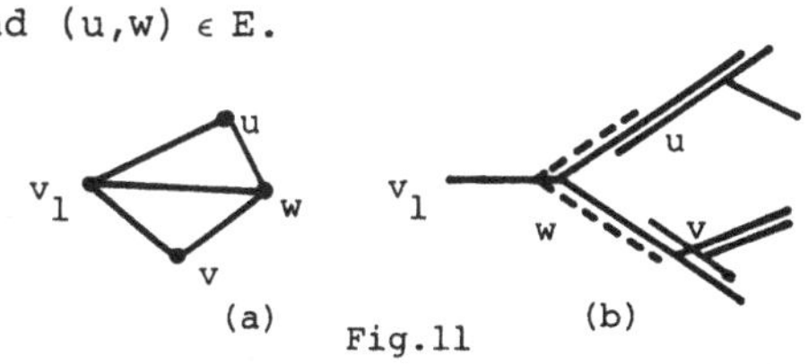

Fig.11

If $(w,v_1)\notin E$, then there exists no intersection model for such a graph and the construction of a model stops. Now assume $(w,v_1)\in E$. Suppose w is to be located on the tree after putting u and v. Then x(w) must be smaller than x(u) or x(v). Thus putting v_1,u,v,w in such a sequence destroyes left-to-right-rule. This suggests putting vertices in lexicographic breadth first order. Actually, the following theorem is given which is an intersection model interpretation of LBFS recognition algorithm for chordal graphs [10].

<u>Theorem 8</u> A rooted tree model for a subtree graph can be constructed by any LBFS sequencing.

LBFS on a graph can be performed in linear time, so the recognition algorithm for chordal graphs [10].

For subtree graphs, the number of dominant cliques is not greater than the number of vertices. This can be used in recognition algorithms for interval graphs and path graphs in the following sections, though it is immaterial for subtree graph recognition.

Unlike the case for circular-arc graphs, the determination of chromatic number of a chordal graph can be performed in polynomial time [11].

5. Path graphs and graph realization problem

Definition A path graph is an intersection graph of simple paths in a tree.

The class of path graphs is a subclass of subtree graphs, and is a superclass of interval graphs.

The above inclusion is strict as is seen from Fig. 12.

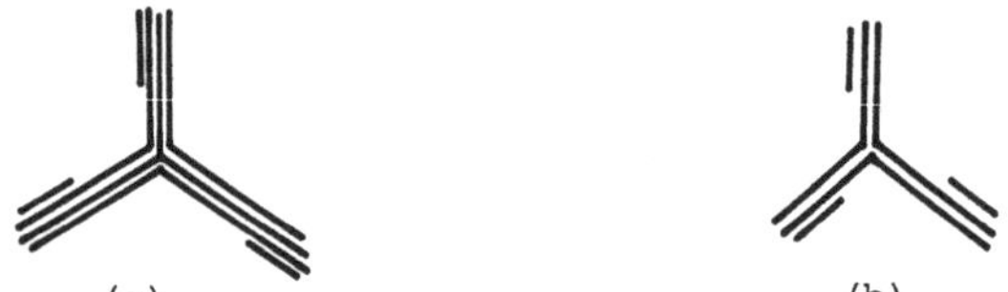

(a) (b)

Fig.12

No fast recognition algorithm for path graphs seems to be reported.

A path graph is a subtree graph and so the set of dominant cliques can be obtained in linear time. As in the case for interval graphs, recognition for path graphs can be reduced to a placement problem of dominant cliques.

Here a placement problem on a tree is defined.

Definition (Linear placement on a tree)

Given a set of n points $S=\{s_1,\ldots,s_n\}$ and a family $\mathcal{S}$ of subsets p_i of S $(i=1,\ldots,k)$, place $s_1,\ldots,s_n$ on an appropriate tree so that elements of every p_i appear consecutively on a path on the tree.

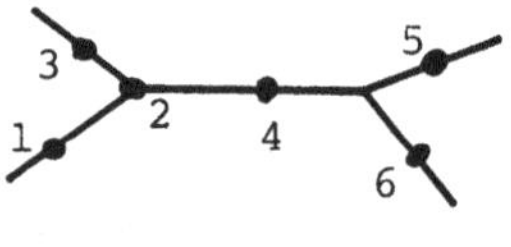

$S=\{1,2,3,4,5,6\}$
$p_1=\{1,2,4,5\}$
$p_2=\{1,2,3\}$
$p_3=\{2,3,4,6\}$
$p_4=\{5,6\}$

Fig.13

Now the recognition for path graphs can be stated using the above definition.

Theorem 9 A subtree graph G is a path graph iff there is a solution for linear placement on a tree problem for which S is the set of dominant cliques and p_i is the set of dominant cliques including vertex v_i, such that full branch point constraint is satisfied. Here full branch point constraint requires that every branch point of the tree has a point $s_j \in \mathcal{S}$.

The last constraint is needed because each S_i represents a dominant clique and $\{S_i\}$ is the set of all dominant cliques.

There is a similar placement problem in graph realization problem.

Definition (Graph realization problem)

Given a 0-1 matrix K, find a graph which has K as the principal part of the fundamental circuit matrix. In a fundamental circuit matrix [I:K], each row corresponds to a circuit, and each column to an edge.

This problem is equivalent to the next placement problem: Place columns of K on a tree so that for every row r, R(r) (the set of columns whose r-th row is 1) appears consecutively on a simple path on the tree. Every branch point must not have a column.

The last constraint is due to the fact that every column represents an edge. (see Fig.14)

$$\begin{array}{cccc} 1 & 2 & 3 & 4 \end{array}$$
$$\begin{bmatrix} 1 & 1 & 0 & 0 \\ 0 & 1 & 0 & 1 \\ 0 & 1 & 1 & 1 \end{bmatrix}$$

(a)

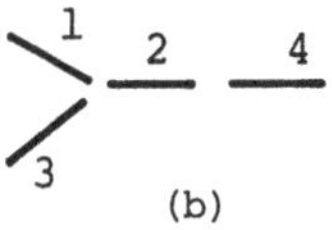

(b)

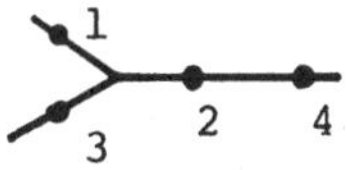

(c)

Fig.14

So to say, graph realization problem is a linear placement on a tree problem under empty branch point constraint.

Thus, path graph recognition and graph realization problem are different only in the constraints on the branch points.

Though there seems no simple reduction between these two problems, the algorithm for graph realization problem in [15][16] seems to be efficiently used for path graph recognition.

In section 4, it is shown that a graph is a subtree graph iff it has no chordless cycle (with more than 3 edges). This is a kind of forbidden graph formulation of graphs. Such a formulation will be given for interval graphs in the following section.

Graph realization problem is known to have such a kind of formulation. However, it seems that no forbidden graph formulation has been given for path graphs.

6. Interval graphs

An interval graph is a subtree graph which has a intersection model whose underlying tree is a line. (i.e. without branch point)

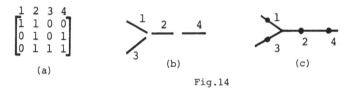

Fig.15

As in subtree graphs, $l(v)$ and $x(v)$ of the model define an ordering of vertices [12]. Using such an ordering, a recognition algorithm for interval graphs can be made [12][13], though no linear time algorithm has been obtained in this direction yet.

Linear time test for interval graphs now available runs in two steps [14]:

1 Perform chordal graph test and obtain a vertex vs. dominant clique matrix.

2 Test the matrix obtained above for consecutive ones property using PQ tree algorithms.

Step 1 can be performed using LBFS and step 2 can be performed in linear time using a sophisticated data structure called PQ trees.

Next is a structure theorem for interval graphs [22].

Definition Three vertices a_1, a_2, a_3, of a graph is called an asteroidal triple if there exist three paths w_1, w_2, w_3 such that for i=1,2,3, (i) w_i connects the two vertices a_j ($j \neq i$) (ii) a_i is not adjacent to any vertices in w_i.

Theorem 10 A graph is an interval graph iff it is chordal and has no asteroidal triple.

In [22], interval graphs are characterized by five kinds of forbidden graphs. No linear time recognition algorithm is given using such a structure yet.

7. Completion problems and isomorphism

Completion problem is to obtain a minimum number of edges to be added so that the augmented graph becomes to have a specified property. Completion problems are studied for several intersection graphs mentioned before.

Theorem 11 Completion problems for interval graphs and path graphs are NP-complete [6][19][20].

Whether other completion problems (for chordal graphs, for circular-arc graphs and for curves-in-the-plane graphs) are NP-complete remains unsolved.

For isomorphism test, the next results are known.

Theorem 12 Isomorphism test for general graphs, isomorphism test for chordal graphs and isomorphism test for path graphs are polynomially reducible to one another [6] [21].

Theorem 13 There is a polynomial time isomorphism test for interval graphs [21].

8. Relations among the classes

Several relations among the various classes are known.

Theorem 14

graphs $\supsetneqq$ curves-in-the-plane $\supsetneqq$ straight-lines-in-the-plane $\supsetneqq$ circle

$\cup\!\!\shortparallel$ (under curves-in-the-plane) $\qquad$ $\cup\!\!\shortparallel$ (under straight-lines-in-the-plane)

circular-arc $\supsetneqq$ Interval

subtree(chordal) $\supsetneqq$ path $\supsetneqq$ Interval

Some explanation would be necessary. In the definition of curves-in-the-plane graphs, each curve has no self-intersecting point and two curves have only finite number of intersecting points. This seems different from the definition of other classes, for example a circular-arc model may have a circle as a subset and the number of intersecting points may be infinite.

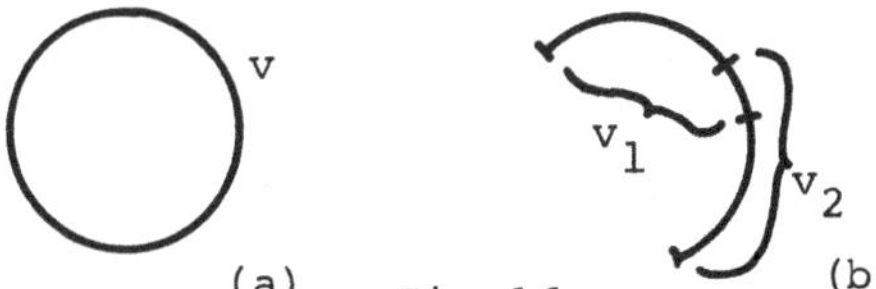

(a) Fig.16 (b)

However these differences are immaterial as is seen below. For a circle in circular-arc model, cutting at some appropriate point does not change the intersection graph. Then draw the model on the plane as in fig.17 (b) so that each arc does not intersect the others. (this is the usual illustration for circular-arc model, though the meaning is quite different). Now modify each circle to obtain necessary intersection by zigzagging sufficiently.

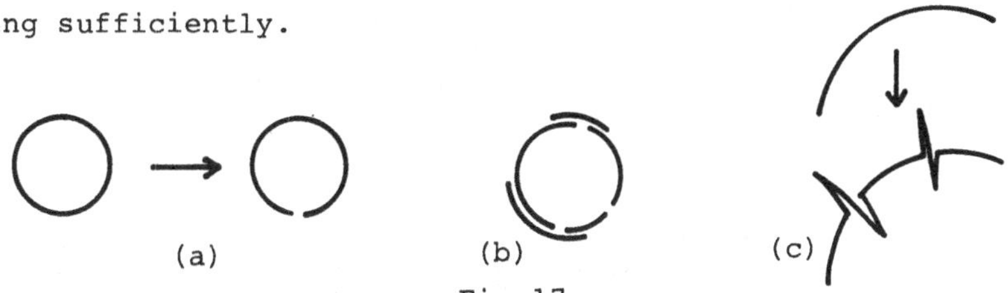

(a) (b) (c)

Fig.17

The same configuration applies to subtree graphs. In this case each subtree is transformed once to a fringing curve as in fig.18(b) (just as in [4]) and then modified to have zigzags to intersect necessary curves.

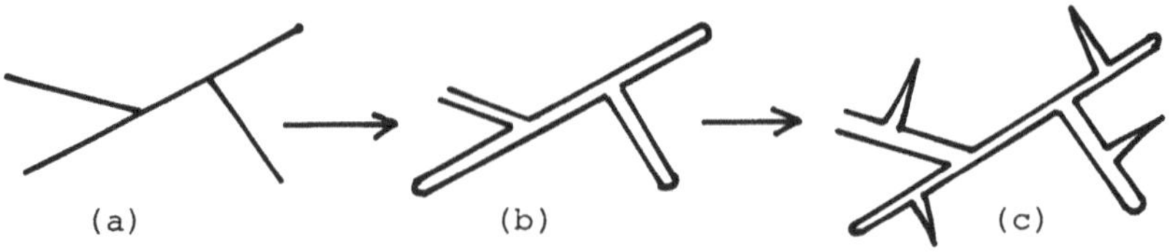

Fig.18

9. Conclusion

Fast recognition algorithms are known for several intersection graphs. However many completion problems are still open.

The author wishes to thank Professor T. Fujisawa for his helpful suggestion and encouragement.

References

[1] F. Harary, Graph theory, Addison-Wesley, Reading Massachusetts (1972).

[2] D.J. Rose, Triangulated graphs and the elimination process, J. Math. Anal. Appl., 32, 597-609 (1970).

[3] T. Ohtsuki, H. Mori, E.S. Kuh, T. Kashiwabara and T. Fujisawa, One-dimensional gate assignment and interval graphs, IEEE tran. on CAS Vol. CAS-26, No.9, 675-684 (1979).

[4] G. Ehrlich, S. Even and R.E. Tarjan, Intersection graphs of curves in the plane, J. Combinatorial theory (B), 21, 8-20 (1976).

[5] S. Even and A. Itai, Queues, stacks and graphs, Theory of machines and computations, Z. Kohavi and A. Paz, ed., Academic Press, New York, 71-86 (1971).

[6] M.R. Garey and D.S. Johnson, Computers and intractability: A guide to the theory of NP-completeness, H. Freeman and Sons, San Francisco (1978).

[7] F. Gavril, Algorithms for a maximum clique and a maximum independent set of a circle graph, Network, 3, 261-273 (1973).

[8] A. Tucker, An efficient test for circular-arc graphs, SIAM J. Comput., Vol.9, No.1, 1-24 (1980) .

[9] F. Gavril, The intersection graphs of subtrees in trees are exactly the chordal graphs, J. Combinatorial theory (B), 16, 47-56 (1974).

[10] D.J. Rose, R.E. Tarjan and G.S. Lueker, Algorithmic aspects of vertex elimination on graphs, SIAM J. Comput., Vol.5, No.2, 266-283 (1976).

[11] F. Gavril, Algorithms for minimum coloring, maximum clique, minimum covering by cliques and maximum independent set of a chordal graph, SIAM J. Comput., 1, 180-187 (1972).

[12] T. Oyamada and T. Ohtsuki, Interval graphs and layout design of MOS arrays, IECE technical report CST75-83 (1975) (in Japanese).

[13] T. Yoshida, An algorithm for obtaining a perfect order of an interval graph, monograph, Osaka University (1976) (in Japanese).

[14] K.S. Booth and G.S. Lueker, Testing for the consecutive ones property,

interval graphs and graph planarity using PQ-tree algorithms J.Computer and System Sciences, 13, 335-379 (1976).

[15] S. Fujishige, An efficient algorithm for solving the graph-realization problem by means of PQ-trees, Proceedings of 1979 ISCAS, IEEE catalog No.79 CH 1421-7 CAS. 1012-1015 (1979).

[16] S. Fujishige, An efficient algorithm for solving the graph-realization problem, IECE technical report CST78-136 (1979) (in Japanese).

[17] A. Lempel, S. Even and I. Cederbaum, An algorithm for planarity testing of graphs, in "Theory of graphs: international Symposium: Rome, July, 1966" (P. Rosenstiehl, Ed.), 215-232, Gordon and Breach, New York (1967).

[18] K.S. Booth, PQ-tree algorithms, Ph.D. Dissertation, Department of Electrical Engineering and Computer Sciences, University of California Berkeley, California (1975).

[19] T. Kashiwabara and T. Fujisawa, An NP-complete problem on interval graph, Proceedings of 1979 ISCAS, 82-83 (1979).

[20] T. Kashiwabara, Y. Masaki and T. Fujisawa, Complexity of intervalization of graphs, IECE technical report CST77-15 (1977) (in Japanese).

[21] G.S. Lueker, Efficient algorithms for chordal graphs and interval graphs, Ph.D. Dissertation, Program in Applied Mathematics and the Department of Electrical Engineering, Princeton University, Princeton N.J., (1975).

[22] C.G. Lekkerkerker and J.Ch. Boland, Representation of a finite graph by a set of intervals on the real line, Fundamenta Mathematicae, 51, 45-64 (1962).

AN EFFICIENT ALGORITHM TO FIND A HAMILTONIAN CIRCUIT IN A 4-CONNECTED MAXIMAL PLANAR GRAPH

T. ASANO
Department of Mathematical Engineering and Instrumentation Physics
Faculty of Engineering, University of Tokyo
Bunkyo-ku, Tokyo, Japan 113

S. KIKUCHI and N. SAITO
Department of Electrical Communications
Faculty of Engineering, Tohoku University,
Sendai, Japan 980

Abstract. This paper describes an efficient algorithm to find a Hamiltonian circuit in an arbitrary 4-connected maximal planar graph. The algorithm is based on our simlplified version of Whitney's proof of his theorem: every 4-connected maximal planar graph has a Hamiltonian circuit.

1. Introduction

The Hamiltonian circuit problem is one of the most popular NP-complete problems, and remains NP-complete even if we restrict ourselves to a class of (3-connected cubic) planar graphs [4,8]. Therefore, there seems to be no polynomial-time algorithm for the Hamiltonian circuit problem. However, for (nontrivial) certain classes of restricted graphs, there exist polynomial-time algorithms [2,3,5]. In fact, employing the proof technique used by Tutte [9], Gouyou-Beauchamps has given an $O(n^3)$ time algorithm for finding a Hamiltonian circuit in a 4-connected planar graph G, where n is the number of vertices of G [5]. Although such a graph G always has a Hamiltonian circuit [9], it is not an easy matter to find actually a Hamiltonian circuit of G. However, for a little more restricted class of graphs, i.e., the class of 4-connected maximal planar graphs, there may be an efficient algorithm. One can easily design an $O(n^2)$ time algorithm to find a Hamiltonian circuit in a 4-connected maximal planar graph G with n vertices, entirely based on Whitney's proof of his theorem [10].

In this paper, we present an efficient algorithm for the problem, based on our simplified version of Whitney's proof of his result. We employ "divide and conqure" and some more techniques in the algorithm. The computational complexity of our algorithm is linear, so optimal within a constant factor.

2. Preliminaries.

We first give some of the graph theoretic concepts needed to understand our algorithm. We use definitions similar to those found in any text on graph theory, e.g.,[6]. A graph $G=(V,E)$ consists of a set V of vertices and a set E of edges. Throughout this paper, n and m denote the number of vertices and edges of G, i.e., $n=|V|$ and $m=|E|$. Each edge is an unordered pair (v,w) of distinct vertices. If (v,w) is an edge, v and w are adjacent and (v,w) is incident to both v and w. A walk of length k with endvertices v, w is a sequence $v=v_0,v_1,v_2,\dots,v_k=w$ such that (v_{i-1},v_i) is an edge for $1 \leqq i \leqq k$. If all the vertices $v_0,v_1,v_2,\dots,v_{k-1}$ are distinct, the walk is a path. If $v=w$ the path is a circuit. A path is sometimes referred as the vertex set. A circuit of length two (or three) is called a 2-circuit (or triangle). A path $v_i,v_{i+1},\dots,v_j$ in the circuit $R=v_0,v_1,v_2,\dots,v_{k-1}v_0$ is called an arc of R, and denoted by $R[v_i,v_j]$ or $R(v_{i-1},v_{j+1})$. A chord of a circuit $R=v_0,v_1,v_2,\dots,v_{k-1}v_0$ is an edge (v_i,v_j) of G such that $|i-j| \neq 1 \pmod k$, that is, an edge joining nonconsecutive vertices v_i and v_j on R. A Hamiltonian circuit (path) of a graph G is a circuit (path) containing all vertices of G. A graph $G_1=(V_1,E_1)$ is a subgraph of a graph $G=(V,E)$ if $V_1 \subseteq V$ and $E_1 \subseteq E$. If $E_1=E \cap \{(v,w) \mid v,w \in V_1\}$, G_1 is an induced subgraph of G. The induced subgraph G_1 is obtained from G by removing vertices in $V-V_1$, and denoted by $G_1=G-(V-V_1)$. A graph G is connected if any two vertices of G are joined by a path. The connected components of a graph G are its maximal connected subgraphs. A cutvertex of a graph is a vertex whose removal increases the number of connected components. A graph G is $(k+1)$-connected if the removal of any k or fewer vertices of G results in a connected graph. The blocks of a graph are its maximal 2-connected subgraphs. A graph is planar if it can be embedded in the plane so that its edges intersect only at their endvertices. A plane graph is a planar graph which is embedded in the plane. A plane graph divides the plane into connected regions called faces. The unbounded region is called the exterior face, and all the others are called interior faces. Each face of a 2-connected plane graph G is bounded by a curve corresponding to a circuit of G, called boundary of the face. We shall sometimes not distinguish between a face and a boundary. A maximal planar graph is a planar graph to which no edge can be added without losing planarity. Note that every face of a maximal planar graph G with $n(\geqq 3)$ vertices is a triangle. A triangle of a plane graph G is said to be a separating triangle if it is not a face of G. Refer to [1,6] for all undefined terms.

Next, introducing Whitney's condition, we describe Whitney's lemma used to establish his theorem.

Let $G=(V,E)$ be a 2-connected plane graph with the exterior face R. Let A and B be two distinct vertices on R. If these G, R, A and B together satisfy the following conditions (W1) and (W2) (called Whiteney's condition, or for short Condition (W)), then we say that (G,R,A,B) satisfies Condition (W):

(W1) All interior faces of G are triangles, and all triangles are faces of G;

(W2) Either

(W2a) R is divided into two arcs $R_1 = R[A,B] = a_0 a_1 \dots a_r$ and $R_2 = R[B,A] = b_0 b_1 \dots b_s$

($a_0 = b_s = A$, $a_r = b_0 = B$), and there are no chords of R joining two vertices on R_i ($1 \leq i \leq 2$), or

(W2b) R is divided into three arcs $R_1 = R[A,B] = a_0 a_1 \ldots a_r$, $R_2 = R[B,C] = b_0 b_1 \ldots b_s$ and $R_3 = R[C,A] = c_0 c_1 \ldots c_t$ for some vertex C on R(B,A) ($a_0 = c_t = A$, $a_r = b_0 = B$, $b_s = c_0 = C$), and there are no chords of R joining two vertices on R_i ($1 \leq i \leq 3$).

We sometimes say "G satisfies Condition (W)" instead of "(G,R,A,B) satisfies Condition (W)" if there is no confusion. It should be noted that the exterior face of K_2 (the complete graph of two vertices) is a circuit of length two under our definition although it is not a circuit under Whitney's definition. Thus K_2 satisfies Condition (W), since K_2 has no interior faces. This observation can greatly simplify the proof of the following Whiteney's lemma, from which his theorem immediately follows.

Lemma 1. [10] Let G be a 2-connected plane graph with the exterior face R, and let A and B be two distinct vertices of R. If (G,R,A,B) satisfies Condition (W), then G has a Hamiltonian path connecting A and B.

Based on the proof of Whitney's lemma, one can easily design an $O(n^2)$ algorithm for finding a Hamiltonian circuit in a 4-connected maximal planar graph G with n vertices. In order to design a linear algorithm, we now introduce Condition (X), which is the same as Condition (W) except for Condition (W2b) above being replaced with the following Condition (X3):

(X3) R is divided into three arcs $R_1 = R[A,B] = a_0 a_1 \ldots a_r$, $R_2 = R[B,C] = b_0 b_1 \ldots b_s$ and $R_3 = R[C,A] = c_0 c_1 \ldots c_t$ for some vertex C on R(B,A) ($a_0 = c_t = A$, $a_r = b_0 = B$, $b_s = c_0 = C$), and there are no chords of R joining two vertices on R_i ($1 \leq i \leq 3$). Moreover, there exists either chord (b_{s-1}, c_k) or (c_1, b_j).

Remark 1. Whenever (G,R,A,B) satisfies Condition (W), we can choose some vertex as C so that G may satisfy Condition (X) (sometimes C may disappear) by scanning vertices on R_3 from C to A or vertices on R_2 from C to B. If (G,R,A,B) satisfies Condition (X), then it clearly satisfies Condition (W) and no chord of R joins C and other vertex (see Fig. 1).

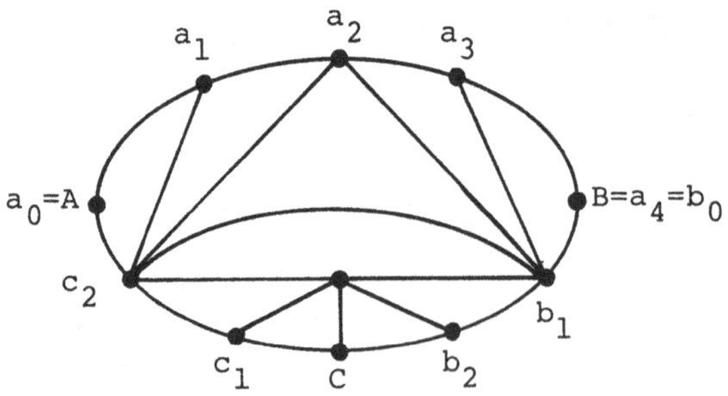

Fig. 1. A plane graph G satisfying Condition (W). If one take c_1 or b_2 as C, then G satisfies Condition (X), since there is a chord (c_2, b_1).

We now obtain the following lemma.

Lemma 2. Let G be a 2-connected plane graph with the exterior face R, and let A and B be two distinct vertices of R. If (G,R,A,B) satisfies Condition (X), then G has a Hamiltonian path connecting A and B.

3. An outline of the algorithm.

This section sketches the idea behind our algorithm. We first apply the linear planar embedding algorithm [7] in order to embed a given planar graph in the plane. Thus we can assume that a 4-connected maximal plane graph G=(V,E) with the exterior face R=1,2,3,1 is given, where 1, 2 and 3 are vertices of G. Clearly (G,R,1,2) satisfies Condition (X), so that G has a Hamiltonian path connecting vertices 1 and 2 by Lemma 2. Thus we can easily obtain a Hamiltonian circuit by combining the Hamiltonian path and edge (1,2). So we may consider only the algorithm to find a Hamiltonian path connecting A and B for a graph G such that (G,R,A,B) satisfies Condition (X). We add one more definition.

Let G be a 2-connected plane graph such that (G,R,A,B) satisfies Condition (X). If a subgraph G' of G satisfies the following conditions (A1)-(A5), then we say that G' satisfies Condition (A):

(A1) G' is a connected spanning subgraph of G;

(A2) G' consists of g blocks G_1, G_2, ..., G_g $(g \geq 2)$ with $(g-1)$ cutvertices x_1, x_2, ..., x_{g-1}, where each x_f $(1 \leq f \leq g-1)$ belongs to exactly two blocks G_f and G_{f+1};

(A3) Neither A nor B is a cutvertex of G';

(A4) A is a vertex of G_1 and B is a vertex of G_g; and

(A5) Let x_0=A and x_g=B, and let Q_f $(1 \leq f \leq g)$ be the exterior face of the plane subgraph G_f of G. Then each (G_f, Q_f, x_f, x_{f-1}) $(1 \leq f \leq g)$ satisfies Condition (W) (see Fig. 2).

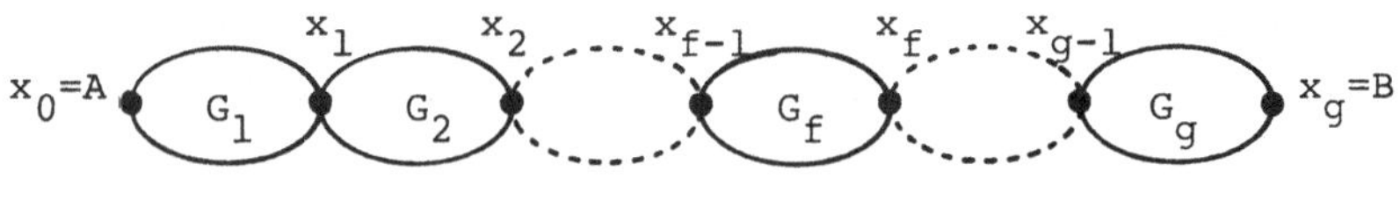

Fig. 2. Graph G' satisfying Condition (A), where each block G_f $(1 \leq f \leq g)$ satisfies Condition (W).

Our Hamiltonian path algorithm now can be outlined as follows:

First delete one or more edges from G so that the resulting graph G' satisfies Condition (A);

next for each G_f $(1 \leqq f \leqq g)$ choose C appropriately so that (G_f, Q_f, x_f, x_{f-1}) may satisfy Condition (X); then obtain a Hamiltonian path $H(G_f, x_f, x_{f-1})$ connecting x_f and x_{f-1} by recursively applying the algorithm for each G_f $(1 \leqq f \leqq g)$; and finally obtain a Hamiltonian path H(G, A, B) by combining all $H(G_f, x_f, x_{f-1})$'s. In Fig. 3 below is an outline of the algorithm written by Pidgin ALGOL [1].

```
procedure HPATH(G,R,A,B):
  begin comment an outline of the algorithm to find a Hamiltonian path in G=(V,E) connecting
  A and B such that (G,R,A,B) satisfies Condition (X). The set of edges marked by the
  procedure is a Hamiltonian path of G connecting A and B;
1 if |V|=2 then (A,B) is a Hamiltonian path of G connecting A and B, so mark (A,B)
  else begin
2      delete appropriate edges from G so that the resulting graph G' satisfies Condition (A);
3      for each block Gf of G' do
          begin comment (Gf,Q̄f,xf,xf-1) satisfies Condition (W);
4         choose C appropriately so that (Gf,Qf,xf,xf-1) may satisfy Condition (X);
5         HPATH(Gf,Qf,xf,xf-1)
          end
       end
  end;
```

Fig. 3 An outline of the algorithm.

Remark 2. We can always execute line 2 because (G,R,A,B) satisfies Condition (X) (we present in Section 4 a method to determine which edges are to be deleted). Noting Remark 1 we can always execute lines 3-5. Thus it is easy to show, by induction on the number of edges of G, that the algorithm correctly finds a Hamiltonian path of G, because G' satisfies Condition (A).

In order to make it easy to analize the time complexity of the procedure HPATH, we define an execution tree.

An execution tree TR(G,R,A,B) for the procedure HPATH(G,R,A,B) is recursively defined as follows:

(i) TR(G,R,A,B) is a rooted tree whose root is (G,R,A,B);

(ii) If $|V| = 2$ then (G, R, A, B) has no sons. Otherwise the (G_f, R_f, x_f, x_{f-1}) is the fth left son of (G,R,A,B) and is the root of the execution tree $TR(G_f, R_f, x_f, x_{f-1})$, where G_f is the fth block of G' obtained from G by the execution of line 2.

Let V(G) denote the vertex set of a graph G. Let EX(G,R,A,B) denote the set of vertices of G which newly appear on the exterior face of G'. Let CV(G,R,A,B) denote the set of vertices of G which newly become cutvertices of G'. Let (F, R_F, A_F, B_F) and (H, R_H, A_H, B_H) be two distinct vertices of the execution tree TR(G,R,A,B). It is clear that if (H, R_H, A_H, B_H) is neither a descendant nor an ancestor of (F, R_F, A_F, B_F) in TR(G, R, A, B), then $V(F) \cap V(H) = \emptyset$. Since G' satisfies Condition (A) we can observe the following fact.

Remark 3. Let (H, R_H, A_H, B_H) be a descendant of (F, R_F, A_F, B_F) in

TR(G,R,A,B), and let x be a vertex of both F and H. Then

(R1) If x is on the exterior face R_F of F then x is on the exterior face R_H of H;

(R2) If x is a cutvertex of F' (F' is the graph satisfying Condition (A), which is obtained from F by the execution of line 2 in HPATH(F, R_F, A_F, B_F)), then x is one of endvertices of the Hamiltonian path of H, that is, $x=A_H$ or $x=B_H$;

(R3) If x is an endvertex of the Hamiltonian path of F (that is, $x=A_F$ or $X=B_F$), then x is not a cutvertex of F' and $x=A_H$ or $x=B_F$.

By Remark 3 we have the following remarks.

Remark 4. Let (F, R_F, A_F, B_F) and (H, R_H, A_H, B_H) be two distinct vertices of the execution tree TR(G,R,A,B). Then

$EX(F,R_F,A_F,B_F) \cap EX(H,R_H,A_H,B_H)=\emptyset$, and

$CV(F,R_F,A_F,B_F) \cap CV(H,R_H,A_H,B_H)=\emptyset$.

Remark 5. Let T(G,R,A,B) denote the time spent by the HPATH(G,R,A,B) for the graph G=(V,E). Let T'(G,R,A,B) denote the time spent by the HPATH(G,R,A,B), exclusive of the time spent by its recursive calls. We claim

$$T'(G,R,A,B) \leqq K\Big(\sum_{v \in EX(G,R,A,B)} d(v) + \sum_{v \in CV(G,R,A,B)} d(v) \Big) \qquad (1)$$

for any (G,R,A,B) satisfying Condition (X), where K is constant and d(v) denotes the degree of vertex v of G. Noting Remark 4 and the fact that G is planar we obtain

$$T(G,R,A,B) \leqq K\Big(\sum_{v \in V} d(v) + \sum_{v \in V} d(v) \Big) \leqq 4K|E| \leqq 12K|V|.$$

Thus (1) implies that the algorithm is linear. We shall verify (1) in Section 5.

4. Proof of Lemma 2.

In this section we give the proof of Lemma 2 which is a simplified version of Whitney's proof of Lemma 1. Since the proof is constructive, we can easily design an algorithm based on the proof.

We proceed to prove Lemma 2 by induction on the number of edges of G=(V,E). Let $m=|E|$. The claim is obviously true if m=1 (that is, $G=K_2$). For the inductive step, we assume that the claim is true for all graphs with at most m−1 edges ($m \geqq 2$). We should show that the claim is true for any 2-connected plane graph with m edges.

Let G be a 2-connected plane graph with m edges. We consider the exterior face R of G as a sequence of vertices on R ordered in a clockwise sense, and denote three arcs of R by $R_1 = R[A,B] = a_0 a_1 \dots a_r$ ($a_0 = A$, $a_r = B$), $R_2 = R(B,C] = b_0 b_1 \dots b_s$ ($b_0 = B$, $b_s = C$), and $R_3 = R[C,A] = c_0 c_1 \dots c_t$ ($c_0 = C$, $c_t = A$). If (G,R,A,B) satisfies Condition (W2a), then R_3 is empty and R_2

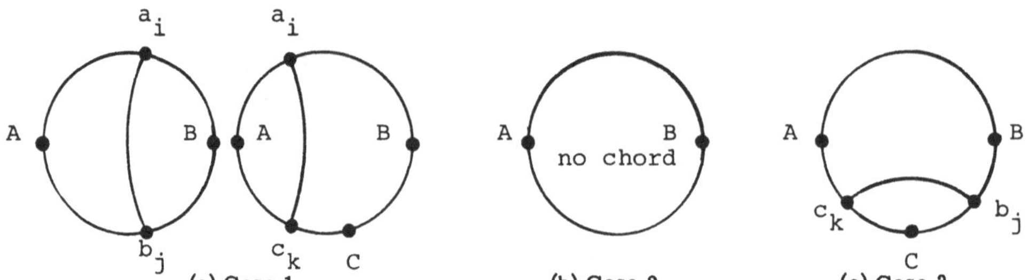

(a) Case 1 (b) Case 2 (c) Case 3

Fig. 4 Three cases in the proof.

=R[B,A], that is, b_s=A. Since (G,R,A,B) satisfies Condition (X), no chord of R joins two vertices on the same arc, and no chord joins vertex C (if any) and a vertex of R. We have three cases according to the types of the chords of R (see Fig. 4).

Case 1. R has a chord of form (a_i, b_j) $(0 \leq i \leq r-1,\ 1 \leq j \leq s-1)$ or (a_i, c_k) $(1 \leq i \leq r,\ 1 \leq k \leq t-1)$.

Case 2. R has no chords. (In this case G satisfies Condition (W2a).)

Case 3 (the remaining case). R has no chords of form (a_i, b_i) or (a_i, c_k), but has a chord of form (b_j, c_k) $(1 \leq j \leq s-1,\ 1 \leq k \leq t-1)$.

Note that vertex C of R disappears in Case 2 since (G,R,A,B) satisfies Condition (X). This is one of the reason why we introduce Condition (X). This fact together with technique finding a Q-chain (defined later) enables us to design a linear algorithm.

Case 1. We can assume without loss of generality that R has a chord of form (a_i, b_j). If R has a chord of form (a_i, c_k) it suffices to interchange the roles of A and B and of c_k and b_j. Suppose that (a_i, b_j) is the chord nearest B among all chords of this form, that is, the circuit $a_i a_{i+1} \ldots a_{r-1} B b_1 \ldots b_j a_i$ has no chord. Now either,

Case (1a), R has no chords other than (a_i, b_j) joining b_j and a vertex on R_1, or

Case (1b), otherwise, that is, R has a chord other than (a_i, b_j) joining b_j and a vertex on R_1. (See Fig. 5.)

We first consider Case (1a). Let $p_0, p_1, p_2, \ldots, p_u$ $(p_0 = a_{i+1},\ p_u = b_j)$ be a sequence of vertices adjacent to a_i such that each (a_i, p_k) is the immediately clockwise edge of (a_i, p_{k-1}) around a_i. Since (G,R,A,B) satisfies Condition (W1), all (p_k, p_{k+1}) $(0 \leq k \leq u-1)$ are edges of G, and there are no edges of form $(p_k, p_{k'})$ $(0 \leq k,\ k+2 \leq k' \leq u)$. Let

$$E_{DEL} = \{(a_i, p_k) \mid 0 \leq k \leq u-1\}.$$

Delete all edges in E_{DEL} from G, and let G' be the resulting graph, i.e., $G' = G - E_{DEL}$. Then G' consists of two blocks G_1 and G_2, one of which contains A and the other B. Both G_1 and G_2 have fewer edges than G. Moreover, let $Q_{11} = a_0 a_1 \ldots a_i b_j$, $Q_{12} = b_j b_{j+1} \ldots b_s$, $Q_{13} = R_3$, and $Q_1 = Q_{11} Q_{12} Q_{13}$, then (G_1, Q_1, A, b_j) satisfies Condition (X), where Q_{11}, Q_{12} and Q_{13} are three arcs (possibly Q_{13} is empty) concerned in this case. Similarly let $Q_{21} = b_0 b_1 \ldots b_j$, $Q_{22} = p_u p_{u-1} \ldots p_0$, $Q_{23} = a_{i+1} \ldots a_s$ (if $p_0 = a_r = B$ then Q_{23} is empty), and $Q_2 = Q_{21} Q_{22} Q_{23}$. Then (G_2, Q_2, B, b_j) satisfies Condition (W). Thus the resulting graph G' of G satisfies Condition (A). Noting Remark 1, we can choose a vertex as C appropriately so that (G_2, Q_2, B, b_j) satisfies Condition (X). By the inductive hypothesis G_1 has a

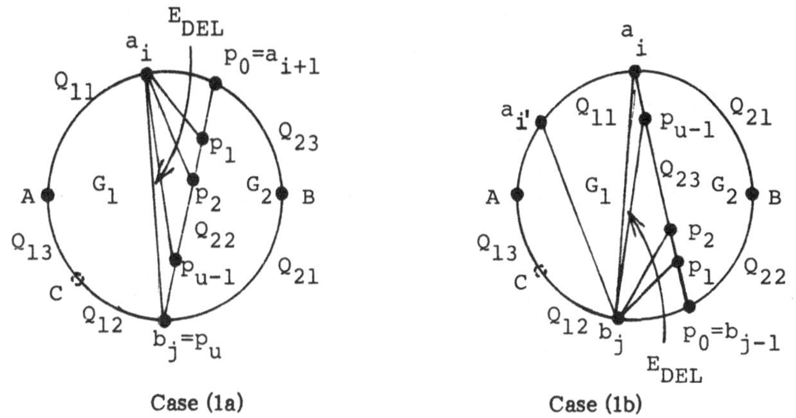

Fig. 5 Case 1, where (a_i,b_j) is the chord nearest B.

Hamiltonian path $H(G_1,A,b_j)$ connecting A and b_j and G_2 has a Hamiltonian path $H(G_2,B,b_j)$ connecting B and b_j. Thus we obtain a Hamiltonian path H(G,A,B) of G connecting A and B by combining $H(G_1,A,b_j)$ and $H(G_2,B,b_j)$.

Next consider Case (1b). In this case let $p_0,p_1,p_2,\ldots,p_u$ $(p_0=b_{j-1},$ $p_u=a_i)$ be a sequence of vertices adjacent to b_j such that each (b_j,p_k) is the immediately counter-clockwise edge of (b_j,p_{k-1}) around b_j. We delete all edges in $E_{DEL}=\{(b_j,p_k)\mid 0\leq k\leq u-1\}$. An argument similar to one in Case (1a) shows that G has a Hamiltonian path H(G,A,B) connecting A and B (see Fig. 5).

Case 2. This case can be considered to be a special case of either Case (1a) with $a_i=A$ and $b_j=b_{s-1}$ or Case (1b) with $a_i=a_1$ and $b_j=b_1=A$ (see Fig. 6). An argument similar to one above works. Note that $G_1=K_2$ satisfies Condition (X).

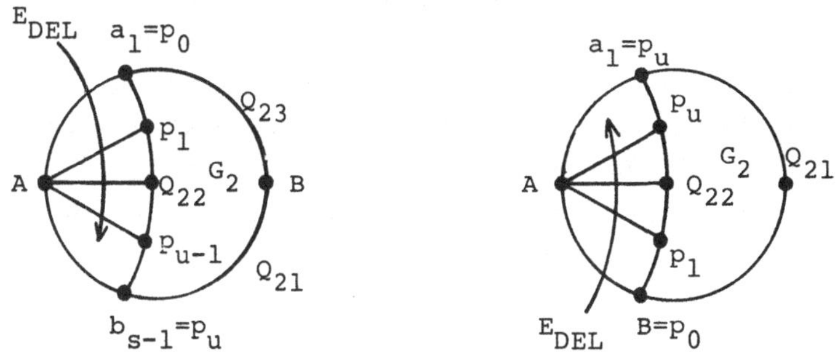

Fig. 6 Case 2.

Case 3. Suppose that (b_j,c_k) is the chord furthest from vertex C of R. Note that b_j is one of $b_1,\ldots,b_{s-1}$ and c_k is one of $c_1,\ldots,c_{t-1}$. Let $Q=q_0,q_1,q_2,\ldots,q_u$ $(q_0=b_j,$ $q_u=a_1)$ be a sequence of vertices which satisfies the following: Each (q_i,q_{i+1}) $(0\leq i\leq u-1)$ is the next edge of (q_i,q_{i-1}) in a couter-clockwise sense around q_i among all edges with an endvertex adjacent to a vertex on

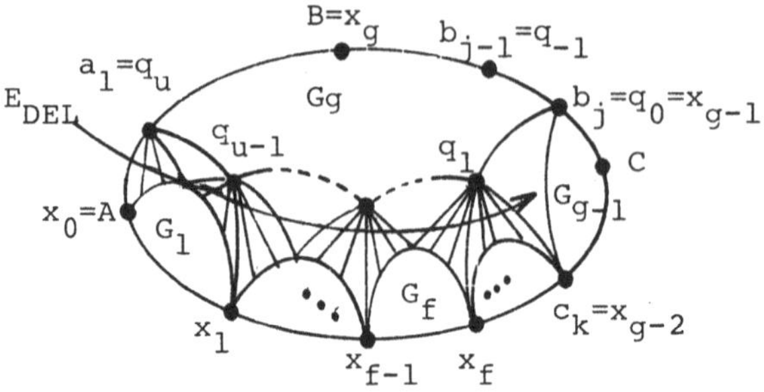

Fig. 7 Q-chain and G' satisfying Condition (A).

R_3, where $q_{-1}=b_{j-1}$. Such a sequence is called a Q-chain of R. The existence of the Q-chain is verified as follows. Since (b_j, c_k) is the chord furthest from C, and every interior face is triangle, there exists a vertex x inside the circuit $A a_1 \dots a_{r-1} B b_1 \dots b_j c_k \dots c_{t-1} A$ adjacent to both b_j and c_k. Thus q_1 always exists (possible $q_1=x$). If $q_1=a_1$ then $q_u=q_1$. Otherwise, let c_{k1} be the vertex furthest from C among all vertices on R_3 adjacent to q_1. Similarly we can easily show that q_2 exists, since there is a vertex inside the circuit $A a_1 \dots a_{r-1} B b_1 \dots b_j q_1 c_{k1} c_{k1+1} \dots c_{t-1} A$ adjacent to both q_1 and c_{k1}. Repeating this argument, we can prove that the Q-chain always exists since a_1 is adjacent to A. Note that any vertex of $q_1, \dots, q_{u-1}$ is not on R, and the circuit $D = q_u a_2 \dots a_{r-1} B b_1 \dots b_j q_1 \dots q_u$ has no chord of form $(q_i, q_{i'})$ $(0 \leqq i,\ i+2 \leqq i' \leqq u)$. Let $E_{OUT}(D)$ be the set of edges adjacent to $q_1, q_2, \dots,$ or q_u outside D, and let

$$E_{DEL} = E_{OUT}(D) \cup CL(q_0, c_k, q_1) \qquad (2)$$

where $CL(q_0, c_k, q_1)$ denotes the set of edges incident to q_0, from c_k to q_1 clockwisely. Let $G'=G-E_{DEL}$, then G' consists of $g(\geqq 3)$ blocks, and satisfies Condition (A) (see Fig. 7). Each block G_f of G' has at most m-1 edges. Noting Remark 1, we can choose a vertex as C of Q_f so that (G_f, Q_f, x_f, x_{f-1}) may satisfy Condition (X), where Q_f $(1 \leqq f \leqq g)$ is the exterior face of G_f and x_f $(1 \leqq f \leqq g-1)$ is the cutvertex of G' belonging to both G_f and G_{f+1} $(x_0=A,\ x_g=B)$. By the inducutive hypothesis, each G_f $(1 \leqq f \leqq g)$ has a Hamitonian path $H(G_f, x_f, x_{f-1})$ connecting x_f and x_{f-1}. Thus we obtain a Hamiltonian path H(G,A,B) of G connecting A and B by combining all $H(G_f, x_f, x_{f-1})$'s.

This completes the proof. Q.E.D.

5. The Hamiltonian path algorithm.

The proof of Lemma 2 leads to an algorithm for finding a Hamiltonian path in a graph satisfying Condition (X). To make the algorithm efficient, we need a good representation of a plane graph. (We assume that a given graph satisfying Condition (X) is already embedded in the plane by a linear planar embedding algorithm [8].) For this purpose we use a list structure whose elements correspond to the edges of the graph. Stored with each edge e=(x,y) are its endpoints x and y, and four pointers $c_1(e)$, $c_2(e)$, $cc_1(e)$ and $cc_2(e)$, designating the edges immediately clockwise and counter-clockwise around the endpoins of the edges. Stored with each vertex x are two edges c(x) and cc(x) incident to x which indicate the starting edge and the final edge of the adjacency list A(x), where c(x) is the immediately clockwise edge of cc(x) around x. Furthermore, we need a representaion of the exterior faces of blocks of a graph. For this purpose we use another list structure together with an array. Each exterior face R of a simple block G has pointers, designating A,B, and C of R, chords of R and so on. Pointers R(A), R(B) and R(C) represent current vertices A, B and C of the exterior face R. The set of chords of R are partitioned into three classes: the set D12 of chords of form (a_i, b_j); the set D13 of chords of form (a_i, c_k); and the set D23 of chords of form (b_j, c_k). The chords of D12 are arranged in nearest order to B. The chords of D13 and D23 are arranged in furthest order from C. R(D12) stores the chord of D12 nearest B. R(D13) and R(D23) store the

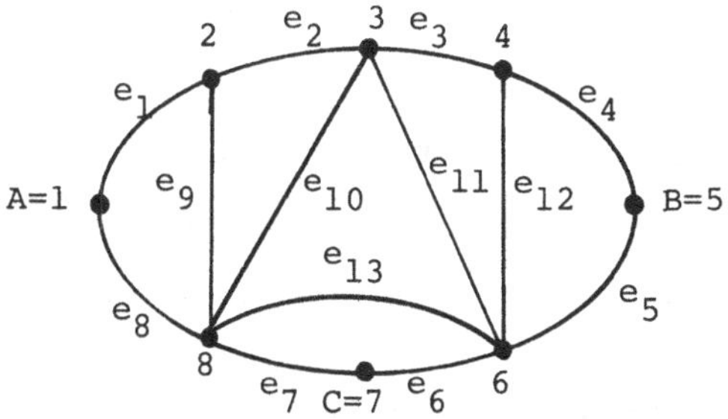

Vertex incidences

	c	cc
1	e_1	e_8
2	e_2	e_1
3	e_3	e_2
4	e_4	e_3
5	e_5	e_4
6	e_6	e_5
7	e_7	e_6
8	e_8	e_7

Edges, neighbors and next chords

	1	2	c_1	cc_1	c_2	cc_2	NEXT
e_1	1	2	e_8	e_8	e_2	e_9	0
e_2	2	3	e_9	e_1	e_3	e_{10}	0
e_3	3	4	e_{11}	e_2	e_4	e_{12}	0
e_4	4	5	e_{12}	e_3	e_5	e_5	0
e_5	5	6	e_4	e_4	e_6	e_{12}	0
e_6	6	7	e_{13}	e_5	e_7	e_7	0
e_7	7	8	e_6	e_6	e_8	e_{13}	0
e_8	8	1	e_9	e_7	e_1	e_1	0
e_9	2	8	e_1	e_2	e_{10}	e_8	e_{10}
e_{10}	3	8	e_2	e_{11}	e_{13}	e_9	0
e_{11}	3	6	e_{10}	e_3	e_{12}	e_{13}	0
e_{12}	4	6	e_3	e_4	e_5	e_{11}	e_{11}
e_{13}	6	8	e_{11}	e_6	e_7	e_{10}	0

Face R and its chords

	A	B	C	D12	D13	D23
R	1	5	7	e_{12}	e_9	e_{13}

Fig. 8 Rerpresentation of a plane graph (G,R,A,B) satisfying Condition (X).

chords of D13 and D23 furthest from C, respectively. Array NEXT(x) stores a next chord in the order above for each chord x of R. Thus the chord of D12 second nearest B is stored with NEXT(R(D12)), and so on. Stored with each vertex are flags, indicating whether or not the vertex is on R or whether or not it is adjacent to some vertex on R. Fig. 8 illustrates such a data structure. Moreover, we set $c(v_i)=(v_i,v_{i+1})$ and $cc(v_i)=(v_{i-1},v_i)$ for each vertex v_i on the exterior face $R=v_0 v_1 \dots v_{k-1} v_0$. Thus R is represented as follows: v_1 is an endvertex of $c(v_0)$ different from v_0; v_2 is an endvertex of $c(v_1)$ different from v_1; and v_0 is an endvertex of $c(v_{k-1})$ different from v_{k-1}. Adjacency list A(v) in a clockwise sense is reprensented as follows: the first vertex of A(v) is an endvertex of c(v) different from v; the second vertex of A(v) is an endvertex of immediately clockwise edge of c(v) around v different from v; and the last vertex of A(v) is an endvertex of cc(v) different from v. Counter-clockwise adjacency list is similarly obtained. Thus we can consider that our data structure contains adjacency lists.

Now we are ready to present the algorithm. In Fig. 9 below is the algorithm to find a Hamiltonian path in a 2-connected plane graph G such that (G,R,A,B) satisfies Condition (X).

procedure HPATH(G,R,A,B):
    begin comment G=(V,E) is a plane graph with the exterior face R satisfying Condition (X).
    Let $R=R_1R_2R_3$, $R_1=a_0,a_1,\dots,a_r$ $(a_0=A,\ a_r=B)$, $R_2=b_0,b_1,\dots,b_s$ $(b_0=B,\ b_s=C)$, and $R_3=c_0,c_1,\dots$
    $\dots,c_t$ $(c_0=C,\ c_t=A)$. If $G=K_2$ then R is a 2-circuit. R has no chords which join vertices on
    $R_i(i=1,2,3)$. If R_3 is not empty, then R has a chord joining either c_1 and some vertex
    on R_2 or b_{s-1} and some vertex on R_3. HPATH(G,R,A,B) finds a Hamiltonian path in
    G connecting A and B, whose edges are marked by HPATH;

```
1      if |V|= 2
2      then (A,B) is a Hamiltonian path of G from A to B so mark (A,B)
3      else if ( R has a chord of forms (aᵢ,bⱼ), or (aᵢ,cₖ) ) or ( R has no chord ) then
                  begin comment Case 1 or Case 2;
4                  if R has a chord of form (aᵢ,bⱼ), or (aᵢ,cₖ)
                   then begin comment Case 1;
5                          wlg we can assume that R has a chord of form (aᵢ,bⱼ) otherwise
                           interchange the roles of A and B and of bⱼ and cₖ in
                           begin
6                          let (aᵢ,bⱼ) be the edge nearest B among such edges;
7                          if R has a chord other than (aᵢ,bⱼ) joining bⱼ and a vertex on
                           R̄₁ then
                                  begin comment Case (1b). Q₁ and Q₂ correspond to the
                                  new exterior faces;
8                                 x:=bⱼ; y:=bⱼ₋₁; z:=aᵢ; CLOCK:=false; Q₂(A):=z; Q₂(B):=B
                                  end
                           else begin comment Case (1a);
9                                 x:=aᵢ; y:=aᵢ₊₁; z:=bⱼ; CLOCK:=true; Q₂(A):=B; Q₂(B):=z
                                  end
                           end
                   end
              else begin comment Case 2. R has no chord;
10                 if b₁ ≠ A then
                           begin
11                         x:=A; y:=a₁; z:=bₛ₋₁; CLOCK:=true; Q₂(A):=B; Q₂(B):=z
                           end
```

12	else begin comment b_1=A;
	x:=A; y:=B; z:=a_1; CLOCK:=false; Q_2(A):=z; Q_2(B):=B
	end
	end;

13	Q_1(A):=A; Q_1(B):=z; Q_1(C):=C;
14	if y=B then Q_2(C):=0 else Q_2(C):=y;
15	if CLOCK then E_{DEL}:=CL(x,y,z) else E_{DEL}:=CCL(x,y,z); comment E_{DEL}=CL(x,y,z) (E_{DEL}=CCL(x,y,z)) is the list of edges incident to x from (y,x) to (z,x) in a (counter-)clockwise sense, where (y,x) $\in E_{DEL}$ and (z,x) $\notin E_{DEL}$;
16	let G'=G-E_{DEL}; comment G' satisfies Condition (A). G' consists of two blocks G_1 and G_2 and z is the unique cutvertex of G';
17	split G' into G_1 A and G_2 B with respect to z;
18	for f:=1 to 2 do begin
19	let Q_f be the exterior faces of G_f;
20	choose Q_f(C) appropriately so that $(G_f,Q_f,Q_f(A),Q_f(B))$ may satisfy Condition (X);
21	HPATH($G_f,Q_f,Q_f(A),Q_f(B)$) end end else begin
	comment Case 3. There is a chord of form (b_j,c_k);
22	let (b_j,c_k) be furthest from C;
23	let Q=q_0,...,q_u (q_0=b_j, q_u=a_1) be the Q-chain of R from q_0 to q_u;
24	let E_{DEL} be the edge set defined in (2) in Section 4;
25	let G'=G-E_{DEL}; comment G' satisfies Condition (A);
26	let x_1, ... , x_{g-1} (x_{g-2}=c_k, x_{g-1}=b_j) be the sequence of cutvertices of G' on R_2 or R_3 from A to B;
27	let G_f be a block of G' containing x_{f-1} and x_f (x_0 = A, x_g = B);
28	for f=1 to g-2 do begin
29	Q_f(A):=x_f; Q_f(B):=x_{f-1};
30	if there is a vertex C_f in G_f adjacent to both q_i and q_{i+1} of the Q-chain in G then Q_f(C) = C_f else Q_f(C)=0;
31	split G_f from G' with respect to x_f; comment G':=G'-(V(G_f)-x_f);
32	let Q_f be the exterior face of G_f; comment $(G_f,Q_f,Q_f(A),Q_f(B))$ satisfies Condition (W);
33	choose Q_f(C) appropriately so that $(G_f,Q_f,Q_f(A),Q_f(B))$ may satisfy Condition (X);
34	HPATH($G_f,Q_f,Q_f(A),Q_f(B)$) end;
35	Q_{g-1}(A):=c_k; Q_{g-1}(B):=b_j; Q_{g-1}(C):=C; Q_g(A):=B; Q_g(B):=b_j;
36	if a_1=B then Q_g(C):=0 else Q_g(C):=a_1;
37	split G' into G_{g-1} and G_g with respect to b_j;
38	for f:=g-1 to g do begin
39	let Q_f be the exterior face of G_f; comment $(G_f,Q_f,Q_f(A),Q_f(B))$ satisfies Condition (W);
40	choose Q_f(C) appropriately so that $(G_f,Q_f,Q_f(A),Q_f(B))$ may satisfy Condition (X);
41	HPATH($G_f,Q_f,Q_f(A),Q_f(B)$) end end end;

Fig. 9 The algorithm for finding a Hamiltonian path.

We now verify the correctness and the time complexity of the algorithm.

Lemma 3. If (G,R,A,B) satisfies Condition (X), then HPATH correctly finds a Hamiltonian path connecting vertices A and B in G.

Proof. Note that HPATH finds an edge set E_{DEL} in G whose removal results in the graph G' satisfying Condition (A). Thus, the correctness of HPATH can be proved by the induction on the number of edges of a graph. Q.E.D.

Lemma 4. If (G,R,A,B) satisfies Condition (X), then HPATH requires O(|V|) time to find a Hamiltonian path connecting A and B in G=(V,E).

Proof. We show that the algorithm reqiures O(|V|) time with the data structure described above. We first establish (1). Let T(G,R,A,B) denote the time spent by the HPATH(G,R,A,B) for the graph G=(V,E). Let T'(G,R,A,B) denote the time spent by the HPATH(G,R,A,B), exclusive of the time spent by its recursive calls. Clearly lines 1-14, 22, and 35-36 require constant time. Let EX(G,R,A,B) denote the set of vertices of G which newly appear on the exterior face of G'. Let CV(G,R,A,B) denote the set of vertices of G which newly become cutvertices. Suppose Case 1 or 2 occurs. Since (x,y) =c(x) or cc(x) we can obtain G' in $O(|E_{DEL}|)$ time by scanning the adjacency list A(x) from c(x) or cc(x) successively. Thus lines 15-17 reqiures $O(|E_{DEL}|)$ time. Line 20 can be done by scanning adjacency lists A(v), where v's are the vertices newly appeared on the exterior face or the new cutvertices. Thus lines 19-20 requires

$$O\Big(\sum_{v\,\varepsilon\,EX(G,R,A,B)} d(v) + \sum_{v\,\varepsilon\,CV(G,R,A,B)} d(v)\Big)$$

time. Suppose next Case 3 occurs. Since $(q_{-1},q_0)=cc(q_0)$ we can find q_1 in $O(d(q_0))$ time by scanning adjacency list $A(q_0)$ in a counter-clockwise sense. Thus line 23 can be done in $O(\sum_{1\leqq i\leqq u-1} d(q_i))$ time, that is, we can obtain Q-chain in $O(\sum_{1\leqq i\leqq u-1} d(q_i))$. Similarly lines 24-27 require scanning adjacency lists $A(q_i)$ for $1\leqq i\leqq u-1$. Lines 33 and 40 can be done by scanning adjacency lists A(v), where v's are vertices newly appeared on the exterior face or the new cutvertices, that is, $v\,\varepsilon\,(EX(G_i,Q_i,Q_i(A),Q_i(B))-R)\cup\{Q_i(A),Q_i(B)\}$. Thus lines 29-33, 37 and 39-40 require

$$O\Big(\sum_{v\,\varepsilon\,EX(G,R,A,B)} d(v) + \sum_{v\,\varepsilon\,CV(G,R,A,B)} d(v)\Big)$$

time. Thus we obtain

$$T'(G,R,A,B) \leqq O\Big(\sum_{v\,\varepsilon\,EX(G,R,A,B)} d(v) + \sum_{v\,\varepsilon\,CV(G,R,A,B)} d(v)\Big)$$

for any (G,R,A,B) satisfying Condition (X). This implies (1). Noting Remarks 3-5 we have $T(G,R,A,B)\leqq O(|V|)$. Q.E.D.

Thus by Lemmas 3 and 4 we obtain the following theorems.

Thoerem 1. If G=(V,E) is 2-connected plane graph and (G,R,A,B) satisfies the condition(X), then HPATH finds a Hamiltonian path joining A and B in G in O(|V|) time.

Theorem 2. There exists a linear time algorithm for finding Hamiltonian circuits in 4-connected maximal planar graphs.

Acknowledgements.

We wish to thank Professor T. Nishizeki for valuable discussions and suggestions on this subjects. This research was supported by the Grant in Aid for Scientific Research of the Ministry of Education, Science and Culture of Japan under Grant: YSE(A) 575215 (1980).

References

[1] A. V. Aho, J. E. Hopcroft and J. D. Ullman, The Design and Analysis of Computer Algorithms, Addison-Wesley, Reading, Mass., 1974.

[2] R. E. Bixby and D. Wang, An algorithm for finding hamiltonian circuits in certain graphs, Mathematical Programming Study, 8(1978), pp. 35-49.

[3] J. A. Bondy and V. Chvátal, A method in graph theory, Discrete Math., 15(1976), pp. 111-135.

[4] M. R. Garey, D. S. Johnson and R. E. Tarjan, The planar Hamiltonian circuit problem is NP-complete, SIAM J. Comput., 5(1976), pp. 704-714.

[5] D. Gouyou-Beauchamps, Un algorithme de recherche de circuit Hamiltonien dans les graphes 4-connexes planaries, Colloques Internationaux CNRS, No. 260 - Problèms Combinatoires et Theorie des Graphes, ed, J.C. Bermond, J.C. Fournier, M. Las Vergnas and D. Scotteau, (1978), pp. 185-187.

[6] F. Harary, Graph Theory, Addison-Wesley, Reading, Mass., 1969.

[7] J. E. Hopcroft and R. E. Tarjan, Efficient planarity testing, J. Assoc. Comput. Mach., 21(1974), pp. 549-568.

[8] R. M. Karp, Reducibility among combinatorial problems, in: R. E. Miller and J. W. Thatcher, eds, Complexity of Computer Computations, Plenum Press, New York, (1972) pp. 85-104.

[9] W. T. Tutte, A theorem on planar graphs, Trans. Amer. Math. Soc., 82(1956), pp. 99-116.

[10] H. Whitney, A theorem on graphs, Annals Math., 32(1931), pp. 378-390.

CHARACTERIZATION OF POLYHEX GRAPHS AS APPLIED TO CHEMISTRY

H. Hosoya
Department of Chemistry, Ochanomizu University,
Bunkyo-ku, Tokyo, Japan 112

Abstract. A polyhex graph represents the carbon atom skeleton of a condensed polycyclic aromatic hydrocarbon, a family of benzene-like molecules. Various methods for characterizing the polyhex graphs are described and discussed, including the topological index, characteristic polynomial, sextet polynomial, etc. Enumeration of the number of the maximum matching (or Kekulé patterns) is also discussed.

1. Introduction

There have been known among the chemists a number of "condensed polycyclic aromatic hydrocarbons (CPCAH)" whose skeletal structures are represented by what the graph-theoreticians like to call as polyhexes or hexagonal animals.

Benzene, C_6H_6, which is the most fundamental molecule among them, is a regular hexagonal molecule and plays as their unit structure.

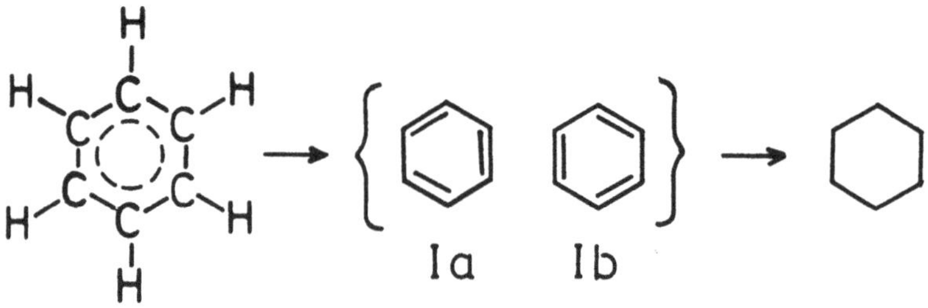

Ia Ib

benzene

Naphthanlene, $C_{10}H_8$, is known as a molecule in which two benzene rings are fused.

naphthalene

II

There are three possible structures for three regular hexagons to be fused into one connected graph as shown below:

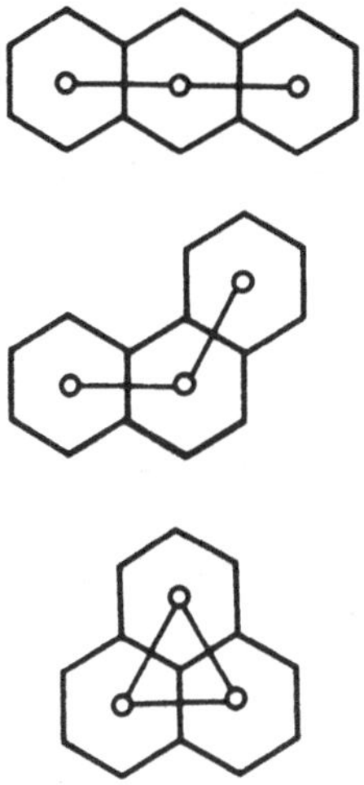

$C_{14}H_{10}$: anthracene III, phenanthrene IV — catahex

$C_{13}H_9$: ------------ V — perihex

Namely, there are three 3-hexagonal animals. However, no stable compound has ever been isolated or synthesized corresponding to the third entry (V), since it has an odd number of points (carbon atoms). Thus in chemical sense, only those polyhexes are called as isomers which have both the same numbers of hexagons and points. Anthracene (III) and phenanthrene (IV) are isomers each other, while compound (V) is not.

The number of isomeric polyhexes (either graph-theoretical or chemical) rapidly increases with the number of hexagons, whose enumeration has been partly accomplished by Harary and Read [1]. Polyhexes are classified into two groups, i.e., catahexes and perihexes, depending that the dual graph is a tree or a non-tree. Graphs I to IV are catahexes, while V is a perihex. Enumeration of the number of perihexes seems to be almost impossible [2].

Generally isomeric compounds have different properties and stabilities. For example, compound III is less stable than IV. The reason for the difference in the stabilities is attributed to the difference in their mathematical properties, mainly in the following two respects. i) The number of the maximum matching or the Kekulé numbers K(G)'s for III and IV are, respectively, 4 and 5 as shown in Fig. 1. ii) The sum of the positive roots of the characteristic polynomial

$$P_G(x) = (-1)^N \det(A - XE)$$

$$= \sum_{k=0}^{N} a_k x^{N-k} \tag{1}$$

is larger for IV than for III, which can be presumed from the absolute values of the determinant of the adjacency matrix A, or of the last term a_N of $P_G(x)$ as

$$P_{III}(x) = x^{14}-16x^{12}+98x^{10}-296x^8+473x^6-392x^4+148x^2-16$$

$$P_{IV}(x) = x^{14}-16x^{12}+98x^{10}-297x^8+479x^6-407x^4+166x^2-25.$$

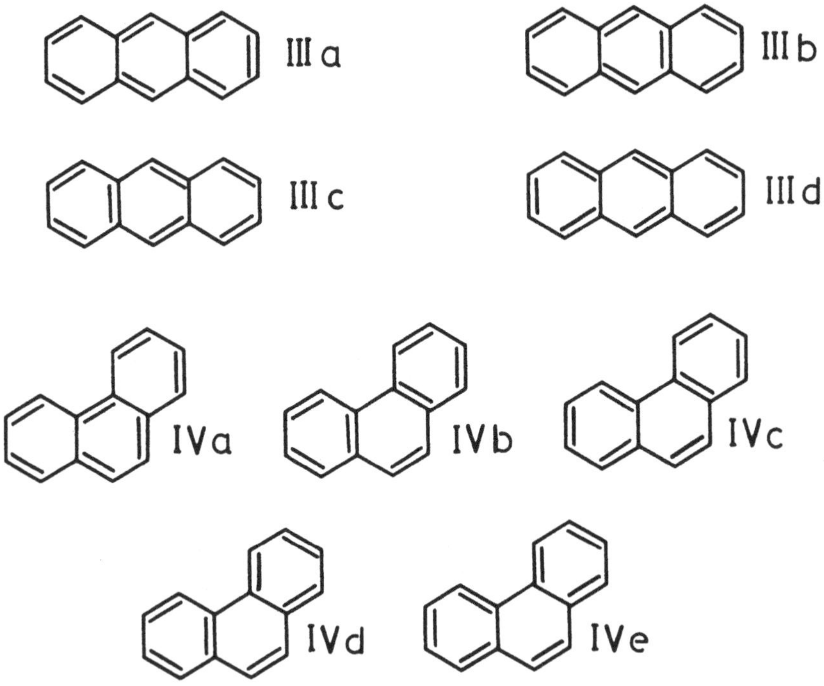

Fig. 1 Kekulé patterns.

Both of the above two facts are interrelated to each other through the following relation. Namely, for a polyhex with an even number (N=2m) of points we have [3]

$$a_N = (-1)^m \{K(G)\}^2. \tag{2}$$

Besides this relation there have been proposed a number of interesting methods for enumerating the value of K(G) for a given polyhex graph, on which we are going to discuss.

2. Topological Index [4,5]

For graph G the non-adjacent number p(G,k) is defined as the number of ways for choosing k disconnected lines, p(G,0) being defined as unity. The number of the maximum matching for G is p(G,m),

$$p(G,m) = K(G) \qquad (m = [N/2]). \tag{3}$$

From now on we are concerned with even polyhexes (N=2m). The Z-counting polynomial $Q_G(x)$ is defined as

$$Q_G(x) = \sum_{k=0}^{m} p(G,k)\, x^k. \tag{4}$$

The topological index Z_G is the sum of the p(G,k)'s, or

$$Z_G = \sum_{k=0}^{m} p(G,k) = Q_G(1). \tag{5}$$

The graph G-ℓ is defined as the subgraph obtained from G by deleting line ℓ, and the graph G⊖ℓ as the subgraph of G-ℓ obtained by deleting all the lines which were adjacent to ℓ in G (See Fig. 2).

Fig. 2 Subgraphs of G.

The inclusion-exclusion principle ensures the recursive relation for p(G,k) as

$$p(G,k) = p(G\text{-}\ell,k) + p(G\ominus\ell,k-1), \tag{6}$$

which gives

$$Q_G(x) = Q_{G-\ell}(x) + x\cdot Q_{G\ominus\ell}(x) \tag{7}$$

and

$$Z_G = Z_{G-\ell} + Z_{G\ominus\ell}(x). \tag{8}$$

A number of interesting methematical properties have been known for these quantities.

3. Characteristic Polynomial

Let the adjacency matrix A of graph G with N points be defined as the N×N square matrix with elements

$$A_{ij} = \begin{cases} 1 & \text{i and j are neighbors} \\ 0 & \text{otherwise,} \end{cases} \tag{9}$$

which gives the characteristic polynomial $P_G(x)$ as in Eq. (1).

The p(G,k) numbers and the sets of the coefficients of $P_G(x)$ for smaller tree [6] and non-tree [7] graphs, and polyhex graphs [8] are extensively tabulated.

4. Sextet Polynomial

Consider a Kekulé pattern as shown in Fig. 1 for a given polyhex. If a set of three circularly arranged double bonds are located on a certain hexagon as Ia, one can get another Kekulé pattern as Ib just by rotating them by 60 degrees. For example, IIIa and IIIb are related to each other as in the relation between Ia and Ib, and we can find many other couplings among the group of Kekulé patterns IIIa-d. Let us call the sets of the three double bonds as shown below respectively as the proper and improper sextets. A couple of the proper and improper sextets in a given hexagon will be called as an aromatic sextet or simply as a sextet.

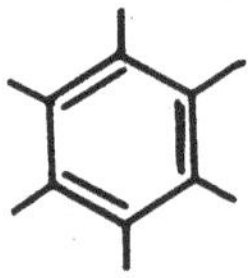

proper sextet

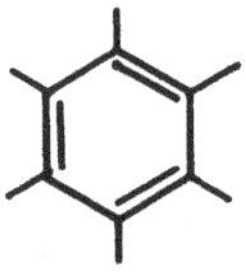

improper sextet

No two sextets are allowed to share a bond. However, it is possible for certain Kekulé patterns to have more than one sextet located on a set of disjoint hexagons. Such disjoint sextets are called to be resonant with each other. It is to be noted here that for certain kinds of Kekulé patterns there is no unique way for choosing a sextet or a set of resonant sextets.

According to Clar [9] let us denote a sextet by a circle and suppress the remaining double bonds to give a <u>sextet pattern</u> as shown below. The above arguments can be expressed in terms of the sextet patterns by taking IVb as an example.

IVb →

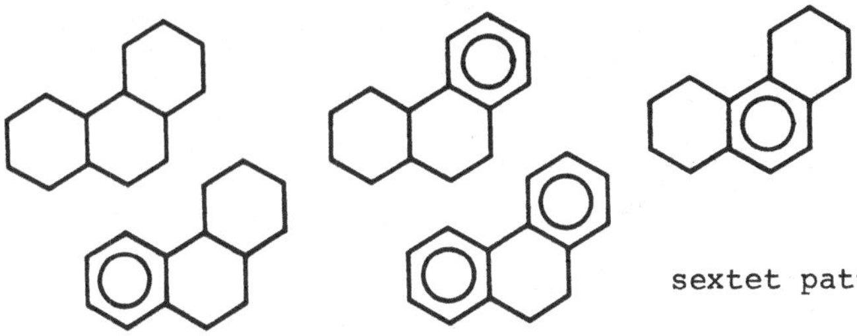

sextet patterns

Here the <u>zero-sextet pattern</u> is also defined that has no circle. It turned out that IVb generates all the posssble sextet patterns for IV.

For a given polyhex, define the <u>resonant sextet number</u> $r(G,k)$ as the number of ways for choosing k disjoint but resonant sextets from G. Then the <u>sextet polynomial</u> $B_G(x)$ is defined as

$$B_G(x) = \sum_{k=0}^{m} r(G,k)\, x^k. \tag{10}$$

For graph IV we have

$$B_G(x) = 1 + 3x + x^2.$$

The present author has shown [10,11] that for catahexes and such "thin" perihexes that have no coronene skeleton as

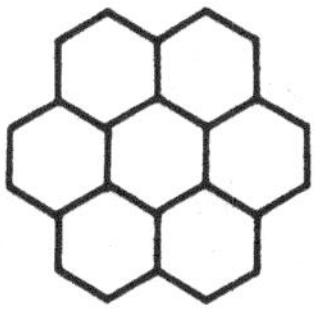

coronene

we have

$$B_G(1) = K(G). \tag{11}$$

5. Clar Transformation and Sextet Rotation

Since the both sides of Eq. (11) are derived from quite different enumeration problems, Eq. (11) is a very important relation. In order to analyze this problem the following two graphical operations are introduced.

Define the <u>Clar transformation</u> C as a simultaneous substitution of all the proper sextets by circles in a given Kekulé pattern k_i followed by the transformation of the remaining double bonds into single bonds,

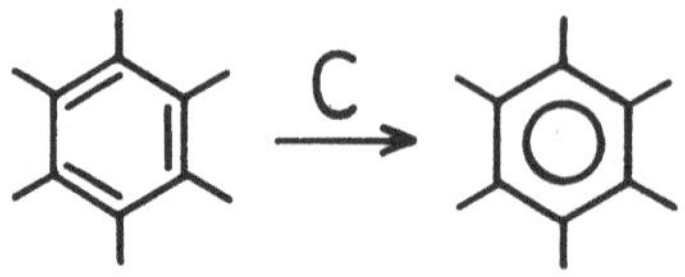

Clar transformation

as exemplified for graph VI in Fig. 3. It can symbolically be written as

$$C(k_i) = s_i. \tag{12}$$

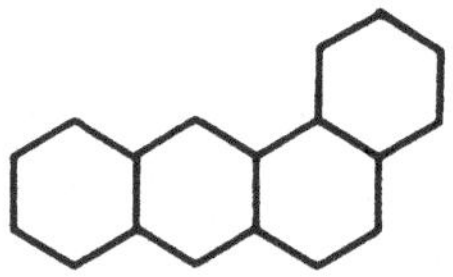

VI

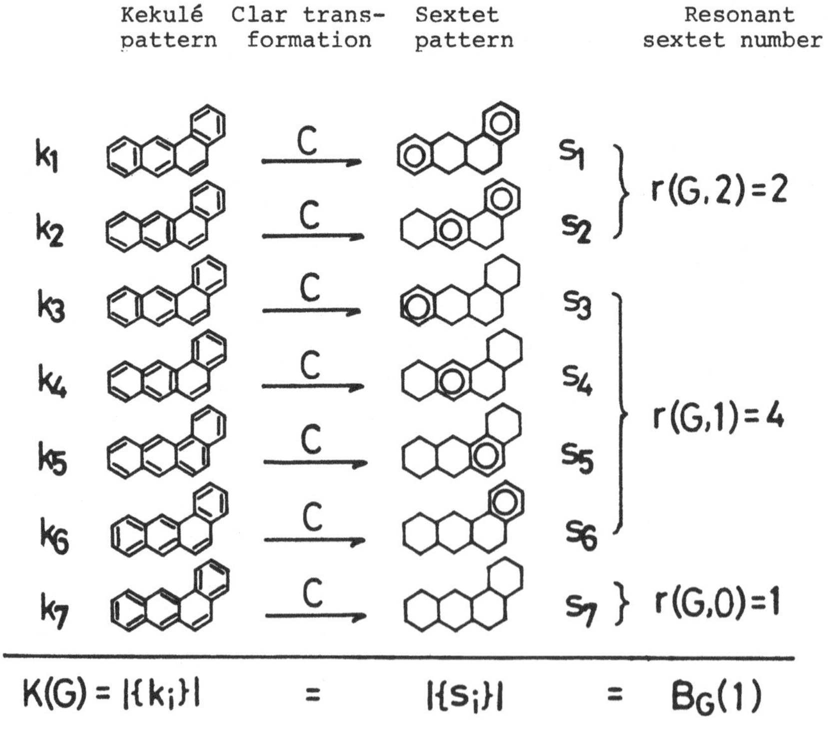

Fig. 3 Clar transformation and resonant sextet numbers.

Define the sextet rotation (R) as a simultaneous rotation of all the proper sextets in a given Kekulé pattern k_i into the improper sextets to give another Kekulé pattern k_j,

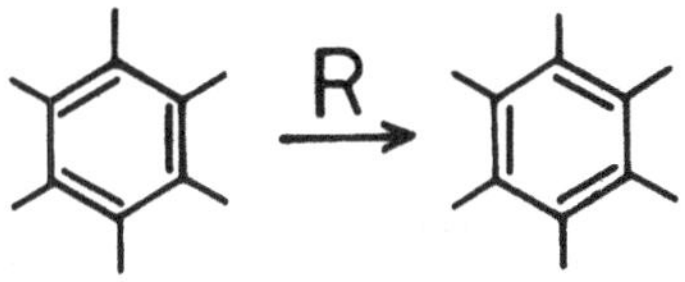

sextet rotation

or symbolically as

$$R(k_i) = k_j. \tag{13}$$

For example, we get $R(k_1)=k_7$ for graph VI. Note that for such k_i with no proper sextet, e.g., k_7 in Fig. 3, one cannot operate the sextet rotation. In this case let us put it down as

$$R(k_i) = \phi,$$

and call such k_i as the root Kekulé pattern.

Similarly the counter-sextet rotation ($\tilde{R}$) is defined as follows:

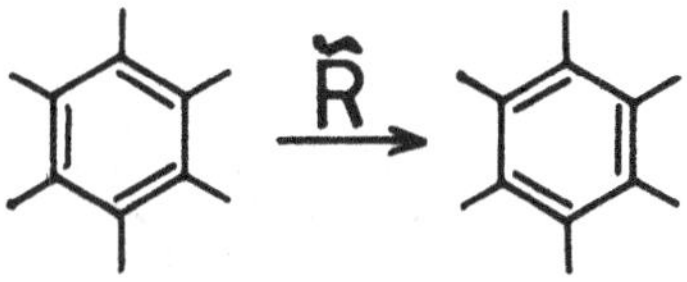

counter-sextet rotation

Note that the operation $\tilde{R}$ is not the inverse of R and vice versa.

Now try to operate the sextet and counter-sextet rotations to the set of the Kekulè patterns for graph VI. The resultant relationship among $\{k_i\}$ for VI is a hierarchical structure and can be expressed by directed rooted trees as shown in Fig. 4, where all the entries in $\{k_i\}$ can find the corresponding nodes including the root. It is to be noted that the two trees obtained by the sextet and counter-sextet rotations are not necessarily isomorphic as exemplified in Fig. 4.

The results obtained in Figs. 3 and 4 are valid for all the catahexes and "thin" perihexes. For "fat" perihexes one has to extend the concept of the sextet to the "super sextet", on which, however, we are not going to discuss here [11].

It has been shown [11] that the proof of Eq. (11) and of the results in Figs. 3 and 4 can be obtained straightforwardly if the following Lemma is proved:

[Lemma] For each polyhex graph, there exists one and only one root Kekulé pattern (a Kekulé pattern with no proper sextet).

6. Coefficients of NBMO

Herndon has proposed an interesting method for enumerating the K(G) value for a polyhex graph by using the coefficients of the non-bonding molecular orbital (NBMO) [12]. However, only the mathematical procedure for obtaining the K(G) value is introduced here.

Given a polyhex graph G with an even number of points. Of course G is bipartite. The component points are either starred (*) or unstarred. Delete from G a point p together with all the adjacent lines. The resultant graph $G \ominus p$ is also bipartite but with an odd number of points. Divide all the points into two groups, namely, the starred {s} and unstarred {r} so that the endpoints belong to {s}. Assign a set of integers ($n_s \gtrless 0$) to all the entries of {s} under the following conditions: (i) The point farthest to the endpoints is given 1 or -1. (ii) The "neighbor-sum" of these numbers for each unstarred point r becomes zero.

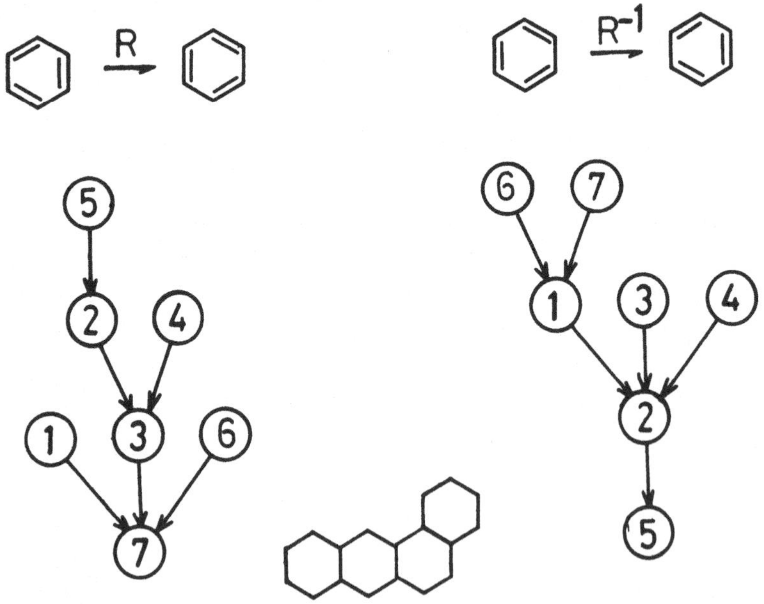

Fig. 4 Hierarchical trees of sextet rotations.

$$\sum_{s}^{\substack{\text{neighbors} \\ \text{of } r}} n_s = 0. \tag{14}$$

Examples are given in Fig. 5 for several subgraphs derived from VI. Take the sum of these numbers for the starred points which were

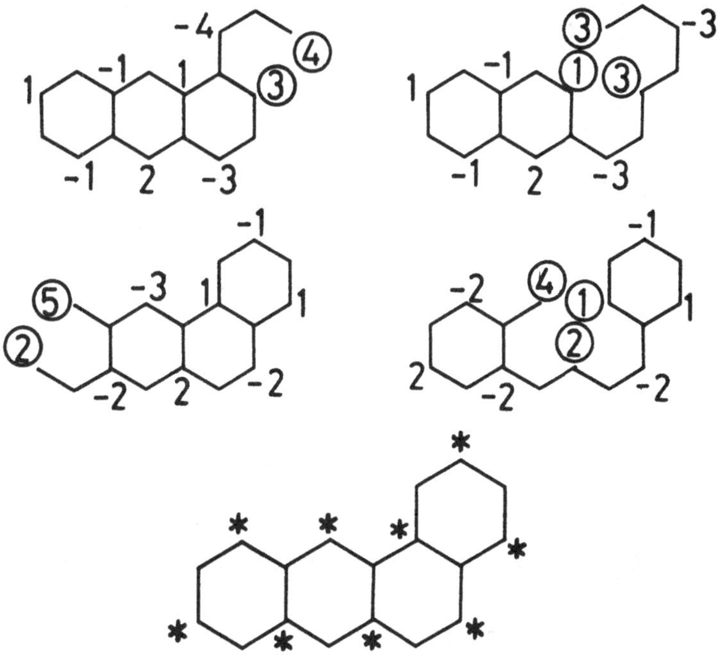

Fig. 5 NBMO and Kekulé numbers.

adjacent to p in the original graph G. As evident from Fig. 5 the (absolute) value of this sum is independent of the choice of p and is equal to the number K(G) of the maximum matching for G. Although this relation is known to be related to Eqs. (2) and (3), a rigorous proof has not yet been obtained. Further study is expected.

7. Several Series of K(G) Numbers

The numbers of the maximum matching K(G) for certain series of graphs are known to form interesting series of numbers. A few examples are shown:

G_n	$K(G_n)$
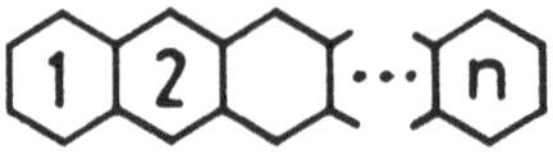	$n + 1$
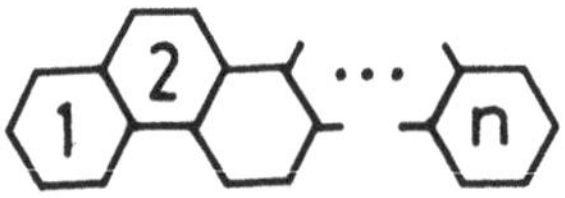	$\dfrac{\left(\frac{1+\sqrt{5}}{2}\right)^{n+2} - \left(\frac{1-\sqrt{5}}{2}\right)^{n+2}}{\sqrt{5}}$
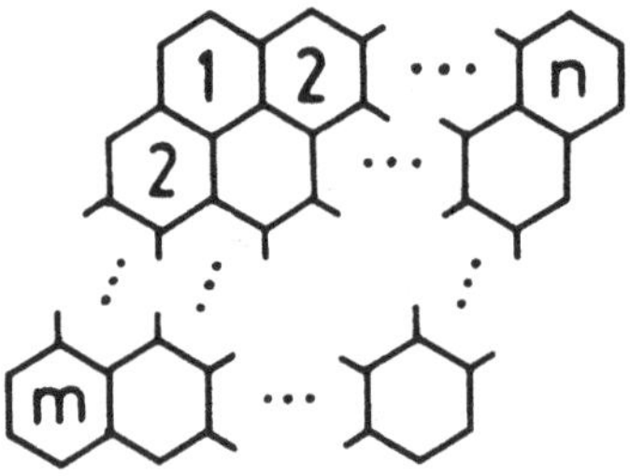	$\binom{m+n}{n}$

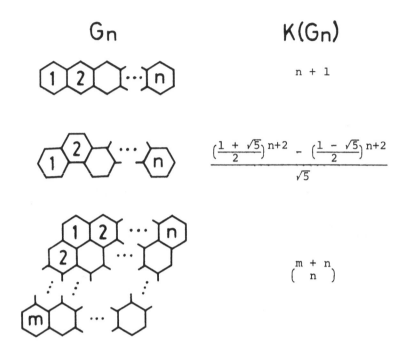

References

[1] F. Harary and R. C. Read, Proc. Edinburgh Math. Soc., Ser. II, 17, 1 (1970).

[2] F. Harary, private communication.

[3] H. C. Longuet-Higgins, J. Chem. Phys., 18, 265 (1950).

[4] H. Hosoya, Bull. Chem. Soc. Jpn., 44, 2332 (1971).

[5] H. Hosoya, Fibonacci Quarterly, 11, 255 (1973).

[6] K. Mizutani, K. Kawasaki, and H. Hosoya, Natural Science Report, Ochanomizu Univ., 22, 39 (1971).

[7] K. Kawasaki, K. Mizutani, and H. Hosoya, Natural Science Report, Ochanomizu Univ., 22, 181 (1971).

[8] T. Yamaguchi, M. Suzuki, and H. Hosoya, Natural Science Report, Ochanomizu Univ., 26, 39 (1975).

[9] E. Clar, "The Aromatic Sextet", Wiley Interscience, London (1972).

[10] H. Hosoya and T. Yamaguchi, Tetrahedron Lett., 1975, 4659.

[11] N. Ohkami, A. Motoyama, T. Yamaguchi, H. Hosoya, and I. Gutman, Tetrahedron, in press.

[12] W. C. Herndon, Tetrahedron, 29, 3 (1973).

THE TWO DISJOINT PATH PROBLEM AND WIRE ROUTING DESIGN

T. Ohtsuki
Dept. of Electronics and Communication Engineering
School of Science and Engineering
Waseda University, Tokyo, Japan 160

Abstract. A new polynomial time algorithm is presented for finding two vertex-disjoint paths between two specified pairs of vertices on an undirected graph. An application of the two disjoint path algorithm to the automatic wire routing is also discussed.

1. Introduction

This paper considers the problem of finding, given an undirected graph $G=(V,E)$ and four vertices s_1, t_1, s_2, $t_2 \in V$, two vertex-disjoint paths, P_1 from s_1 to t_1 and P_2 from s_2 to t_2. The more general problem, called disjoint connecting path or discrete multi commodity flow, of finding pairwise disjoint paths between pairs of vertices is NP-complete [1] and remains NP-complete for planar graphs [2]. The complexity of this problem is open for any fixed $k \geq 3$, but can be solved in $O(|E|)$ operations if $k=2$ and G is planar or chordal (triangulated) [3]. Also, an $O(|V| \cdot |E|)$ time algorithm for the general two path problem has been presented very recently [4].

In this paper, a different $O(|V| \cdot |E|)$ time algorithm is presented for solving the two disjoint path problem on general undirected graphs. The outline of the algorithm is described in Section 2 and its complexity is considered in Section 3. Finally, an application of this algorithm to the computer-aided wire routing design is discussed in Section 4.

2. The Two Disjoint Path Algorithm

In what follows, the two disjoint path problem under consideration is abbreviated by TPP. The convention "TPP is true (false)" is also used to indicate the existence (nonexistence) of the desired pair of paths, respectively. The set of vertices constructing a path P is also denoted by P and the set of edges constructing it is denoted by E(P). Sometimes the notation P(s,t) is used to indicate a path with source s and sink t. For two vertices $u,v \in P$, the subpath of P between u and v is denoted by P[u;v]. Throughout this paper, disjoint means vertex-disjoint.

Let $G_o = (V_o, E_o)$ be a given undirected graph. Without loss of generality, we assume that G_o is 2-connected. The outline of the presented algorithm is as follows.

Step 1. Find two disjoint paths between $\{s_1,t_1\}$ and $\{s_2,t_2\}$. We assume that two paths $P(s_1,t_2)$ and $Q(s_2,t_1)$ are found, otherwise TPP turns out to be either true or false.

Step 2. Find all the bridges $\mathcal{B} = (B_1, B_2, \ldots\ldots)$ with respect to $P \cup Q$, where a bridge B is either i) a single edge $e = (x,y) \in E_o - E(P) - E(Q)$ with $x,y \in P \cup Q$ or ii) a maximal subgraph of $G = (V, E_o - E(P) - E(Q))$ with at least one vertex $x \in V_o - P - Q$ such that, for every other vertex y of B, there exists a path R(x,y) without intersecting P or Q except at y. An example of the set of bridges is shown in Fig. 1.

An attachment of a bridge B is its vertex which belongs to $P \cup Q$. The set of bridges with every attachment on P or on Q is denoted by $\mathcal{B}^P$ or $\mathcal{B}^Q$, respectively. The set of bridges with attachments on both P and Q is denoted by $\mathcal{B}^{PQ}$.

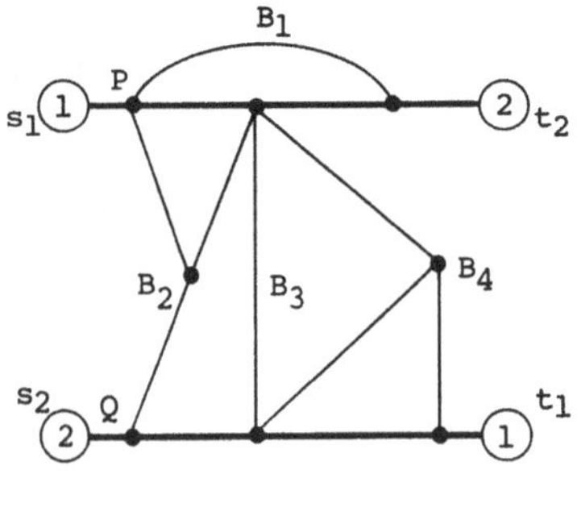

Fig. 1. Set of bridges.

Step 3. If there exist three vertices a, b, c on P in this order and two bridges $B_i \in \mathcal{B}^{PQ}$ and $B_j \in \mathcal{B}^P$ such that $b \in B_i$ and $a, c \in B_j$, replace the subpath P[a;c] of P so as to go through B_j as shown in Fig. 2 and update the set $\mathcal{B}$ with respect to the new P. This operation is repeated until no such pair of B_i and B_j exists. Perform the same operation for path Q.

<u>Step 4</u>. Discard all the bridges in $\mathcal{B}^P$ and $\mathcal{B}^Q$. Henceforce we may assume that all the bridges belongs to $\mathcal{B}^{PQ}$. Therefore TPP is true if there exist two disjoint paths $P_1(a,d)$ and $P_2(b,c)$ without traversing $E(P) \cup E(Q)$, where a, b, c, d are distinct bridge attachments such that s_1, a, b, t_2 are in this order on P and s_2, c, d, t_1 are in this order on Q. A pair of bridges (B_1,B_2) is <u>alternating</u> if B_1 and B_2 include $P_1(a,d)$ and $P_2(b,c)$ as above, respectively (see Fig. 3).

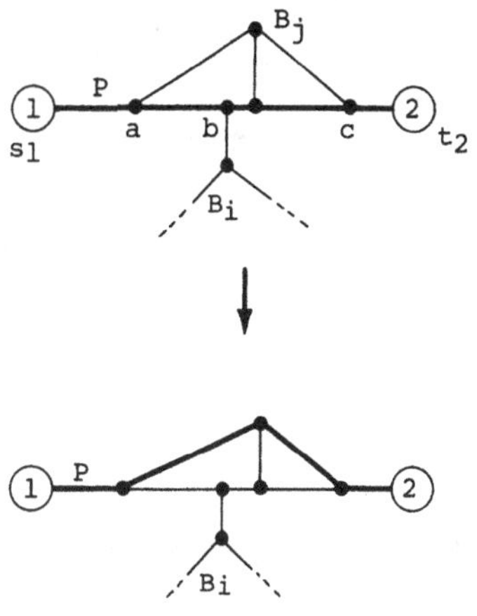

Fig. 2. Elimination of $\mathcal{B}^P$.

<u>Step 5</u>. If there exists an alternating pair of bridges, then TPP is true. Otherwise go to the next step.

<u>Step 6</u>. It is assumed that there exists at least one bridge having two or more attachments on each of P and Q, since otherwise TPP is obviously false. Discard all the bridges not possessing the above property.

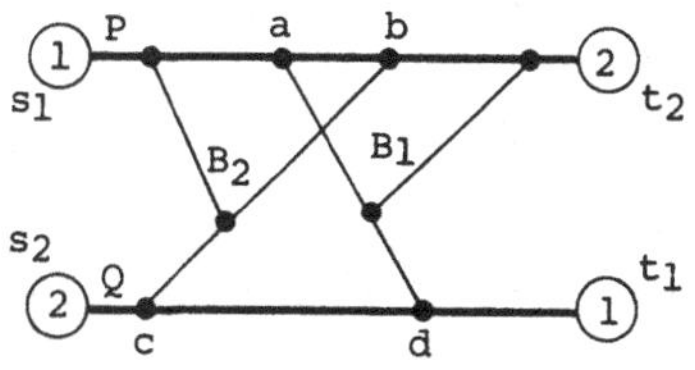

Fig. 3. Alternating pair of bridges.

For each bridge $B \in \mathcal{B}$, let a and b (c and d) be its attachments on P(Q) closest to s_1 and t_2 (s_2 and t_1), respectively, and $G_o(B)$ be the section graph of G_o determined by the vertices of $B \cup P[a;b] \cup Q[c;d]$ (see Fig. 4). For each bridge B, call the binary recursive function $f(G_o(B),P[a;b],Q[c;d])$ and let $\mathcal{B} \leftarrow \mathcal{B} - \{B\}$. TPP is true if f = "yes" and false if f = "no" for every $G_o(B)$.

The binary recursive function $f = (G,P,Q)$ is defined as follows. G is a graph with two disjoint paths $P(s_1,t_2)$ and $Q(s_2,t_1)$ specified. Furthermore G has a single bridge with respect to $P \cup Q$ containing attachments s_1, s_2, t_1, t_2. f returns "yes" ("no") if two disjoint paths $P_1(s_1,t_1)$ and $P_2(s_2,t_2)$ exist (do not exist). Without loss of generality we assume that G is 2-connected.

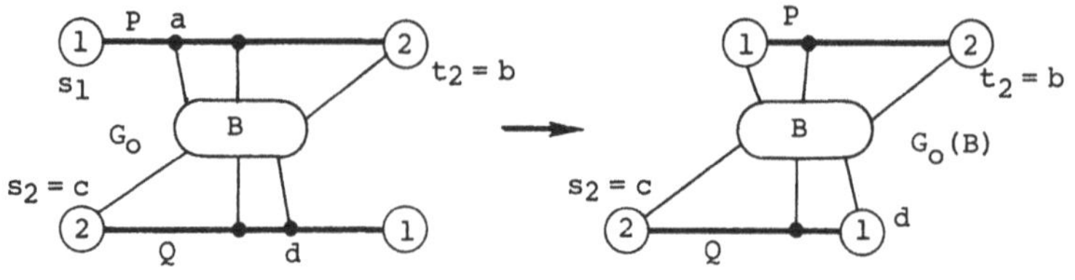

Fig. 4. Section graph $G_o(B)$.

The following steps (Steps 7 - 14) are performed in f.

Step 7. Find a path $P'(s_1,t_2)$ which is disjoint with $P(s_1,t_2)$ and $Q(s_2,t_1)$. Existence of P' is clear from the definition of bridge.

Step 8. Find all the bridges $\mathcal{B} = \{B_1, B_2, \ldots\ldots\}$ with respect to $P \cup Q \cup P'$ by means of the same operation as in Step 2.

Step 9. Perform the same operations as Steps 3, 4 with respect to P', and pertinently update the path P' and the set $\mathcal{B}$. Note that each bridge must have an attachment on $P' - \{s_1,t_2\}$ and another on $P \cup Q - \{s_1,t_2\}$.

Step 10. If there exists a bridge $B_i \in \mathcal{B}$ having an attachment $a \in P - \{s_1,t_2\}$ and another attachment $b \in Q$, then return "yes", otherwise go to the next step. Note that TPP is true if such a bridge exists. This can by proved by recalling that B_i also includes another attachment $c \in P' - \{s_1,t_2\}$ and the 2-connectivity assumption. Fig. 5 illustrates how to extract a desired pair of paths.

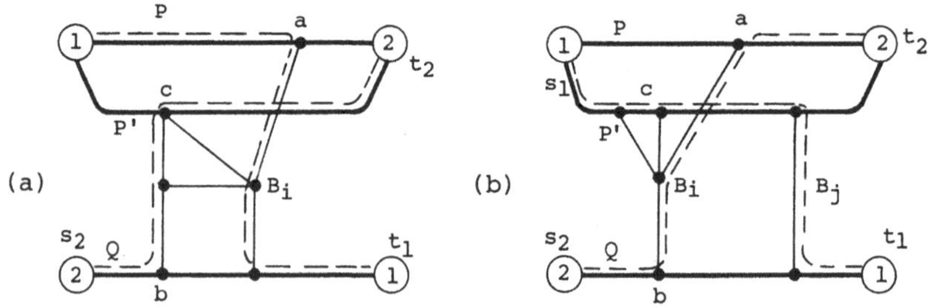

Fig. 5 Extraction of two paths in Step 10.

Step 11. Now we may assume that each bridge has either all the attachment on $P' \cup Q$ or all of them on $P \cup P'$. The set of bridges of the former (latter) type is denoted by $\mathcal{B}^{I}(\mathcal{B}^{II})$.

If there exists an alternating pair of bridges in $\mathcal{B}^{I}$, then return "yes". Otherwise go to the next step.

<u>Step 12</u>. For each bridge $B \in \mathcal{B}^{I}$ having two or more attachments on each of P' and Q, call $f(G(B), P'[a;b], Q[c;d])$, where a and b (c and d) are the attachments on P'(Q) closest to s_1 and t_2 (s_2 and t_1), respectively, and return "yes" if f = "yes". If f = "no" for every such bridge or if no such bridge exists, go to the next step.

<u>Step 13</u>. Let x and y be attachments of bridges of $\mathcal{B}^{I}$ closest to s_1 and t_2, on P' (It is necessary that s_1, t_2, x, y are distinct). If there exists an alternating pair of bridges B_i, $B_j \in \mathcal{B}^{II}$ such that B_i has an attachment $u \in P'[x;t_2] - \{x,t_2\}$ and B_j has an attachment $v \in P'[s_1;y] - \{s_1,y\}$, then return "yes". Otherwise go to the next step. The extraction of desired paths is illustrated in Fig. 6. It should be noted here that some bridges of $\mathcal{B}^{I}$ include two disjoint paths $M(x,s_2)$ and $N(y,t_1)$.

<u>Step 14</u>. Let x and y be as in Step 13. For each bridge $B \in \mathcal{B}^{II}$ having an attachment $u \in P'[x;t_2] - \{x,t_2\}$ and another attachment $v \in P'[s_1;y] - \{s_1,y\}$, perform the following operations, or if no such bridge exists, return "no".

If B has an attachment in $P'[s_1;x] - \{s_1,x\}$, let $s_1^* \leftarrow s_1$ and $x^* \leftarrow x$. Otherwise let $s_1^*(x^*)$ be the attachment on P(P') closest to $s_1(x)$ and update bridge B by discarding subpaths $P[s_1;s_1^*]$ and $P'[s_1;x^*]$ except $\{s_1^*,x^*\}$. By means of the same argument for $P'[y;t_2]$, we specify vertices t_2^* and y^* corresponding to s_1^* and x^*, respectively.

Consider the section graph G' of G determined by the vertices of $P[s_1^*;t_2^*]$, $P[x^*;y^*]$ and B (see Fig. 7). Call $f(G', P[s_1^*;t_2^*], P'[x^*;y^*])$ and return "yes" if f = "yes". If f = "no" for every such bridge, then return "no".

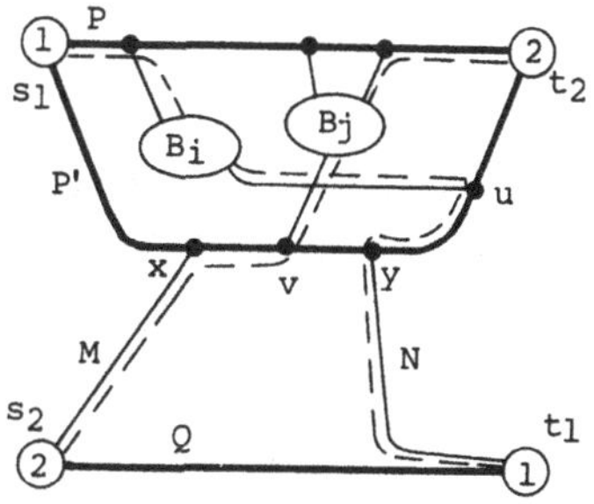

Fig. 6 Extraction of two paths in Step 13.

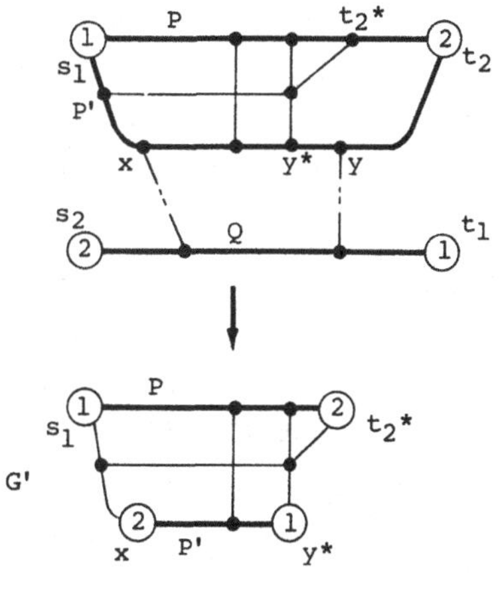

Fig. 7. Section graph G'.

3. Complexity Analysis

We have not explicitly discussed computer implementation of the algorithm, which is a long and tedious description. However its complexity can be easily evaluated unless we insist on very strict analysis

Henceforce linear means $O(|E|+|V|)$. The algorithm consists of operations in the main routine (Steps 1 - 6), which are performed once and those in the recursive procedure f (Steps 7 - 14). First we show that all the steps are performed in linear time if we neglect the statements of recursive calls.

Step 1 is performed by applying flow techniques [5]. It is linear since only two augmentation paths are required. Step 2 is performed by means of an obvious modification of the well-known graph search technique, which is linear. Step 3 is also done by means of a modification of the graph search technique. Its straightforward implementation requires $O(|V|\cdot|E|)$ time. To guarantee linearity of Step 3, we need a careful implementation so that each edge is not traversed no more than some constant time in the graph search. The implementation and its linearity proof are complicated and are not given here. Step 4 requires trivial operations only and obviously is linear.

The term "bridge" is the same as that appears in the planarity testing [6],[7], except that it is defined here with respect to some paths instead of a cycle. Thus the operation in Step 5 to find a pair of alternating bridges can be viewed as a part of the linear planarity test algorithm [8].

Step 6 is obviously linear except for the recursive call of f, and the linear 2-connectivity test algorithm [9] can be used. To find a path $P'(s_1,t_2)$ in Step 7 can also be done in linear time by using the graph search. We do not give the complexity analysis of Steps 8 - 14, since the operations therein are obvious modifications of those in Steps 1 - 6.

What remains to be shown is that the depth of recursive calls is bounded by $O(|V|)$, which yields the conclusion that the whole algorithm terminates in $O(|V|\cdot|E|)$ time. We only consider the edges or vertices of graph $G=(V,E)$ at the first call of f, since the number of operations related to the other edges is bounded by some constant. If an edge or a vertex of G belongs to an subgraph $G'=(V',E')$ of G which is extracted in Step 12 or Step 14, then it is clear that $|V'|<|V|$. Hence the number of such subgraphs including a specific edge or vertex is of $O(|V|)$, and so is the depth of recursive calls, which implies that the presented algorithm runs in $O(|V| \cdot |E|)$ time.

4. An Application to Wire Routing

The TPP is related to "wire routing", which is an important portion of the layout design of LSI's, printed circuit boards (PCB's) or hybrid IC's. In computer aided wire routing design, the constraints on the way in which the connections of signal nets should be carried out are very often modeled by an underlying graph, usually a grid, such that the only routes allowed are those using its edges. Graph-theoretically, the routing is equivalent to or even harder than the Disjoint Connection Path (Discrete Multi-Commodity) Problem, which has been shown to be NP-complete [1].

The almost all existing layout design systems [e.g.,10] are based on the following strategy. First we try to connect as many signal nets as possible by using an automatic router, which very rarely gives a complete (100 %) connection. The so-called "maze-type" algorithms [11] are often used in automatic routers, in which the signal nets (or pin pairs) are connected one by one by means of a graph search technique until no more signal net can be connected without intersecting already-routed ones. Next the partial design is improved by means of manual interaction through graphic displays or digital plotters, where the designers' experience and intuition play an essential role. The complete connection, if succeeded, goes through to a digitizer and a design rule check program. It goes without saying that such a design methodology costs much design turnaround time and can involve errors due to manual operations.

Recently a new interactive design system for PCB, which provides us with error-free wiring pattern, has been proposed [12]. The design turnaround time of wire routing can be remarkably decreased if the TPP algorithm is implemented on such a design system. Suppose we have connected k nets $\{N_1, N_2, \ldots\ldots, N_k\}$ using a maze-type algorithm and (k+1)th net N_{k+1} cannot be connected. This implies the existence of "boundary" which separates a pin (terminal) s from another pin t of net N_{k+1}. Graph-theoretically, "boundary" is a minimal set S of vertices, called minimal s, t separator, such that every path between s and t includes at least one vertex in S. With an obvious modification of a maze-type algorithm, we can list up the vertices in the boundary S [12]. Now it is clear that we must change the route of at least one net in $\{N_1,N_2,\ldots\ldots,N_k\}$ in order to obtain a complete connection, if it exists. The TPP algorithm is used to check whether (k+1) nets $\{N_1,N_2,\ldots\ldots,N_{k+1}\}$ can be connected by rerouting only one of $\{N_1,N_2,\ldots\ldots,N_k\}$. Namely, the TPP algorithm with respect to the pair (N_i,N_{k+1}) is applied for each $N_i \in \{N_1,N_2,\ldots\ldots,N_k\}$, where all the vertices included in the (n-1) nets $\{N_1,\ldots\ldots,N_{i-1},N_{i+1},\ldots\ldots,N_k\}$ are prohibited to be used.

In the routing design of linear bipolar IC's and thic film hybrid IC's, usually a single layer is provided for wire connection. So the linear TPP algorithm for planar graphs [3] can be used. On the other hand, we should use the TPP algorithm for a general graph when LSI's or PCB's with multi-layer technology are concerned.

Example. Fig. 8(a) shows a graph (single-layer grid) representing the constraints for connecting nets $N_1,N_2,\ldots\ldots,N_6$. This example is far simpler than those appear in practise, but suitable to demonstrate how the TPP algorithm is applied. The number, say i, in a circle indicates a pin of net N_i. A typical automatic router connects nets $N_1 \sim N_5$ as indicated by the solid lines. It is observed that net N_6 cannot be connected unless we reroute some of $N_1 \sim N_5$. Now the graph search algorithm for connecting N_6 extracts a boundary consisting of six vertices indicated by × in Fig. 8(b), where the vertices corresponding to pins are neglected. By removing the route for N_5(removing N_4 fails) and applying the TPP algorithm with respect to net pair (N_5,N_6) on the subgraph shown in Fig. 8(c), we discover the connection as indicated by

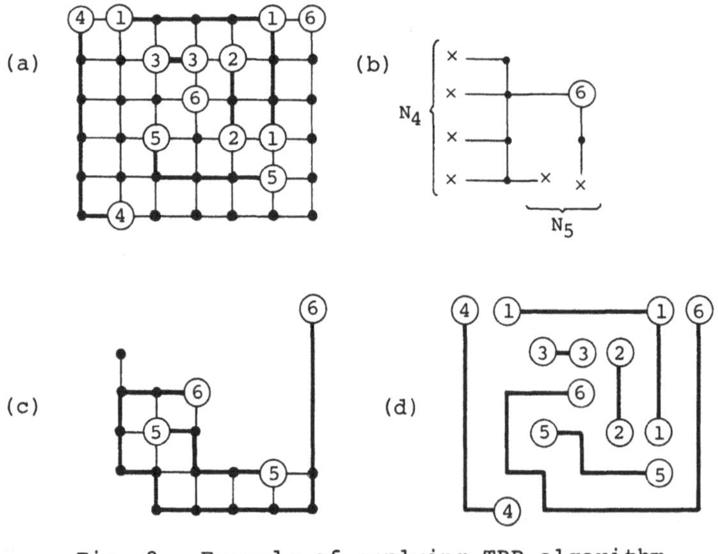

Fig. 8. Example of applying TPP algorithm.

the solid lines. Note that the vertices on the connection routes for $N_1 \sim N_4$ and their incident edges are removed when considering the pair (N_5, N_6). The complete connection for $N_1 \sim N_6$ is shown in Fig. 8(d).

Acknowledgment. This work was supported by the Grant in Aid for Scientific Research of the Ministry of Education, Science and Culture of Japan under Grant: Cooperative Research (A) 435013 (1980).

References

[1] Karp, R.M., "On the complexity of combinatorial problems", Networks 5, pp. 45-68 (1975).

[2] Lynch, J.F., "The equivalence of theorem proving and the interconnection problem", ACM SIGDA Newsletter 5 : 3 (1975).

[3] Perl, Y. and Shiloach, Y., "Finding two disjoint paths between two pairs of vertices in a graph", J. Assoc. Comput. Mach. 25, pp. 1-9 (1978).

[4] Shiloach, Y., "A polynominal solution to the undirected two paths problem", ibid. 27, pp. 445-56 (1980).

[5] Even, S. and Tarjan, R.E., "Network flow and testing graph connectivity", SIAM J. Comput. 4, pp. 507-18 (1975).

[6] Auslander, L. and Parter, S.V., "On imbedding graphs in the sphere", J. Math. Mech. 10, pp. 517-23 (1961).

[7] Fisher, G.J. and Wing, O., "Computer recognition and extraction of planar graphs from the incidence matrix", IEEE Trans. CT-13, pp. 154-63 (1966).

[8] Hopcroft, J.E. and Tarjan, R.E., "Efficient planarity testing", J. ACM 21, pp. 549-68 (1974).

[9] Tarjan, R.E., "Depth-first search and linear graph algorithms", SIAM J. Comput. 1, pp. 146-60 (1972).

[10] Johnson, D.R., "PC board layout techniques", Proc. 16th Design Automation Conf., pp. 337-43 (1979).

[11] Lee, C.Y., "An algorithm for path connections and its applications", IRE Trans. EC-10, pp. 346-65 (1961).

[12] Mori, H., et. al., "BRAIN: An advanced interactive layout design system for printed wiring boards", to be presented at the IEEE Internat. Conf. on Circuits and Computors (1980).

Vol. 77: G. V. Bochmann, Architecture of Distributed Computer Systems. VIII, 238 pages. 1979.

Vol. 78: M. Gordon, R. Milner and C. Wadsworth, Edinburgh LCF. VIII, 159 pages. 1979.

Vol. 79: Language Design and Programming Methodology. Proceedings, 1979. Edited by J. Tobias. IX, 255 pages. 1980.

Vol. 80: Pictorial Information Systems. Edited by S. K. Chang and K. S. Fu. IX, 445 pages. 1980.

Vol. 81: Data Base Techniques for Pictorial Applications. Proceedings, 1979. Edited by A. Blaser. XI, 599 pages. 1980.

Vol. 82: J. G. Sanderson, A Relational Theory of Computing. VI, 147 pages. 1980.

Vol. 83: International Symposium Programming. Proceedings, 1980. Edited by B. Robinet. VII, 341 pages. 1980.

Vol. 84: Net Theory and Applications. Proceedings, 1979. Edited by W. Brauer. XIII, 537 Seiten. 1980.

Vol. 85: Automata, Languages and Programming. Proceedings, 1980. Edited by J. de Bakker and J. van Leeuwen. VIII, 671 pages. 1980.

Vol. 86: Abstract Software Specifications. Proceedings, 1979. Edited by D. Bjørner. XIII, 567 pages. 1980

Vol. 87: 5th Conference on Automated Deduction. Proceedings, 1980. Edited by W. Bibel and R. Kowalski. VII, 385 pages. 1980.

Vol. 88: Mathematical Foundations of Computer Science 1980. Proceedings, 1980. Edited by P. Dembiński. VIII, 723 pages. 1980.

Vol. 89: Computer Aided Design - Modelling, Systems Engineering, CAD-Systems. Proceedings, 1980. Edited by J. Encarnacao. XIV, 461 pages. 1980.

Vol. 90: D. M. Sandford, Using Sophisticated Models in Resolution Theorem Proving.
XI, 239 pages. 1980

Vol. 91: D. Wood, Grammar and L Forms: An Introduction. IX, 314 pages. 1980.

Vol. 92: R. Milner, A Calculus of Communication Systems. VI, 171 pages. 1980.

Vol. 93: A. Nijholt, Context-Free Grammars: Covers, Normal Forms, and Parsing. VII, 253 pages. 1980.

Vol. 94: Semantics-Directed Compiler Generation. Proceedings, 1980. Edited by N. D. Jones. V, 489 pages. 1980.

Vol. 95: Ch. D. Marlin, Coroutines. XII, 246 pages. 1980.

Vol. 96: J. L. Peterson, Computer Programs for Spelling Correction: VI, 213 pages. 1980.

Vol. 97: S. Osaki and T. Nishio, Reliability Evaluation of Some Fault-Tolerant Computer Architectures. VI, 129 pages. 1980.

Vol. 98: Towards a Formal Description of Ada. Edited by D. Bjørner and O. N. Oest. XIV, 630 pages. 1980.

Vol. 99: I. Guessarian, Algebraic Semantics. XI, 158 pages. 1981.

Vol. 100: Graphtheoretic Concepts in Computer Science. Edited by H. Noltemeier. X, 403 pages. 1981.

Vol. 101: A. Thayse, Boolean Calculus of Differences. VII, 144 pages. 1981.

Vol. 102: J. H. Davenport, On the Integration of Algebraic Functions. 1–197 pages. 1981.

Vol. 103: H. Ledgard, A. Singer, J. Whiteside, Directions in Human Factors of Interactive Systems. VI, 190 pages. 1981.

Vol. 104: Theoretical Computer Science. Ed. by P. Deussen. VII, 261 pages. 1981.

Vol. 105: B. W. Lampson, M. Paul, H. J. Siegert, Distributed Systems – Architecture and Implementation. XIII, 510 pages. 1981.

Vol. 106: The Programming Language Ada. Reference Manual. X, 243 pages. 1981.

Vol. 107: International Colloquium on Formalization of Programming Concepts. Proceedings. Edited by J. Diaz and I. Ramos. VII, 478 pages. 1981.

Vol. 108: Graph Theory and Algorithms. Edited by N. Saito and T. Nishizeki. VI, 216 pages. 1981.